7/15

W9-BAI-482

THE
QUEEN

"The quest stands upon the edge of a knife. Stray but a little and it will fail. But hope remains if friends stay true."
—J.R.R. Tolkien, *The Lord of the Rings*

THE

QUEEN

*The Epic Ambition of Hillary
and the Coming of a Second "Clinton Era"*

Hugh Hewitt

**CENTER
STREET**

New York Nashville Boston

The excerpts from *National Review* articles "Abedin Goes for the Power Save" by Charlotte Hays and "The Huma Unmentionables" by Andrew C. McCarthy are used with permission.

Center Street
Hachette Book Group
1290 Avenue of the Americas
New York, NY 10104
www.CenterStreet.com

Printed in the United States of America

RRD-C

First edition: June 2015

10 9 8 7 6 5 4 3 2

Center Street is a division of Hachette Book Group, Inc.

The Center Street name and logo are trademarks of Hachette Book Group, Inc.

The Hachette Speakers Bureau provides a wide range of authors for speaking events. To find out more, go to www.HachetteSpeakersBureau.com or call 866-376-6591.

The publisher is not responsible for websites (or their content) that are not owned by the publisher.

Library of Congress Control Number: 2015938233

ISBN: 978-1-4555-6251-0

For Doctor Larry Arnn and all my other teachers

Table of Contents

The Dedicatory Letter

Madame Secretary:

It is the 500th anniversary of the publication of The Prince *by Niccolo Machiavelli, give or take a year. Machiavelli addressed his short essay on ruling "To the Magnificent Lorenzo Di Piero De' Medici," who was then, as you are now, the leading member of a long-powerful family that had recently returned to power after a period of exile from it. The Medici were busy planning their new appointments and policies when Machiavelli delivered his book, accompanied by the wish that the "gone and back again" Medici power brokers would succeed even more spectacularly than they had in their first era of rule.*

Machiavelli had been a senior official in the government overthrown by the return of the Medici, and had in fact been imprisoned and tortured by them. Upon release, however, he did not seek a quiet life but rather to continue with a role in the great game of ruling. As Charles Krauthammer wrote in his spectacularly successful memoir of 2013, Things That Matter, *politics is indeed sovereign in this world, and Machiavelli wanted to be back in the midst of the use of power.*

Politics is sovereign in this world, and only theology competes for a level of interest among general readership. But for theology to matter, it must be true that there is a God of some sort. Politics matters whether or not there is a God. The "Great Gamble" referred to by Blaise Pascal that challenged non-believers to consider the consequences of their denial could also be applied to those disinterested in politics: They gamble that it will never be about them. Sometimes that gamble goes disastrously against them. The Germans in 1931 and all the Jews of Europe not long thereafter. The Iranians in 1977. The Ukrainians in 2014. Suddenly, the maelstrom.

There is so much to say about politics, but much of it is carried away by events. Remarkably, Machiavelli's advice remains very relevant five centuries later. I suspect you have read The Prince, *just as I know you have read Saul Alinsky's* Rules for Radicals.* *I also suspect that you harbor contempt and envy, bordering on hatred, for President Obama — something like the searing contempt your husband feels for him detailed in* Game Change *by Mark Halperin and John Heilemann. That rage, reported by Halperin and Heilemann in such acute detail ("an off-the-rack Chicago pol" I believe they report Bill calling the soon-to-be new president)— is profound, and I just can't believe Bill had it and you didn't. You two don't think him very smart, do you? You suspect it but cannot say it, and you tried to get to his college and law school transcripts for that reason: to show the world he had been lifted up, not clawed his way up as you and Bill have. Many people suspect this but cannot say*

* See page 16

it, and even now the very able Axelrod and the not-so-gifted Jarrett and the rest protect this flank carefully. (See the complete transcript of my interview with Axelrod, part of which is referenced below). Those who say such things on my side of the aisle are not believed to be sincere, but merely jealous, or in some cases racist. But what you seem to suspect is a lack of intellectual capacity is often revealed in his speeches and his conversations that, when unscripted, are trite compilations of slogans and self-serving, self-pitying gasps for fealty. The Crusades? Really, how it must make you cringe.

It must gall you still that he beat you. It must motivate you to run to replace him and then snub him, make his people crawl. To erase his victory. To use the greatest megaphone in the world to announce to the world that Chance the Gardener has left the building. Not too quickly, of course. Slowly, carefully. A thorough erasing takes time and must be done gently or you will tear the paper.

"Sometimes, Hugh," Willie Brown, then a Speaker of the California Assembly, said to me in a feigned hushed tone before a greenlight-on camera in 1992, "I have to admit that what I enjoy most is simply the raw exercise of power."

So did Machiavelli. So does your husband. So apparently do you. You could no more not seek to be president than George W. Bush could have walked away in 2004, or Barack Obama in 2012. You have wanted to be president before. The desire doesn't go away. To it is added your amazing personal drive to defeat, if only by accomplishment, the loser that bested you and then made you work for him. You wanted the job once and haven't stopped wanting it. You need it, in fact.

I was told about that desire in 1978 by Richard Nixon when I joined his staff as a 23-year-old ghost writer.

You had helped force Nixon from the Oval Office you seek to occupy. I think it is ironic in that this, perhaps my last book on politics, for I have nothing more to write that I haven't already written in a dozen previous books, I am addressing a member of the team who, in arranging the deposition of RN, opened many doors for me in the years ahead. Perhaps this is a long-delayed, thank-you gift, though the crisis brought about by the partisan savaging of Nixon set the country off on the course that opened the door to Khomeini. Yes, Archibald Cox, Sam Dash, Leon Jaworski, the old racist Sam Ervin, Richard Ben-Veniste, etc. etc.—they all own part of Khomeini's legacy. Of course they didn't know. But you cannot topple heads of government and heads of state of the world's greatest power without setting off earthquakes. The Qaddafi adventure taught you everything about unintended consequences you didn't already know, didn't it? We will have to talk about your collapse that night. You may not want to admit it, but it is the central issue of the campaign, that and the disappeared emails and the "private" server and the doings of your legions of off-the-books operatives.

All of those stories, and many more, simply pale next to the night of Benghazi.

You. Went. Home. Or were sent home. It was the latter wasn't it? No matter. That dam will hold. The emails are gone, right? They are gone, aren't they? Even if that is true, what may not hold are the walls around the details of the call you placed to Gregory Hicks that night, and the other things—things that Obama and perhaps Axelrod and almost certainly Valerie Jarrett know. Valerie has enough of your emails on other topics to, well, to assure that you are not going to be trashing her at least until the Inaugural Oath is sworn and perhaps not even then.

So you helped run off Nixon. You let Mubarak topple. You killed off Qaddafi. Look at the mess you left in Yemen, in Syria, in Iraq, in Lebanon, in Ukraine. In, well, everywhere.

People of your party worry that fracking will set off tremors. They do not worry about what it means to depose a president of Egypt or Libya, much less a hated Republican. They should. You should.

I don't expect that you would ever read this little book after your election, so I am publishing it before the contest, which I fervently hope you will not only lose but lose in spectacular fashion, as you do not deserve the office given your reckless, feckless tenure at the Department of State and the wreckage you and the president have wrought, the disaster upon disaster you left behind. (I am not assuming your election, of course—far from it. Think of this book as a sort of "contingency plan" should you somehow win, in spite of your record, the sort of contingency plan you did not have in place in Benghazi on 9/11—of all dates—in 2012.) Thus I write it in such a way to maximize any help it might give to your GOP opponent, but also in such a way as to help you govern should you somehow win, as you are clearly not ready to govern. I do not claim to be disinterested or pretend objectivity that none have, or very few believe in (and for the handful who do believe in such a thing, genuine contempt for their faculties must be recorded). If you read this it will be because it made a stir by its title and its reception, its promotion, and because we share a close friend in common, who may or may not give it to you with his genuine assurance that, while I am wrong, I am not rotten. He might point to my on-air friendships with many of your long-time friends and admirers, like historian Jonathan Alter or columnist E.J. Dionne, or to in-depth interviews I have conducted with Axelrod and other leading lights of your party. People whom you know will vouch for me. For whatever reason, you will read it.

If you do in fact win, then, well perhaps you will recall a few things from these short pages. There are obvious things you ought to do to win, and I expect you will do some of them, and once done, will recall their efficacy if not their unique origin with me, and revisit some of the other suggestions. Some of these are substantive. Some are stylistic. Some are designed to assure your star shines far brighter than Obama's, which won't be hard if you don't set fire to the White House.

Here is what Machiavelli wrote to Lorenzo 500 years ago:

"Take then, your Magnificence, this little gift in the spirit in which I send it; wherein, if it be diligently read and considered by you, you will learn my extreme desire that you should attain that greatness which fortune and your other attributes promise."

In the same spirit, with the same level of candor, I offer you The Queen.

July 8, 1971
Berkeley

Dear Saul,

When is that new book coming out--or has it come and I somehow missed the fulfillment of Revelation? I have just had my one-thousandth conversation about <u>Reveille</u> and need some new material to throw at people. You are being rediscovered again as the New Left-type politicos are finally beginning to think seriously about the hard work and mechanics of organizing. I seem to have survived law school, slightly bruised, with my belief in and zest for organizing intact. If I never thanked you for the encouraging words of last spring in the midst of the Yale-Cambodia madness, I do so now. The more I've seen of places like Yale Law School and the people who haunt them, the more convinced I am that we have the serious business and joy of much work ahead, --if the commitment to a free and open society is ever going to mean more than eloquence and frustration.

I miss our biennial conversations. Do you ever make it out to California? I am living in Berkeley and working in Oakland for the summer and would love to see you. Let me know if there is any chance of our getting together --2667 Derby #2, Berkeley 415-841-5330.

There were rumors of your going to SE Asia to recruit organizers. Is the lack of imagination among my peers really so rampant as that suggests or did you get yourself a CIA-sponsored junket to exotica?

I hope you are still well and fighting. Give my regards to Mrs. Harper. Hopefully we can have a good argument sometime in the near future.

Until then,
Hillary

PART I

CHAPTER I

Setting the Bar High:
Questing For a New "Clinton Era"

At the end of his opening chapter, Machiavelli tells Lorenzo why a prince like Lorenzo ought to listen to a commoner like Machiavelli. This excerpt may explain why a senior Democratic stateswoman, former First Lady and recipient of the best advice from the most skilled advisors of the left ought to listen to a radio talk show host of the center-right:

> "Nor do I hold with those who regard it as a presumption if a man of low and humble condition dare to discuss and settle the concerns of princes; because, just as those who draw landscapes place themselves below in the plain to contemplate the nature of the mountains and of lofty places, and in order to contemplate the plains place themselves upon high mountains, even so to understand the nature of the people it needs to be a prince, and to understand that of princes it needs to be of the people."

The best-positioned person to advise you on how to win the presidency is probably Karl Rove, but he doesn't dare help you openly (though whether he might help you quietly depends on the nominee of the GOP...more on this later.) Thus the very first transcript I include in Part IV is from Rove, and immediately after that, selections from conversations with Axelrod and Newt Gingrich, two other American political geniuses who, however flawed, won big when winning big was necessary. Every word of all those transcripts was selected from millions of words in my archive of 25 years of interviews, for you and your team. Bring a highlighter to Section IV.

I think you are shrewd enough to accept help from anyone if the advice or observation is actually helpful and not a poison pill, regardless of who provides the insight or the nudge. Whether or not my suggestions are poison pills will be for you to decide, but very few people know the base of the GOP better than the ten talk show hosts with at least a decade of experience talking with that base, and I don't see Rush, Sean, the Great One, Laura Ingraham, Glenn, Bill, Dennis, Michael or Mike stepping forward to help you. That leaves me, 15 years into the medium, 25 into broadcasting, and a veteran of the Reagan Era, even of his White House, a time long ago still fondly remembered as perhaps the last "great age" of America. It is the sort of era you would have named for you, I suspect.

There is no "first Clinton era" you care to recall, is there? Now the term "Clinton era" means that agonizing period of scandal and embarrassment, for which you have many paybacks to deliver. Oh, your husband amuses himself and the Democratic base by talking about the balanced budget, but we know the score. It was really about his pants and America's defenses towards al Qaeda being down, and his concessions on welfare reform and the numbers of pardons delivered as he waved what he thought was a last goodbye to the Oval Office. Marc Rich, well, there is a problem for the campaign.

A sorry record for an eight-year presidency, and one that began with a Democratic majority in both houses of Congress. No "HillaryCare" from them, but your husband did sign the now-reviled "Freedom Restoration Act" in 1993, which birthed the much-beloved-on-the-right *Hobby Lobby* Supreme Court decision in 2014, just as Bill signed the "Defense of Marriage Act" in 1996. He was for the modern equivalent of segregation—according to your party—before he was against it. Some presidency. As George Will said at the time, "He may not have been the worst president, but he was the worst man to ever hold the presidency." Some era.

There could be a "Hillary Era," however—a "second Clinton era," that would stand in quite a distinctly different category than your husband's puissant eight years of small beer, big headlines, and welfare reform. Oh, Bill is a gifted political act, like Neil Diamond is a gifted stage act, and like Diamond will always be welcome at Red Sox games. Bill can always get a labor crowd thumping.

But Reagan's death prompted an outpouring of genuine sadness and a shudder through the world such as passes only when one of the great ones dies. Nixon got the same shake, and not because of love, though there was from some much of that, but because of genuine significance. 41 won't. 43 will. 44 will get the respectful silence owed the office and an outpouring of affection from everyone who saw in his election the truth that in America anyone can become president. But achievements as president? Well, the eulogies will be short in that regard. One wonders if the Nobel Peace Prize will come up? The bottom line: If 45 wants to be the equal of 40, there are things that must be done.

To own "Clintonian" in the way Jackson owns "Jacksonian" and Jefferson owns "Jeffersonian," you will have to do big things. Not talk of them as Obama has done again and again. Things no one dreams of doing, but which could be done. You can do them. They would not be good for the Republicans as it would permanently end their role in American politics, and it is possible they would not be good for the Americans over 50 alive today, because they would be unsettling. But they might be good for the country long-term. If you wish to dominate an era as Reagan did, you have to steal from the other party their best parts and people, as Reagan did, as Nixon did. You have to co-opt. Certainly you cannot stick with the disastrous ideological choices of the Obama-Jarrett years. (And yes, you should begin to use that phrase about as soon as the ballots are in, perhaps having Bill do it before the Inauguration, and you thereafter. Not often. Just here and there, always with a smile.)

We begin at the beginning: The oldest rule of politics: Unify your side. Divide your opponents.

A newer rule of politics: Tell everyone exactly what you intend to do. (See Part III on "Transparency" for more details.)

Here, in five ideas, is what you should do, and what the GOP ought to be preparing to see you do (but won't, because they have never been much on the imagination front, have they?). And not just to win in 2016, but to establish a long, enduring—very, very, long enduring—second Clinton Era.

These five ideas/proposals would certainly form a core of your campaign that would make you unbeatable, so here are the five things I suggest you make central to your campaign:

1. A constitutional amendment abolishing the Electoral College and substituting in its place a direct election of the president by popular vote.

2. A constitutional amendment abolishing the two term limit on the presidency.

3. A constitutional amendment mandating that 5% of GDP be spent on the Pentagon's budget, with safeguards that the money actually be spent on soldiers, sailors, airmen and Marines and the equipment they need, and not on absurd "tack-ons" like "green energy" production for military bases. Rebuild the military and detach it from the GOP, and do so before a coup becomes a reality in the next forty years.

4. An ironclad commitment to massive development of our own energy resources, via fracking onshore and select development of new offshore resources, via out-of-sight platform drilling. Campaign on authorizing the Keystone XL Pipeline, once you have the nomination. What is Mr. Steyer going to do? Disown you? The left will think you're posturing. Some in the center will be seduced. Cite the statistic that for every energy job created, four are generated downstream of it. Sell the true statement that "Energy is freedom," and cite the knowledge you gained as Secretary of State of the Third World's desperate need for energy to alleviate poverty and power growth.

This will be the hardest of all the backflips you must accomplish, a full-throated embrace of the fossil fuels you are on record as saying are destroying the planet. And like Canadian figure skater Kevin Reynolds' first ever "double quad" on ice in a competitive event in 2010, it will be unprecedented and very difficult to seize a GOP core position and persuade your side it was necessary and indeed worth doing.

5. A near-complete amnesty for all illegal immigrants coupled with an ironclad commitment to the immediate construction of a long, double-sided, high fence covering at least half the length of the 2,000-mile, Mexican-American border. The GOP has long failed to understand how to make this dual commitment work, to see in it the easiest way to hit the sweet spot. To your supporters on the left assure them the gate in the fence will be wide. Open it soon after construction is complete. Then close it prior to 2020. Then open again thereafter. With the majorities you build in your demographic surge you can put forward the Constitutional amendment removing term-limits on the presidency.

Now that is a Clinton Era with genuine historic significance.

These five proposals would energize the left beyond any measure we have seen in the past (including the Obama '08 campaign), while peeling off the serious hawks and the biggest money interests of them all in the energy business. They would also effectively enlist nearly every Spanish-speaking American in your cause, yet give border-security conservatives the sole thing they have long asked for and been repeatedly denied by the establishment GOP, which fears building a long, strong, double-sided border fence because they believe it risks their being called racist. That fear of that branding is deeper within the GOP even than a fear of return to minority status in the House and Senate, which failure on border security will surely bring them.

To repeat: The oldest rule of politics: Unify your side. Divide your opponents.

A newer rule of politics: Tell everyone exactly what you intend to do.

I will come back to each of these five proposals in detail in a later chapter, but absorb them all in one big gulp for a moment and see what your reaction might be.

The left hates the Electoral College and sees in it a deeply unfair exclusion of concentrated minority votes in large, urban settings. Campaign for the fulfillment of one-person, one-vote, via an amendment. Let the GOP defend the work of a few hundred white landowners of the late-18th century, half of whom owned slaves and thought nothing of it.

Take up the record of FDR in his third and fourth term. Ask why Reagan ought to have been denied a third term (his disease did not manifest until late 1992, and old Reaganauts will love you for saying so). And why not Bill in 2000, or Barack in 2016? The old retainers of them will think, if only for a moment, back to what might have been, enjoying the emotional jolt of thinking that you are saying they would have won, enjoying the prospect of a comeback in the implication, unstated, that you would like some veterans of past eras around you.

You can rhetorically disqualify yourself from a third term in a gentle way. But do not make the amendment applicable only to those who follow you. Bring up your age and candidly suggest that even though you feel better than you ever have, Karl Rove's solicitous concerns aside, you won't know until 2024 what you'd like to do or not do. It is an older, smarter, healthier America, and you are too old, too smart and too healthy to say that if a moment needed a third term, you would not try for it. Seniors will love the idea that you are explicitly stating that 78 years old is not too old to be president, much less 70. Young people will admire your candid ambition balanced by your candid assessment of the very low likelihood of such an event. But even if many object, stand on the principle, which ought to be applicable to you: If it is good for the country, it is good for everyone who might be touched by the return to the original design. (Throwing a bone to the Framers, whose electoral college you are trashing at the same time.)

As for point three, defense hawks are deeply worried, and rightly so. Truth be told, they are in genuine play if Senator Rand Paul is on the ticket, and perhaps even Senator Ted Cruz. The officer corps—present and past—know how deep the president has cut. The folks who count nukes know what has happened to the deterrent. The folks who watch the PRC know what a regional hegemon is—a superpower about to push aside its old superior within four days sailing off its coast, and they know this is what the ChiComs have achieved on President Obama's watch—your watch.

So take a large slice of them from the GOP by committing the country to Defense Department budget seriousness, and destroy the GOP's hope to beat you with one stroke if Senaor Paul (and perhaps Senator Cruz) is the nominee or the Veep. (Senator Cruz appears to be moving to shield himself from this vulnerability even as Senator Rubio is being lifted on the public's deep and growing concern over safety, but Senator Paul remains a unique and to no small number of conservatives uniquely appealing candidate who easily has the "highest floor" of all the GOP field. He will never be swept from the field, the convention, or the headlines of the fall of 2016.)

To your friends you can explain there is much that can be done from within the Pentagon's budget that they would applaud, much that has been done for years. But if the cost of a huge majority is a few more aircraft carriers and nuclear submarines and a full complement of F-35s, then put them on the table. Secure the soccer moms, who are security moms first. Answer critics of Benghazi with an explanation they will accept and which will not injure you: That the military assets needed that night were not nearby and not available to come to the aid of the besieged.

Put on the table the rejection of the anti-energy absolutism of the left as well. Tom Steyer is your Sister Souljah, and he does not have to live in the heat of Mumbai without air-conditioning, which requires electricity, which requires nukes or coal, and he does not cook on open stoves in huts across Africa. Invite him to recognize that the American economy needs its own and Canada's oil and natural gas, the pipelines to bring it safely to refineries, new refinery capacity to make it useable, and new fields to exploit offshore before the PRC arrives with massive platforms off our own coast. Be an energy realist, and in one para-graph of an acceptance speech slow if not halve the rush of money from energy interests to the GOP. Give them pause, turn a few. Make it impossible to compete with your dollars. If you must wink at the Greens, don't let anyone see you do so, but in reality you will have to do this anyway. The only way to pay for the debt Barack ran up is with a severance tax on energy, and few will object when that is added to the package post-inauguration.

Now on the border fence you will find some loud opposition within your party, to which you reply "Hezbollah" with a knowing look. "We are not afraid of robust immigration from Mexico and Central and Southern America," you exclaim, "but four years with access to the highest classified intelligence available in the world has persuaded me of the absolute need for airtight border protection. We must have con-trol of the border in an era of the Islamic State longing for WMD that travel in small containers that can kill millions. We must be serious about traffickers in tunnels and terrorists entering via well-worn trails. Every passable mile of the 2,000-mile border must be addressed by using union labor to build a humane but effective, doubt-sided high fence, which does not end the threat but helps limit it. We must do other things as well, including freeing up ICE resources by regularizing the vast, vast majority of the 14 million here without documents. Those who do not step forward to accomplish regularization will be the few we want ICE to find and deport, and we will."

Defense spending, energy development and border security pro-vide you with a trio of "Nixon to China" initiatives that leave the GOP in shambles as it presses towards 2016, while your first two amendments give you the Clinton Era writ large. You will change the rules of the greatest game of all, the history of the Republic's fundamental law, and for what you will say is a "high purpose," which since you and Bill equate you and your family's destiny as the highest purpose will not be insincere so much as it is purposefully misleading. "Go big or go home" is the cliché, but it is a cliché with special import here.

Not for the cautious, but what did caution get you in 2008? What caution will get you in 2016 is scrutiny. And that you cannot afford. Read closely what David Axelrod told me in February of this year. Read and reread that transcript excerpt in Part IV. Dwell on the fact that it was Axelrod who rightly warned you against the "milk and cookies" fiasco of 1992, when you offended every stay-at-home mom in America. Now Axelrod is warning you against the warm embrace of the "Hillaryworld" cocoon. You need diversion and enthusiasm: the former away from your largest ambitions, the latter for your already boring campaign.

And you have been running the worst campaign in history to date—the awful memoir, the even worse book tour, the stilted, wooden appearances even with patsies from the left side of the already left-wing MSM. Three and out. Three and out. Three and out. Dull, dull, dull. And then there are the whispers of Elizabeth Warren growing every day, of any alternative, because you are old and boring. Stale. Past your "sell-by" date. Your "server" presser was the worst of any major figure in memory since Nixon's "I am not a crook," and your semi-annual tweets are making you look as foolish as a ninety-year old trying to Skype.

So, change everything when you give a Fourth of July speech in 2015, and again as you approach Iowa, and again on the stage in Philadelphia. Again and again, shock the electorate, and get the journos back on their toes at your appearances and talking late into the night in the bars: "What will she say next?"

About the server, all you can say—in a variety of ways and often beginning immediately—is this:

> "The public knows the difference between private and public and
> the public trusts me. The right wing nutters don't, but the public
> does. I won't be bullied, browbeaten or berated by every would be
> Javert on the Fox News Channel. Read my lips: It was fine to have
> the server. Fine to delete my own personal emails. Legal to act as
> I did and actually prudent to do so given the crazies who seem to

breed in the dark corners of the world with increasingly sophisticated means of stealing everything online that isn't deleted. The advantage of having been around the block in D.C. and around the world as Secretary of State is I know my opponents domestically and my enemies abroad, and I will not—will not—let them dictate my life, my campaign and certainly not the security of the United States."

This rhetoric is playing a pair of fours as though they were a straight flush, but it is your only play. If sustained focus attaches to the peril in which you placed the country by running your "homebrew," well then your goose is cooked. You know that the PRC, Putin, the mullahs and the nut in North Korea probably have every single email you sent or received from that server, but they will play a game of waiting until you are in 1600 to float them, and you won't hesitate to send a message back, "big time" as Dick Cheney would say. That is actually your appeal to some on my side.

But if a conservative operative did the dirty deed and pilfered your private server's files before you purged them? Well then W's DUI in 2000 is going to seem like a very small speed bump compared to what you will hit when early voting begins in 2016 and the bad actors drop your private emails into the world wide inner tubes. You have no choice but to pretend this threat doesn't exist and persuade everyone in Democrat land that it is a fantasy novel, an episode from *House of Cards* deemed too far out even for Netflix watchers.

In the meantime, the best defense is a hurry-up offense. Get going on the substance of your campaign, the really big ticket items, and go bold. And that begins by addressing your greatest known weakness. (The server and its ripple effects go into the category of what Rumsfeld would call "known unknowns." Much as you might hate to do so, you really ought to read Rumsfeld's Rules. The man knows his way around D.C. and his advice is non-partisan.)

CHAPTER 2

Your Greatest Weakness

You were a failure at the State Department, and you know this better than anyone else, save perhaps Bill. President Obama is nothing if not capable of hiding the truth from himself so he won't bring this up as it implicates his abysmal record. And no senior Democrat will breathe a word of your failure within earshot of you or anyone with any conceivable access to you. You are surrounded by flatterers, who want position in your administration. No one, except perhaps Bill, will bluntly discuss with you just how bad a hash you made of it.

Benghazi was just the pinnacle of your incompetence, but it tops the mountain of mistakes you have made and draws attention to them all: Russia, China, Egypt, Syria, Libya, Venezuela, Haiti, Honduras, but especially Iran. All a hashed-up series of improvisations based on a general theory that if you were not part of W's gang of bullies, everyone would like you, that Putin and Medvedev just needed some attention, the PRC some charming, the Arab nations a dose of freedom to become mini-Israels. You believed that "Twitter Revolution" nonsense, even after the mullahs in Teheran sent their shock troops out in scooters to mow down the Green Revolution demonstrators.

You should have known early on that the president would mishandle every convulsion, ignore every ally, treat with every "new force" he could tell himself owed it all to him. The Nobel Peace Prize for a rank amateur who had never handled one crisis much less negotiated a successful end to a war served only to inflate an already dirigible-sized ego and lead the amateur into catastrophe after catastrophe. How that medal must have galled Bill. How that record now burdens you.

Because you didn't put up a fight. You went along for the ride. Racking up the miles, doing nice work for women and girls in most places and doing your best not to let Barack cut and run on the women and girls in Afghanistan, Iraq, Iran and especially Syria, where they are dead now by the tens of thousands.

What a mess. *Hard Choices*, indeed. Disastrous choices. Deadly choices that grow more obvious in their terrible consequences with every beheading and burning video from the Islamic State and every body bag in the Ukraine.

Then you compounded the problem with an insipid, cliché-filled pyramid of dense text, and made a screeching audiobook of it, a fountain of material for your enemies. If Webb runs against you (be very attentive to an attack from that quarter as he isn't remotely like your ordinary politician) he will be giving out copies of your audiobook. I have been playing segments for months, like every talk show host plays your laugh track. You know how hideous your voice and your laugh is, but you know as well you cannot change your voice and your laugh. So you recognize it for one of the things that cannot be changed, and you blame it on genes and habit. But for God's sake minimize it. Fire the audiobook genius.

Here is exactly what you must do with your record at State as soon as the field is cleared and Joe Biden dispatched and every other pretender—save Webb, who will have to be beaten thoroughly or perhaps promised the Pentagon as Secretary of Defense early on. You will have to blame it all — not what you inherited in the form of the Bush wars and the worldwide economic panic—but all that followed January 2009, the endless series of foreign policy fiascos, on the president's epically incompetent staff, especially Valerie Jarrett.

About the Bush wars, these will have a political benefit for you still if you are accurate about the record. Know the numbers of troops deployed in each theater on day one of your tenure, the casualty count when you took over (and since), the dollar cost, the loss of civilian life in Iraq, even the incipient rumbles of revolution in Syria as you took over Foggy Bottom. Many within the GOP will welcome the recounting of the failures of foreign adventures, and as the Rand Paul forces will almost certainly have been vanquished in the GOP primary, they will find much to cheer in your calibrated blasts at W's invasions. If you have followed the advice in chapter one and adopted recommendation three, you will have nicely fed the hawks with promises of future resources, while stroking the feathers of the neo-isolationist doves with references to where "adventurism" leads and leaves the country.

So you "embraced the suck" while at State and did what you could. Yes, your own staff botched the reset button, but for everything else point to Jarrett's insanely jealous and amateurish approach to Holbrooke and everyone else on your team that effectively neutered every one of your initiatives. You will have to hang her out to dry, a narrative the Democrats will want, but one that must be done ever so carefully as I discuss below. You cannot ever cut off the president as McCain did Bush in 2008. We know that W did not exactly suffer as McCain floundered in the last two months of the campaign. We both know W actually thought the country would be better served by the best possible Barack than by the almost certain McCain. I know because he told a group of talkers on the last Wednesday of his presidency to go easy on the new guy—that the new president would grow into the job. Like his initial assessment of Putin, W's initial assessment of Obama was far, far off the mark. W's greatest fault was his always generous assessment of people and motives. This won't of course hobble you, but it hobbled him.

You can't allow yourself to be blamed for President Obama's utter lack of skills. Sarah Palin was better equipped to take on the management of the world than this bumbler, and you know that to be true. Increasingly, the country understands it as the position of the country slips further and further into chaos and irrelevance.

President Obama's incompetence and the damage it has done to the country and indeed the world is the anvil around your neck. How to break it, especially after that awful book you put your name on?

First, break it. Make a big speech detailing the failures of the past three years, contrasting them with the failures of the first four years, and urging people to do the math. If you and Gates and Jones hadn't been there, if the D-Team had been in charge from day one, who knows what would be facing us now? You kept the sanctions on Iran as long as you could. You wanted a Status of Forces agreement with Iraq, a long term commitment to the Afghans, and would have supported striking Assad, but for Jarrett, Jarrett, Jarrett and her Rasputin-like hold on an insecure, in-over-his-head president. That's the ticket. That's the position you will have to take in the months after the nomination is secure and the foreign fires rage out of control.

And the memoir? You will have to explain it succinctly. It was necessary to help minimize the damage and the danger. The world could not know with 30 months left on the ticker just how detached and incompetent this president is. You tried with the memoir—again—to buck him up. Again. You are hesitant to discuss it further even now for the transition to capable hands is still six months away. But help is on the way. The A-Team, the Kosovo/Balkans team,t is coming. Bill is coming. Holbrooke is dead but there are scores of competent foreign policy pros who were locked out by Valerie. This time there won't be a hack in the West Wing pulling the strings and insisting on Secret Service protection. Jarrett drove out Rahm, then Pete Rouse, then Bill Daley, then Jack Lew, then Robert Gates. You and Panetta held out the longest, as long as you could, and tried to keep the curtain down with the heaviest of velvet folds with your memoir, but now the truth must be told.

You cannot completely turn on Obama until Obama is turned out. But you can let it be known that the truth is not flattering. Especially the truth about Benghazi, the truth you have never spoken, but which you have never have been asked to reveal either. Take credit for intimidating the GOP and the Manhattan-Beltway media elite, but set up your telling. You cannot dismount the campaign and stick the landing with a broken leg, no matter the miracle of the Japanese Olympian from 1992.

You will have to deal with Benghazi. Here is how you do it: Blame the president. Tell everyone he and his team made every call that night. Valerie. Valerie. Valerie. It will, to borrow from Kissinger, "have the added benefit of being true."

CHAPTER 3

What to do about Bill, Now and Later

This is the question you face every day, but you must make one choice about how to deal with it and how to answer it in public, and then stick with that answer. Announce your decision and—at least until the end of the campaign—stand by it. Repeat it often. Make sure you have provided the voters clarity. They can accept whatever you decide, but not ambiguity on what everyone knows is a core issue.

With regards to Bill, you have three choices.

You can tell people he will have no role other than that which you served in his administration: a trusted advisor handling ad hoc matters as needed, perhaps as an emissary to the Middle East, or as a companion to Barack and W in raising funds for the inevitable disaster relief efforts.

You could also tell them that Bill will have a defined role and then define it. Again, you might make good use of him as your Secretary of State—unusual, but perfectly acceptable. And very few talented people will accept the job anyway given Bill's penchant for the spotlight and his almost certain thrusting of himself into every controversy.

Finally, you can say he will effectively be co-president, much as Gerald Ford and Ronald Reagan once briefly negotiated such a plan when Ford had defeated Reagan for the 1976 GOP nomination and was attempting to hold the future president in the then-current president's arc of influence.

You should make your choice of options one, two or three based solely on what increases the likelihood of your election. Without winning, it is all academic. After winning, it can be changed. On election night, if you would like, though that would not be prudent assuming you want a second term. If you carry any secret desire to humble him as he once humbled you, it will have to be on election night 2020, not election night 2016, and by then your grandchild (perhaps grandchildren, may you be so blessed) will probably hold you back from that—and Chelsea's future as well. You can write a book, one to be published only when your youngest grandchild is 30, if you want to humble him.

But as for getting elected, it seems to me that your best choice is your third choice, for this is what a crucial part of the electorate will want, and while some will resent it—hard-left feminists, for example—they will have no choice but to accept it and learn later that the perfect exercise of the feminist ideal is to use the man to win the office, then use the man to keep the office and indeed change the office in a way he never could or did. To surpass his "achievements," and by not a small margin—that will satisfy the feminists, and history.

So, how to tell people of your intention on this score? A formal speech, one that people will refer to even as they refer to, say, George W. Bush's "We meet here in the middle hour of our grief" speech at the National Cathedral following the attack of 9/11, or FDR's "We have nothing to fear but fear itself," or Richard Nixon's "Checkers" speech as a candidate for the vice presidency in 1952 or RN's "Great Silent Majority" speech in the middle of the Vietnam War. The speech in which you announce Bill's future role should be associated with a place and given at a time in the campaign—early fall of 2015, or even later, say January 2, 2016—when it does not seem a desperate move, but a calculated one.

I suggest Seneca Falls for obvious reasons. At the place where women gathered to launch their demand for political equality, you will speak about sharing power with a man, even though a well-crafted address will leave no doubt about who will be in charge.

And I suggest a specific time: about a month before the first ballot is cast in Iowa soon after the New Year's Eve hangovers are gone and the media bigs are back behind their desks. The mess Barack has made of nearly everything requires that you show a willingness to do new things, bold things, and the practical consequences of this timing will be to impact—indeed overwhelm—all other political messaging cresting towards the new election season. If you announce beforehand that the new year will begin with a new speech about a new approach, all of December will be frozen and not just by the weather and ordinary holiday activities. Every political reporter will be asking "What will she do with Bill?" By promising them an answer at a set time, you will effectively freeze the campaign for a crucial period of the time. But the timing is only a bonus. The real benefit is in the many messages you will deliver that night.

On that day—announce the speech and reserve the venue for 8 p.m. eastern—have an aide first enter and place a chair next to the lectern from which you will speak to a crowd of all women and from which you will not move until the end of your remarks, and then have the aide exit. Allow the commentators to chatter and anticipation to build. Then enter alone to sustained applause. Bask in it. Glory in being a woman in Seneca Falls on her way to the nomination.

At the end of the applause, thank the audience. Then smile and simply say, "No, this chair isn't for Clint Eastwood," and allow the laughter and standing ovation to roll on and on. When it quiets, say the chair is for the most important man in my life and the man who reclaimed two term presidencies for the Democrats for the first time since FDR, Bill Clinton."

Then Bill will enter to rapturous applause, you two will embrace, kiss and wave. This will bring the house down, and you should hold the moment as long as possible.

Then, with Bill still standing next to you, you say "Have a seat honey." He will look abashed, people will shriek with laughter and applause, and then as only the master theater man could, Bill will look amused, shrug his shoulders, tilt his head to you and sit. He will not say a word this night.

And here are the words I think you should speak:

"Friends, I have come here, to this place, to briefly address a very large question: What should a woman do with her husband when she is the president and he has been the president?

"It is a serious question, going as it does to a central principal of American constitutional government: accountability. The Framers intended one man—and it was most definitely a man then—to be accountable for the operation of the executive branch. If he failed, he was to be impeached. My husband has some experience with that process. (Nervous laughter to be expected. You smile and so does he.)

Now, I am seeking that office, and believe of all Americans I am best prepared to exercise its duties. One has to believe this to run for the job or one is irresponsible. The job is too great, the times too dangerous, to seek the office for reasons of vanity or gain or simple fame. You have to believe that you are the best qualified eligible person on the planet.

"It may be that Bill or Barack are better qualified than I to hold this job again. This possibility is one reason why, as you have heard me say in another place, that I will seek the repeal of the Constitution's two-term limit, never intended by the Framers, but put there by Republicans jealous of FDR after that great American's death. We needed FDR in 1944. We could have used Bill in 2000. Oh, could we have used Bill in 2000? But neither Bill nor Barack are eligible, and I believe myself more qualified than my friend Joe and my other friends who seek the job. The voters will decide.

"But Bill here gives me a particular advantage that I wish to discuss today as well as a source of some concern for many Americans. They do not like him, in some cases. For others, they like me more than Bill and feel Bill will overpower my views. They worry that I will be overshadowed or somehow diminished.

"Let me tell you straight out. I will be president and not Bill. But he will be the second most powerful person in the government—more powerful than my vice president, more powerful than

my secretary of state, more powerful than my attorney general or
the leaders of my party in the Congress. In this flat, firm declaration I am leveling with you and I hope you honor this candor with
consideration of my argument.

"Bill simply knows more about governing in a constitutional
manner than anyone else I know well enough to rely upon with
absolute certainty of straightforward advice and with an absolute
guarantee that he will be there when I need him. President Obama
has served nobly and well, and his family deserves the time he
owes them now. His daughters are no doubt going to be as happy
as Chelsea was when her dad finally got to be a full-time dad to
her, even though college loomed. I know I can rely on President
Obama for advice.

"And I know I can rely on President Bush for the same. We do
not often agree. But we do agree on the greatest men and women
of this country, the extraordinary bravery and sacrifice of the men
and women who serve it, and of the need for strength abroad and
principled, transparent decision-making at home. President Bush
can ride a mountain bike better than I, but I think I can deliver the
average speech with a touch more flare than he. We will see. He is
a friend, though not a political ally. And if I am inducted into the
presidents' club, I will call on him.

"Strong women do not fear the advice of strong men, or
of strong women. Golda Meir, Margaret Thatcher, Michelle
Obama—each of these amazing women never hesitated to seek the
best counsel as they made their way through intensely challenging
public lives.

"And neither will I, which brings me back to Bill.

"Bill will in fact be a co-president in all but title and official duties. If I am elected, Bill won't be able to sign—or veto—bills Congress sends me, or to order even one troop to take one step. But he
will be my right arm and my very strong right arm. He will speak
for me, and if and when he gets that speaking wrong (and that will
surely happen as no one truly can channel another's thoughts 24/7),
I will correct the record but be clear in doing so that Bill Clinton

remains my right arm, far above my other advisors, far above the role any First Spouse has filled, save perhaps Edith Wilson when she acted in secret.

"There will be no secret acting here. I am leveling with you now so that no one can later say I did other than this. My Seneca Falls speech on Bill will be a reminder to you all that when I send him to sit opposite Vladimir Putin or any other world leader, he does so with an authority unique in American history at least since Harry Hopkins traveled the globe for FDR. And that will be a very good thing.

"Thank you and see you in Des Moines!"

CHAPTER 4

The Islamist Radicals and Your Response

Would that you could collect and burn every copy of Lawrence Wright's *The Looming Tower*, the most important book written since 9/11 about 9/11, by a credentialed man of the left and superstar of *The New Yorker*. The book is a triple indictment of your candidacy.

First, it illumines in minute detail the many and repeated failures of your husband to see the growing threat looming throughout his presidency. The evidence of al Qaeda's plans was always there in the open, declared repeatedly by bin Laden and Zawahiri—published openly, repeated often and with emphasis. Your husband's national security "team" was as inept and toothless as his legal and political team arrayed against Ken Starr was brilliant and ruthless. All of his incompetence comes flowing out in an accelerating avalanche of damning detail. 9/11 was his fault. Wright knows it. Any reader of *The Looming Tower* knows it.

Of course not many Americans have read it, even though it won the Pulitzer, even though Wright is a man of the left, as credentialed as possible for left-wingers given his lofty perch at *The New Yorker*. How he came to write this book-length indictment has never failed to surprise me. His integrity must be absolute. How your husband must hate him for constructing this damning narrative.

But that is only the first part of the problem the book presents. The second part is that it was in print and highly praised before you began your tenure at State. Everything you needed to know was there, in print, in every bookshop in America. If you have ever read this book, you have given no sign. You aren't much of a reader to begin with, especially not of books with the name Lewinsky in the index. Wright does not dwell on that unfortunate affair or the pain it caused you, but his integrity obliged him to note that many in the Muslim world judged your husband's orders to attack Sudan and Afghanistan in the aftermath of the African embassies bombings to be an effort to simply divert attention from his mistress's exposure.

However uncomfortable some sections are, the book is so necessary and so compelling and so available and so praised that for you not to have read and absorbed its lessons—well, that is the second strike. You avoided learning what needed to be learned after 9/11, even though you represented New York, even though you lived in DC, even though you accepted the job of secretary of state. Malpractice on this level is stunning. How could you allow yourself to be so careless about the inner workings of one of our five deadliest enemies (the others being Iran, the PRC, Russia and North Korea)? Sunni fundamentalism expressed in taqfiri jihadism is frightening, but you swore an oath. If the public becomes aware of your laziness in responding to the attacks of 9/11 and in preparing to lead Foggy Bottom, it will be hard to defend.

The third strike is your pathetic response to the Arab Spring in Egypt, Libya and throughout the Arab world. You really did act the fool. *A video?* When we deal with responding to Benghazi later, we can cover in more detail that specific collapse of credibility, but *The Looming Tower* lays bare your ignorance of the enemy as late as September of 2012.

So, what to do?

First, of course: read the book, a few times. Know the names. Master the narrative of Qutb and bin Laden. Have at your fingertips the specifics of the missed opportunities to foil the 9/11 attack. Understand and be able to recount all of the many dysfunctions of your husband's regime.

Now, here is the key. Invite Wright to dinner, and in the presence of some friendly journalists. Off the record, of course. But let it be known that you know his work. Co-opt the New York media elite even more profoundly than they already are co-opted by demonstrating an attachment to work of the caliber of Wright.

This cadre of key influencers is not enormous: Remnick, Kristof, Friedman and a few others. Break bread with them and talk knowingly of the difficulty of balancing the realities of Wright's research with the necessity of protecting our Saudi friends. Refer without specifics to the host of compromises that must be made to maintain the fragile networks of scattered agents of influence. Pretend, in other words, to have long ago read and absorbed all this knowledge Wright provided, and to have been acting on it as only a seasoned and far-seeing diplomat could have.

Condemn the lassitude of your husband's era. Hint, even, that Bush could not be blamed for the mess he was handed. Imply again and again how you tried, again and again, to get President Obama to at least allocate 30 minutes to this specific threat, but that his vision of a remade world around a rapprochement with Iran mediated by Turkey and/or Egypt killed your attempts to bring some realism to his flights of Nobel Prize-induced fantasy.

Bluntly declare yourself to have been foiled in the effort to combine the reality of Bush's backbone and almost animal understanding of threat with the deftness of Kissinger-like sophistication in dealing with our triple-faced "allies," only to be burdened with an incompetent amateur as your boss. "Recall the worst editor you ever had. . ." and trail off, allowing them to fill in the blanks and thus establish Obama in their minds as the problem of the past eight years.

The president's time is almost past. Your *New Yorker* friends will not miss him. He did not deliver for them, not even an occasional dinner. He golfs! He does not read! He is in their collective view—shudder— not very smart, but smart enough to have fooled them all. Conned, they will be willing to abet your rewrite of the Wright gap.

Boldness here matters, and not just with Wright, but with every intellectual of standing who knew scores before they were posted. This was a great strength of W.'s. He dined-in with writers: Jay Winik, Victor Davis Hanson. Yes, even Wright. The Beltway press could never bring itself to the collective admission of an intellectual curiosity vastly superior to that of Obama's and near the equal of your husband's though not so eclectic. Bush focused on war as you ought to have done, and now must pretend to have done.

It will work. But you must get started.

After Wright, you must pursue and seduce—always with the court scribblers close at hand—the very best writers on the long war: Robin Wright, Robert Kaplan, Dexter Filkins. These are three of the more serious people who saw it all unfolding, who traveled the world to get a first-hand glimpse. They are admired on my side as well as yours. Bring them in. Sit them down. Read their books or at least summaries prepared by eager interns, but best to actually read them. Add to their number the greatest foreign correspondent of our era, the *New York Times'* John Fisher Burns. Have Burns come from London, or better, go to him on the obligatory trip to our most important ally. Be seen as knowing—in the eyes of the Manhattan-Beltway media elite and the conservative intelligentsia both—who realizes the score on the war.

Add to the list Jessica Stern and J.M. Berger, whose *ISIS: The State of Terror* seems likely to be the book of choice for those in your party who will want to at least pretend to have read something on the rise of this al Qaeda variant that makes the first generation fanatics seem almost civilized by comparison.

This is the secret to a successful presidency. There are people who know how the real world works, who have records of anticipating its evolution, and who have written and thought about these things. They will all come to you. They will all tell you what you ought to already know but don't. It is so easy to acquire what you need and to insist that it be delivered in whatever form you find most fitting.

Imagine asking for 30-minute lectures by such authors as these, with dinner guests of the sort named. Ask and obtain the right to videotape, for your library— and perhaps for use at a key, crucial moment in the campaign—the evidence of your studiousness on the subject of the greatest fear.

You flunked State Department 101. Now you must persuade people that you have made up for the error. Get started.

CHAPTER 5

"Huma"

A book that tiptoes past your hardest problems does you no good. This chapter will sting, and will produce some false controversy. I expect you to denounce it, but you should follow its advice.

I suggest before you read this you revisit the July 30, 2013, *Politico* story by Andrea Drusch entitled "How Close Are Huma Abedin and Hillary Clinton," which begins:

> "As a student at The George Washington University in 1996, Huma Abedin began working as a White House intern assigned to then first lady Hillary Clinton. The two have been together since, with Abedin traveling the country as Clinton's "bodywoman" throughout her 2008 Democratic Presidential nomination campaign. She later became Clintons's deputy chief-of-staff at the State Department, and still works for her transitional team, assisting the former secretary of state's move back into her private life. Here's 17 pictures that describe their 17 years together so far."

Anyone who scrolls through the pictures will instantly and forever understand that Huma is indeed "your second daughter" as she has often been described. She is known as that, and also as the tortured, deeply humiliated wife of sociopath Anthony Weiner. The latter status might even make her sympathetic and thus more useful to your cause, and even help explain your closeness as she has suffered the same sort of public humiliation that you have, a sort of humiliation that puts iron into the soul even as it floods red into the cheeks.

If she was just the unofficial second daughter and the shattered, but-stronger-for-it good wife as well as hyper-competent experienced aide, Huma would be a valued member of the team. But you and I and indeed hundreds already know the problem. And soon thousands will, and in the course of the campaign, millions. She could cost you the election. She must be out until after you are in, and in a very public way. First, just to let you know the most precise statement of your problem, I have obtained permission from Andrew McCarthy and the *National Review* to reprint the entirety of McCarthy's article—"The Huma Unmentionables,"—from July 23, 2013, which appeared only a week before the *Politico* slide show of your inseparability.

McCarthy is no crank, though you will have to paint him as one. He prosecuted and convicted the "Blind Sheik." He is among the most knowledgeable of Americans on the Islamist threat, and he has a standing that while it can be dented and smeared, cannot be destroyed because he is a good man, a fantastic lawyer, an experienced prosecutor and a steady television and radio presence.

The "Charlotte" that McCarthy refers to in the key article printed below is Charlotte Hays, a *National Review* writer disgusted by Huma's resolute backing of her husband's bizarre sexting behavior. Charlotte had written a short post, "Abedin Goes For The Power Save," that read in its entirety:

> "The star of Anthony Weiner's press conference yesterday was the sexting mayoral aspirant's wife Huma Abedin. Abedin didn't just stand by her man. While Carlos Danger, as he calls himself when sending lewd messages to women, cowered, Abedin took the mike and publicly forgave her husband for his transgressions, including the latest in the news. Just so you know what Ms. Abedin is publicly forgiving, Mark has linked to the relevant material. I'd like to think a good wife would have urged Weiner to call it quits. What was clear, at least to this observer, however, is that Abedin had a mission beyond common decency: the preservation of a power couple's political viability. The former Hillary Clinton aide had no shame.

Abedin has won accolades from sympathetic Democrats and has no doubt ensured her own political future, elective or appointive, if not that of her ludicrous husband. It was a moment when one glimpsed the raw ambition of today's New Class political culture. I say: Bring back Silda Spitzer, who merely stood in pained shame as her husband confessed his hooker habit. But shame is so yesterday. If Abedin wants to forgive her husband, that's fine by me, though next time—and there will be a next time—I beg her to do it in private. She has given standing by your man a bad name."

McCarthy then posted in response to Hays the detailed article reproduced in its entirety below, and the exchange between Hays and McCarthy anticipates the broader narrative struggle that will define your campaign should Huma be a part of your inner circle now or during the presidency. Someone will raise the Hays complaint of Huma and Weiner, and someone else will write: "That's nothing, what about her Brotherhood ties?" In the era of the Islamic State, the second narrative is the killer, especially given your ineptitude on all matters Muslim during your tenure at State. Read McCarthy's piece carefully, and ask yourself—really ask yourself—what will voters think when it is read repeatedly aloud over network television and talk radio, emailed to millions and millions again and again? It was written *before* IS began its rampage. It is the time bomb:

"Charlotte's revulsion over Huma Abedin's calculated 'stand by your man' routine is surely right. Still, it is amazing, as we speculate about Ms. Abedin's political future, that the elephant in the room goes unnoticed, or at least studiously unmentioned.

Sorry to interrupt the Best Enabler of a Sociopath Award ceremony but, to recap, Ms. Abedin worked for many years at a journal that promotes Islamic-supremacist ideology that was founded by a top al-Qaeda financier, Abdullah Omar Naseef. Naseef ran the Rabita Trust, a formally designated foreign terrorist organization under American law. Ms. Abedin and Naseef overlapped at the *Journal of Muslim Minority Affairs (JMMA)* for at least seven years.

Throughout that time (1996–2003), Ms. Abedin worked for Hillary Clinton in various capacities. Ms. Abedin's late father, Dr. Zyed Abedin, was recruited by Naseef to run the *JMMA* in Saudi Arabia. The journal was operated under the management of the World Assembly of Muslim Youth, a virulently anti-Semitic and sharia-supremacist organization. When Dr. Abedin died, editorial control of the journal passed to his wife, Dr. Saleha Mahmood Abedin — Huma's mother.

Saleha Abedin is closely tied to the Muslim Brotherhood and to supporters of violent jihad. Among other things, she directs an organization – the International Islamic Committee for Woman and Child. The IICWC, through its parent entity (the International Islamic Council for Dawa and Relief), is a component of the Union for Good (also known as the Union of Good), another formally designated terrorist organization. The Union for Good is led by Sheikh Yusuf al-Qaradawi, the notorious Muslim Brotherhood jurist who has issued fatwas calling for the killing of American military and support personnel in Iraq as well as suicide bombings in Israel. (As detailed here, the Obama White House recently hosted Qaradawi's principal deputy, Sheikh Abdulla bin Bayyah, who also endorsed the fatwa calling for the killing of U.S. troops and personnel in Iraq.)

Like Sheikh Qaradawi, who helped write the charter for the IICWC, Saleha Abedin is an influential sharia activist who has, for example, published a book called *Women in Islam* that claims man-made laws enslave women. It reportedly provides sharia justifications for such practices as female-genital mutilation, the death penalty for apostates from Islam, the legal subordination of women, and the participation of women in violent jihad. Dr. Abedin has nevertheless been hailed in the progressive press as a "leading voice on women's rights in the Muslim world" (to quote *Foreign Policy*). What they never quite get around to telling you is that this means 'women's rights' in the repressive sharia context.

Back to daughter Huma. In the late mid to late Nineties, while she was an intern at the Clinton White House and an assistant

editor at *JMMA*, Ms. Abedin was a member of the executive board
of the Muslim Students Association (MSA) at George Washington
University, heading its "Social Committee." The MSA, which has
a vast network of chapters at universities across North America, is
the foundation of the Muslim Brotherhood's infrastructure in the
United States. Obviously, not every Muslim student who joins the
MSA graduates to the Brotherhood—many join for the same social
and networking reasons that cause college students in general to
join campus organizations. But the MSA does have an indoctrina-
tion program, which Sam Tadros describes as a lengthy process
of study and service that leads to Brotherhood membership — a
process "designed to ensure with absolute certainty that there is
conformity to the movement's ideology and a clear adherence to its
leadership's authority." The MSA gave birth to the Islamic Society
of North America (ISNA), the largest Islamist organization in the
U.S. Indeed the MSA and ISNA consider themselves the same organization. Because of its support for Hamas (a designated terrorist
organization that is the Muslim Brotherhood's Palestinian branch),
ISNA was named an unindicted co-conspirator in the *Holy Land
Foundation* case, in which several Hamas operatives were convicted
of providing the terrorist organization with lavish financing.

As I've recounted before, the MSA chapter to which Ms.
Abedin belonged at George Washington University has an in-
triguing history. In 2001 [to be clear, that is after Ms. Abedin
had graduated from GWU], its spiritual guide was . . . Anwar
al-Awlaki, the al-Qaeda operative who was then ministering to
some of the eventual 9/11 suicide-hijackers. Awlaki himself had
led the MSA chapter at Colorado State University in the early
nineties. As Patrick Poole has demonstrated, Awlaki is far from
the only jihadist to hone his supremacist ideology in the MSA's
friendly confines. In the eighties, Wael Jalaidan ran the MSA at
the University of Arizona. He would soon go on to help Osama
bin Laden found al-Qaeda; he also partnered with the Abedin
family's patron, Abdullah Omar Naseef, to establish the [afore-

mentioned] Rabita Trust—formally designated as a terrorist organization under U.S. law due to its funding of al-Qaeda.

Ms. Abedin served as one of Secretary of State Clinton's top staffers and advisers at the State Department. As I've previously detailed, during that time, the State Department strongly supported abandoning the federal government's prior policy against official dealings with the Muslim Brotherhood. State, furthermore, embraced a number of Muslim Brotherhood positions that undermine both American constitutional rights and our alliance with Israel. To name just a few manifestations of this policy sea change:

- The State Department had an emissary in Egypt who trained operatives of the Brotherhood and other Islamist organizations in democracy procedures.
- The State Department announced that the Obama administration would be 'satisfied' with the election of a Muslim Brotherhood–dominated government in Egypt.
- Secretary Clinton personally intervened to reverse a Bush-administration ruling that barred Tariq Ramadan, grandson of the Brotherhood's founder and son of one of its most influential early leaders, from entering the United States.
- The State Department collaborated with the Organization of Islamic Cooperation, a bloc of governments heavily influenced by the Brotherhood, in seeking to restrict American free-speech rights in deference to sharia proscriptions against negative criticism of Islam.
- The State Department excluded Israel, the world's leading target of terrorism, from its 'Global Counterterrorism Forum,' a group that brings the United States together with several Islamist governments, prominently including its co-chair, Turkey—which now finances Hamas and avidly supports the flotillas that seek to break Israel's blockade of Hamas. At the forum's kickoff, Secretary Clinton decried various terrorist attacks and groups; but she did not mention Hamas or attacks against Israel — in transparent deference to the Islamist governments, which echo the Brotherhood's position that Hamas is not a terrorist organization and that attacks

against Israel are not terrorism.

- The State Department and the Obama administration waived congressional restrictions in order to transfer $1.5 billion dollars in aid to Egypt after the Muslim Brotherhood's victory in the parliamentary elections.

- The State Department and the Obama administration waived congressional restrictions in order to transfer millions of dollars in aid to the Palestinian territories notwithstanding that Gaza is ruled by the terrorist organization Hamas, the Muslim Brotherhood's Palestinian branch.

- The State Department and the administration hosted a contingent from Egypt's newly elected parliament that included not only Muslim Brotherhood members but a member of the Islamic Group (Gamaa al-Islamiyya), which is formally designated as a foreign terrorist organization. The State Department refused to provide Americans with information about the process by which it issued a visa to a member of a designated terrorist organization, about how the members of the Egyptian delegation were selected, or about what security procedures were followed before the delegation was allowed to enter our country.

- On a trip to Egypt, Secretary Clinton pressured General Mohamed Hussein Tantawi, head of the military junta then governing the country, to surrender power to the parliament dominated by the Muslim Brotherhood, and the then–newly elected president, Mohamed Morsi, a top Brotherhood official. She also visited with Morsi; immediately after his victory, Morsi had proclaimed that his top priorities included pressuring the United States to release the Blind Sheikh. Quite apart from the Brotherhood's self-proclaimed 'grand jihad' to destroy the United States . . . the group's supreme guide, Mohammed Badie, publicly called for jihad against the United States in an October 2010 speech. After it became clear the Brotherhood would win the parliamentary election, Badie said the victory was a stepping stone to 'the establishment of a just Islamic caliphate.'

As more recent events remind us, this is not an exhaustive account of Obama-administration coziness with the Muslim Brotherhood. It is just some of the lowlights.

When a handful of House conservatives tried to draw the attention of the State Department's Inspector General to some of these matters—wondering how on earth someone with Ms. Abedin's background could have qualified for a top-secret security clearance—they were castigated by the Obama White House and the Beltway Republican establishment. As reaffirmed in the last 24 hours, Ms. Abedin's connections to prominent Islamic-supremacist figures and groups are deemed unsuitable for public discussion— Egyptians may be able to eject the Muslim Brotherhood. But in today's Washington, it is raising questions about the Muslim Brotherhood that gets you run out of town.

Naturally, what did get Washington chattering was a scandal far more typical in Clinton circles—the lucrative arrangement Ms. Abedin struck with Mrs. Clinton's State Department that allowed her, after returning from maternity leave, to draw a $135,000 ... salary while remaining in New York, not actually working at Foggy Bottom, and moonlighting as a 'strategic consultant' for an outfit called Teneo–founded by Bill Clinton's chum Doug Band. What a racket. The marriage to Huma Abedin, a Clinton insider, enables Anthony Weiner to resurrect a debased career and deflect attention from his psychotic antics even as he continues them. The marriage to Anthony Weiner, a prominent Jewish progressive, enables Huma Abedin to deflect attention from her associations with various Islamic supremacists even as, during her tenure as a top State Department official, American policy embraces Islamic supremacists.

But let's not discuss that.

A note for your campaign team: You must begin the discrediting of Andrew McCarthy immediately, and scream whenever and at whoever books him that he is a bigoted anti-Muslim and a crank. Of course he is not. He is the man who put the Blind Sheik away for good and knows the subject area of Islamist radicalism better than anyone. He is, in short, the best sort of patriot. But this is the sort of article that condensed and repeated on television throughout your campaign, even if you take the necessary step outlined below, could kill your campaign. You see, Mrs. Clinton, Huma is a problem. A serious one as the country emerges from its Obama-induced haze into an era of Islamic State-induced resoluteness about national interest and national security. She will not pass unnoticed through the next 15 months. Indeed, the "McCarthy perspective" is already well known, and while understood to be dangerous to one's social status to discuss, it is nevertheless passing from email to email like Samizdat used to circulate in the Soviet Union. Officially, it is ignored by the ruling class, read by the ruling class, even more widely read by the elites surrounding them, and of course by the world at large.

You may sincerely believe that Huma has nothing to do with the Muslim Brotherhood, or that its members are misunderstood reformers who were wrongly tossed from power in Egypt because of the Sisi coupists for selfish reasons and not because they are Sharia absolutists rejected by a country-wide convulsion of fear and disgust. It really doesn't matter what you think. What matters is that the campaign will turn on national security and you cannot have Huma anywhere near it, especially as you will be obliged to denounce Islamist extremism again and again and again and to pronounce your failed policies in Libya, Egypt, Turkey and above all Iraq and Iran to be the eye-opening doses of reality that have made you the perfect person to be tougher on the Islamist threat than any of the Republican rookies lining up to take you on.

This is a delicate dance, but one that cannot even begin until Huma is well and truly exiled. Again, a public speech will be necessary, like the one that you needed to locate Bill for the chattering class on their ever-changing map of the DC power grid. Huma must be off of it.

This "staffing speech" will have to be made, the one in which you trumpet how "girl power" will truly flow in the West Wing, in which you name your core staff. It will also conspicuously deal with Huma. It must.

Its timing depends upon when the issue of who will run the trains first begins to appear in the world of Mike Allen. You will disguise it as a speech on transition planning, which Mitt Romney turned into not only an acceptable but a necessary enterprise, and one to be discussed publicly like the hyper-experienced, responsible presidential image you will campaign on. Tucked into that speech you will see this paragraph:

> "Many have asked what role Huma Abedin will have in my administration. They know of our long and deep friendship. It is in fact a love that comes from the same source, though, of course, not of the same depth or intensity as my love for Chelsea and Char-lotte. Huma is a wonderful, wonderful, strong woman, who has helped me a great deal. But she will not be a part of this campaign or my administration. This is not because of the slanders against her as a secret agent of the Muslim Brotherhood traded in by fanatical anti-Muslim extremists like Andrew McCarthy and Frank Gaffney. No, Huma is not being cast out because of the alleged sins of her parents or her youthful writings. She is simply on a different course in her life, one that simply will not include another weary-ing stretch at my side. Her husband failed in his bid for mayor of New York. It is my hope that Huma succeeds in hers. No, she has not committed to such a run, but it is my earnest hope that this most capable young leader begin her own career, not continue to serve mine."

There. Done and done. Everyone will know why you have exiled Huma: she cannot be Caesar's wife on an issue in which everyone near you will have to be Caesar's wife. You cannot credit the allegations, but you cannot ignore them either. So you just denounce them even as you cast her out.

There will be tears. There always are. But this is the presidency. And you must win if you are to create a "Clinton Era."

Which brings us to your vice president, and the very, long game.

CHAPTER 6

Your Vice President

Vice presidents have posed problems since George Washington puzzled over what to do with John Adams. Your political ancestor, Aaron Burr, schemed to deny the White House to Jefferson, to whom he had pledged absolute support.

More recently, W was so well-served by Cheney that the idea of the super-competent "non-successor" as adjunct to the inexperienced but promising youngster was re-energized. The trouble is party succession. Cheney was never an option as Bush's replacement, and the GOP suffered for years and years because of it, even during Vice President Cheney's greatest moments of contribution. There was no unifying force as the GOP was obliged to endure the intrigue between John McCain and Mike Huckabee that blocked Mitt Romney from an Iowa primary win, and then one in West Virginia. Either would almost certainly have kept the widely acknowledged (quite a feat), least trustworthy person in today's politics, Charlie Crist, from delivering a victory in Florida's 2008 primary to McCain and with it the 2008 GOP nomination. Had Cheney been replaced by anyone but McCain in 2004, W's re-election would have been easier and 2008's many GOP fiascos avoided.

Now, the unique circumstances of Obama's selection of Biden are unlikely to ever recur, and never had a president been as reckless with a selection as Obama was with Biden (except that McCain's selection of Palin was its equal in terms of pushing forward an incredibly unprepared-to-be-president individual too near the Oval Office). The Biden-Palin debate will forever remain the low mark of American politics, screaming out at history: This was the best they could do after 200 years of practice—a lovable dolt and a wholly unprepared governor from a minor state?

No, you will have to be like W. Jeb, Rubio, Cruz or Walker will have to be like W, as well.

Truth be told, any of those four—indeed, any GOP nominee not named Bush or Romney—ought to ask Romney to serve as their VP for their *first* term, and *only* for their first term—thus borrowing the 2012 GOP nominee's immense credibility, fundraising lists, and organizational expertise for a first term—and yet assuring the loyalty of all would-be successors through the selection of VP Romney's replacement in the summer of 2020. Indeed, this move is so obvious that we will know the quality of your opponent by how early he embraces the selection publicly. If he does not, we will know their fault line is insecurity, and you can act on that through the campaign.

Your choice is much more difficult, because, truth be told, your proposal to amend the Constitution to remove the two-term limit on the presidency will pass Congress and be ratified by the states (for in it is contained the promise of a return of Obama, fire on the fuel of his acolytes' many altars) and this will greatly complicate the family succession. Chelsea will easily win her Senate seat when you appoint Senator Gillibrand to the Supreme Court, and she will be ready for the VP slot when your time is complete, whether at the end of a second or a third term. Whom could you trust to keep the bargain to name her when the time comes?

Of course, you could name her yourself, if a third term at 77 was plausible. By that point re-election will be assured by the changes made to citizenship and registration laws. But assume the worst: You die or are incapacitated before you have the opportunity to elevate Chelsea to the Naval Observatory.

(The critics of this book will think the idea of Chelsea as senator, much less VP, far-fetched. The whole idea of "family succession" will be mocked as absurd, dismissed as similar to the fever-swamps warnings about your husband refusing to leave in 2000 and the current round of internet nuttiness about President Obama's intentions to declare martial law and stay past January of 2017. The scoffers ignore how the speed of events has accelerated, as well as the deep desire for stability in DC court life, and how these will combine to declare your radical proposals to be bold "breakthroughs" promising an end to "gridlock" once they are unveiled. These are the same fools who thought Obama as president far-fetched in 2004, and have forgotten that they scoffed then. They thought you as president far-fetched in 2009, and have forgotten that they scoffed then. They thought amnesty for illegal aliens by executive order far-fetched in 2011, and have forgotten that they scoffed then. The same scoffers who though the Islamic State the "jayvees," and never dreamed a sitting Secretary of State could or would maintain her own e-mail server vulnerable to a hundred foreign intelligence agencies and yet not only get away with it but gleefully delete what she chose not to turn over to the record keepers at State!

We are in revolutionary times when social media can be manipulated to first encourage and then bless any innovation, especially one as popular as "daughter power" meets the ultimate Tiger Mom. No, the problem is not the plausibility of Chelsea as senator and beyond, but the reliability of your first selection in keeping the commitment made, one three-on-one meeting between yourself, Bill, Chelsea and the nominee that will have to be conducted in absolute secrecy, recorded only by you, and reduced to writing, and sequestered away in a vault with keys available only to the family. An interesting meeting that will be. You and Bill can choreograph it, of course. Not even heavy lifting. But, oh, to watch it.)

You have three choices really, and only one upon close examination.

On the surface, Minnesota Senator Amy Klobuchar is qualified to be president, and the old woman/young woman ticket is the only way to generate real energy for your candidacy among anyone other than your purple-hat gang dying to see one of the original feminist cadre be first to close the door on an all-girls meeting with the president. But the problem is she will want to be president and not be replaced down the road by Chelsea. She would refuse the conditioned nomination. She might even go rogue. She has ambition too, and smarts, and she doesn't need you to catapult past obstacles. Too untrustworthy. She could leave the meeting and announce your demand. She really could. She can afford to play a longer game for the biggest prize. No, you need someone who can be relied upon to agree to the deal and keep it secret should you collapse at your desk, even as American constitutionalism collapses around you.

There is young Julian Castro, and clearly Obama was pointing you there when he named the former mayor of San Antonio to be Secretary of Housing and Urban Development. The nerve. (But you do have to consider the opportunity he created for you, and put aside the spite that, at least for a time, people would say you owed your ticket to his careful management of the succession via the elevation and credentialing of a Latino who otherwise didn't exist in 2013 as a ticket energizer in 2016.)

But what deals has Obama struck with Castro, deals as secret as the one you propose to offer your nominee? Think on that a long time. Press him hard, again and again in the interview process. Put him under oath. Perhaps even flutter him. Fluttering a potential nominee has never been done. But tell them it is routinely done, but has been kept secret to protect the reputations of Biden and Ryan, and has been required ever since Palin was the vice presidential nominee. She did not disclose her daughter's pregnancy in McCain's slapdash circus. How will your potential running mates know? They can refuse and go rogue, but eyebrows will go up if they decline, not because you asked.

Even if there is no secret deal, the problem with Castro is he is a lightweight and we all know it: the mayor of San Antonio plus three years at HUD. There is a Palin factor here. No crises. No achievements. No hard interviews. Just all sparkle. He appears hardly curious at all and he has wasted his time at HUD thus far, and anyone who has struggled to buy or refinance a home in the past few years can be persuaded to blame him in the general election. Plus there is that name, "Castro." Say goodbye to Florida, no matter how many Univision and Telemundo ads you run that say "Not that Castro." And besides, the GOP is poised to nominate Bush, Walker, Rubio or Cruz though some of the second tier could make the jump as circumstances swirl—but every plausible GOP nominee—will have a short list of three potential Veeps: Romney, Rubio or Cruz. Romney would be the safest choice for the young senators should they win the ring, or underfunded dark horses. In the end, Bush or Walker will pick Rubio or Cruz. Your selecting a Latino VP will be cancelled out by a Latino GOP presidential nominee or a number two who is a Latino. Your ties to Latino voters will have to be forged by the specific promises you make on the campaign trail, bound up with the fence (with the very wide gate), and worked over and over again by the SEIU with the promise of a "livable minimum wage."

No—your only real choice for Veep is my Harvard classmate, former Massachusetts Governor Deval Patrick. To the question: "Will he stay bought?" We have to answer: "Yes." He will be 60 when he enters the Observatory. He will live the career capper. He can make a fortune for two years at 64 or 68 when he exits en route to becoming president of Harvard (and yes, put that on the table when you talk). It is easy to arrange. It can be all but formalized by your pal Drew Gilpin Faust before you begin the serious campaigning and vetting. His backstory is tricky, but can be managed to great acclaim when generally known. He is a winner. And he will stay bought. Plus he brings Mephistopheles himself, Axelrod, back to the team and in full genius mode, a Gatling gun of phrasing and himself eager to settle scores with Valerie.

Should you topple over and Vice President Patrick suddenly becomes President Patrick, he will name Chelsea immediately if your demise comes late enough to have gotten her to the Senate. The only risk will be if you exit before Breyer steps down to clear the way for a Gillibrand appointment, and Chelsea's succession. But there is risk in every plan. More StairMaster please if you are going to worry about death or disability in year one. Besides, Bill can go all Edith Wilson if need be, though a full *Weekend at Bernie's* is beyond even his considerable talents at deception. No 25th Amendment maneuvers for your number 2, not with Bill having your back and Rahm looming behind the Chief of Staff's desk again, free of the anchor that was Valerie Jarrett driving him to distraction every day.

Does Deval take the deal? What else can he do? Otherwise he is done. He may think Harvard is coming his way, but you can disabuse him of that. Harvard won't go where a president with all the government's contracts won't allow it to go. And if Deval says no, there goes the office in Harvard Hall, which is his North Star. He can't be the first black president. But he can be the world's greatest university's first black president. Use the leverage and get the deal.

And get one good cut in on Obama at the same time. His rival, elevated. All of President Obama's unspoken insecurities unloosed at once: That he's David Axelrod's favorite client, the genuinely deeply talented one, the one who really came from nothing. A real lawyer, like Michelle, one who actually practiced law and could find a courtroom. A genuine executive and genuine achiever, a real Harvard man—from the College not a grad school—and one who will reopen all of the president's deepest insecurities about having been an affirmative action admit at Occidental, a "transfer" to Columbia and a reach even for HLS at the height of its "outreach," the affirmative action selection for "president" of the law review, and all of the worries about his real grades and "achievements" exposed as fodder for future biographers of the worst president ever. On the surface it will be all smiles and backslaps, but oh the dagger will be sharp. Vice President Patrick will also of course energize the African-American vote to compensate for the otherwise inevitable fall off that will come with the retirement of Barack Obama. The announcement will enrage the president, though of course he will have to keep a pyramid's silence—forever. Wonderful that. Payback is hell.

Obama set out to transform America. He never knew he was transforming it into a Clinton dynasty that will last and last. How long can Chelsea go? As long as she wants, of course, within the forms, until a grandchild—whichever one makes sense—all thanks to that amendment and the platform you built around it. An America without a Clinton to lead it? Unthinkable by 2030, because of that new amendment. To which we turn now.

CHAPTER 7

"Let the People Decide": PART I
The Secondary Plank That Is the Centerpiece

All great campaigns require a slogan, and the slogan needs a platform on which to rest.

"Hope and change" was as vacuous as they come. But the panic of 2008 was all that Obama really needed, and Sandy, Candy and ORCA's collapse on Election Day gave him 2012. Slogans didn't really matter. Everyone knew he was a "first," and everyone knows you will be as well.

But your two amendments—abolishing the Electoral College and repealing the 22nd Amendment—will need a unifying elevator pitch, and the obvious will serve: "Let the People Decide."

The appeal of demolishing the College is self-evident, and I deal with it in the next chapter. But repealing the 22nd is tricky, because it is so self-serving, and thus you will have to take it on transparently, and acknowledge as much. Indeed, the key to winning is to ride your ambitions like a war horse of old. The 22nd is straightforward and so too will be its repeal:

> Section 1. No person shall be elected to the office of the President more than twice, and no person who has held the office of President, or acted as President, for more than two years of a term to which some other person was elected President shall be elected to the office of the President more than once. But this article shall not apply to any person holding the office of President when this article was proposed by the Congress, and shall not prevent any person who may be holding the office of President, or acting as President,

during the term within which this article becomes operative from holding the office of President or acting as President during the remainder of such term.

Section 2. This article shall be inoperative unless it shall have been ratified as an amendment to the Constitution by the legislatures of three-fourths of the several states within seven years from the date of its submission to the states by the Congress.

The "Wikipedia history" of the 22nd (as of the writing of this book) is adequate to the stump:

Historians point to George Washington's decision not to seek a third term as evidence that the founders saw a two-term limit as a bulwark against a monarchy, although his Farewell Address suggests that he was not seeking re-election because of his age. Thomas Jefferson also contributed to the convention of a two-term limit when he wrote in 1807, "If some termination to the services of the chief Magistrate be not fixed by the Constitution, or supplied by practice, his office, nominally four years, will in fact become for life." Jefferson's immediate successors, James Madison and James Monroe, adhered to the two-term principle as well. In a new political atmosphere several years later, Andrew Jackson continued the precedent.

Prior to Franklin D. Roosevelt, few Presidents attempted to serve for more than two terms. Ulysses S. Grant sought a third term in 1880 after serving from 1869 to 1877, but narrowly lost his party's nomination to James Garfield. Grover Cleveland tried to serve a third term (and second consecutive term) in 1896, but did not have enough support in the wake of the Panic of 1893. Cleveland lost support to the Silverites led by William Jennings Bryan, and declined to head the Gold Democrat ticket, though he did endorse the Gold Democrats. Theodore Roosevelt succeeded to the presidency upon William McKinley's assassination and was himself elected in 1904 to a full term, serving from 1901 to 1909. He sought to be elected to a (non-consecutive) term in 1912 but lost to Woodrow Wilson. Wilson himself tried to get a third term

in 1920 by deadlocking the convention. Wilson deliberately blocked
the nomination of his Secretary of the Treasury and son-in-law,
William Gibbs McAdoo. However, Wilson was too unpopular even
within his own party at the time, and James M. Cox was nominated. In 1940, Franklin D. Roosevelt became the only president to
be elected to a third term; supporters cited the war in Europe as a
reason for breaking with precedent.

In the 1944 election, during World War II, Roosevelt won a
fourth term but suffered a cerebral hemorrhage and died in office
the following year. Thus, Franklin Roosevelt was the only President
to have served more than two terms. Near the end of the 1944
campaign, Republican nominee Thomas E. Dewey, the governor
of New York, announced support of an amendment that would
limit future presidents to two terms. According to Dewey, "Four
terms, or sixteen years, is the most dangerous threat to our freedom
ever proposed."

The Republican-controlled 80th Congress approved a 22nd
Amendment in March 1947; it was signed by Speaker of the House
Joseph W. Martin and acting President pro tempore of the Senate William F. Knowland. Nearly four years later, in February
1951, enough states ratified the amendment for its adoption. While
excluded from the amendment's restrictions, then-President Harry
S. Truman ultimately decided not to seek another term in 1952.

Not so simple as it has been presented for years, eh? Sure, FDR was
the only man to succeed in his ambitions, but others wanted to. And
Jefferson was a nut about some things. The simple truth is that FDR
provoked the 22nd Amendment, and his death cleared the way for it.
The Framers knew what they were doing. A term limit limits the power
of the presidency in the second term, and that cripples the presidency
from almost the moment the second term begins and almost absolutely
in years seven and eight of a two-termer. The president can only act
constitutionally if he has both the House and Senate under the control
of his own party with him and then only haltingly. President Obama's
adventures in extra-constitutional governance have hurt you every

day and will tarnish his already sorry reputation, but he was a desperate lame duck with nothing to show for all his hope and change so he strained and strained to find anything, to his ultimate derision by historians and to your advantage in framing the argument for change. No president with the prospect of a third term needs to act as unconstitutionally as President Obama has as a lame duck.

You will be proposing to end that second-term " lame duck" status, and you will be wonderfully able to harness the Obama supporters to their man's potential return as well as run against Bush again, citing how your husband would have far exceeded the miserable Gore campaign in 2000, and how he would have anticipated and prevented al Qaeda's attacks, avoided Florida 2000 with a clear cut win, and avoided the horrors of the Roberts Court's assault on campaign finance reform.

People have forgotten the final two years of your last tenure at 1600. They have forgotten Marc Rich and the FLMN terrorists, the tawdriness, and of course, most of the impeachment narrative. They do know your husband had sex in the Oval Office with Monica and lied about it, but the new culture finds that almost charming and lying about it refreshingly honest. No, you can reinvent the history of then to suit now, and that reinvention should be that the 22nd Amendment stopped Bill's recovery, the war on Al Qaeda before it got out of hand under Bush, and many other ills.

Blame all of W's perceived faults and more on the 22nd, and pivot to the obvious injustice done to Obama by the same device. Push the repeal with a smile and a non-denial denial about your own ambitions: "I'll be 69 when I am sworn in, so you won't have to worry about me seeking a third term. But say circumstances were such that the people wanted me—ha, ha, ha, imagine that!—why shouldn't the people decide? If I ran and got thumped, what a lesson on limiting ambition that would be. And why shouldn't Barack be eligible to be reelected again to the office he ran so well?"

Every day this discussion will fuel the news cycle, pushing all of the "return" narratives of Bill and Barack. Even among GOPers, a sense that if they get it right with Rubio or Cruz, why would they want to blow it? The illusion of permanence—Rove fell for it. I have fallen for it (see the subtitle of my 2006 book, *Painting the Map Red*), it tempts all political pundits, strategists and historians. They want the grand plan for realignment so that a party dominates an era. But realignments are done, broken by the new realities and the new threats. In fact, only Julius and Augustus Caesar saw clearly the need to replace a broken system or change within the republic with an ordered succession, which they promptly set about doing while respecting the forms all along the way through the "Roman Revolution."

You need the Amendment to order your succession, to prevent any more GOP comebacks and any more rank amateurs like Obama. What you will be about is organizing a third American century by providing it with a long run of prepared leaders, beginning with you and followed by Chelsea.

But all in the open and the golden apple of stability will be bordered by the silver frame of the people's right to choose unfettered by the dead white legislators of the 1950s, who cooked up the 22nd. You will be on the side of the Framers as well as the people, except of course where the Framers defaulted to an Electoral College clearly born of a different age of travel and balancing of regional interests. Appropriate to an age of slavery, not rebirth, the College must be the principle target of your campaign and to that we turn next.

But remember, in every speech, demand repeal of the 22nd. Every speech. It must be a mandate, and if the GOP controls the House against you in 2017, campaign on it and only it through 2018. "Let the people decide" will rocket along for a decade to come until every check on the people's majoritarian impulses is gone, and with them, the checks on you.

CHAPTER 8

"Let the People Decide": PART 2
Abolishing the Electoral College

You are about building a dynasty and a new way forward for the United States, Madame Secretary, and that cannot be done with the Electoral College in place. It was intended to buffer the young republic from the winds of powerful factions and would-be kings, and it has worked well—too well, in fact. Now it stands astride progress yelling, "Stop! Pay attention to Kansas and Colorado and New Hampshire and New Mexico," and a host of lightly populated nowhere places, with almost no cultural treasures and hardly any of the elites, who in fact run the country from Washington, DC, San Francisco and Silicon Valley, Los Angeles and New York. It is time to cut the anchor and run with the wind. So you should say, and so you should campaign.

Having spent 30 years in various media outlets defending the Electoral College, let me confess that it is the hardest thing to do on my side of the aisle. Candor is almost always preferred to misdirection. But candor regarding the College is almost always ineffective and sometimes disastrous. The College protects small-town and rural America from the countries' big cities. While true, that defense can easily be misunderstood as protecting the largely Anglo populations in small towns and rural America from the largely minority populations of the big cities.

You will want to pluck that chord—carefully. Most Americans, including most Americans of color, are worn out by the politics of race. And while every explosion of racial conflict, whether in Missouri with Michael Brown, Florida with Trayvon Martin, New York City with Eric

Garner or anywhere else, cause ratings to soar for the networks that heavily invest in breathless coverage, the fact is the spectacle attracts the aggrieved on all sides of the issues, not merely those who believe America "has a race problem." We will return to your tricky triangulation on the issue, but know that it flows beneath the Electoral College conversation as well.

No, you must direct your ire and the campaign against the College towards the Red States and work to keep the small Purple or Blue States in the fold with a wink and a nod. Do so via a number of devices, but do not begin this phase of the campaign until after the nomination is secure. Iowa and New Hampshire especially will not cotton to anti-small state talk, but for them we have solutions once the caucuses and primary are behind us.

The College is so weird to most Americans that most of your argument is already made. Challenge defenders to answer "Why North Dakota with more cows than people and oil than common sense ought to be able to have three electoral votes when Washington State, home of so much that matters—and I don't mean just the Seahawks—and the Buckeye State have thirty times the people and less than eight times the political punch of either of the Dakotas or Montana or Wyoming?" Feel free to throw in punches at Dick Cheney here, the all-purpose Beelzebub for campaign 2016, as Wyoming's greatest contribution to the Union over the past two centuries and hardly justifying half the electoral power of New Hampshire.

The trick will be to pit the smallest, most deeply Red States, rhetorically, against the bluest, nearly-as-small states, thus framing the grievance as small state v. micro-state, not big cities against the small towns and farmers. Voters must understand you to be specifically for them, even though you are for yourself and the *familia*.

Now, envy is a useful thing to harness on your behalf, but envy never completely trumps self-interest. Recall the referendum on Scottish independence in September of 2014. Its rise to parity in the polls, to near victory until the last two weeks, was fueled by the envy of the small against the large.

Ultimately, however, the economic self-interest of the small ultimately trumped the envy and resentment Scots felt against the English. When banks and manufacturers threatened to bolt Scotland en masse, that self-interest—even among some previously independence-minded Scots—became of greater importance to voters there than the near certain-to-have-been-fleeting joy of punching John Bull in the snout. The hangover of the celebration, Scots concluded by a large margin, wasn't worth the party.

Defenders of the College will attempt to paint its greatest virtue as stability and the risks of the popular vote election of the president as too great and too precarious by far to try. To which you must calmly and repeatedly reply: "I trust the people," adding, "Communication in the new era of social media make all voters equally powerful in all places," and "The amending process is slow and deliberate, and can be trusted to balance out all the pros and cons, and in the process, educate the world about governance and constitutionalism just when it needs it most."

Add, "What critics of my proposal to abolish the College note how 'Abolish the College' flows off the tongue—I have reserved the domain name and Twitter handle, fail to grasp when they charge that instability will follow the success of the Amendment, is that a byproduct of the amendment process will be an increase in constitutionalism across the globe and a rise in international stability as countries see how change ought to be accomplished."

CHAPTER 9

5%

Recall that in Chapter 1, I laid out your core, five-part platform. Now we must focus on part three of that platform which involves national security as expressed through the national defense:

> "A constitutional amendment mandating that 5% of GDP be spent on the Pentagon's budget, with safeguards that the money actually be spent on soldiers, sailors, airmen and Marines and the equipment they need, not 'green energy' production for military bases. Rebuild the military and detach it from the GOP, and do so before a coup becomes a reality in the next forty years."

"Another constitutional amendment," some of your advisors will groan. But this is the GOP-splitting, election-guaranteeing bold stroke that can detach a significant part of the GOP from a party flirting with isolationism and alarming its previously most reliable voting bloc, the national security conservatives.

In case you doubt my bona fides in talking about this group of conservative voters, please know that I began my career as a ghostwriter for Richard Nixon during his exile in San Clemente, the Elba of America, as he worked on *The Real War*, which was a realpolitik manifesto published for the 1980 election, one which then-candidate Reagan found useful to be photographed carrying.

Eighteen years after scribbling away for RN, I penned an article for the then-young *Weekly Standard*, entitled "Our Six Party System," which

I reproduce in part here 17 years later because it provided an accurate map to the parties in 1998. And while the names of key players have changed, the map of the parties is still the same...but you can permanently rearrange it:

> "EACH OF OUR MAJOR POLITICAL PARTIES is really three smaller parties stacked in a pyramid. The chart below is a handy reference guide. The critical challenge for each party's elite is to attend to its base. These days, the base of the Republican pyramid is cracked.
>
> This base is what I call the Party of Faith, the legions of Americans who believe in "the laws of Nature and of Nature's God." The fact that they practice religion is what defines them. Overwhelmingly Christian, they go to church, read Scripture, and organize their social lives around interactions with other believers. Faith in God and the attempt to obey His will is at the center of their lives.
>
> The Party of Faith has its own subculture. Its most prominent political leaders are Dr. James Dobson of Focus on the Family and Gary Bauer of the Family Research Council, but there are numerous others, too, including Pat Robertson, Chuck Colson, and, increasingly, the dozen or so pastors of the new mega-churches, like Southern California's Chuck Smith, Greg Laurie, and Rick Warren. When and if these leaders serve notice on the GOP's elite that the Republican party no longer represents them, the threat will be real. If the base's support for the GOP collapses, the Republicans' ability to contend with the Democratic party will be gone overnight.
>
> But there's another reason the Democrats would easily prevail if the GOP were separated from its base: In the middle tier of the party pyramids, the Democrats again have the advantage.
>
> The Party of Wealth has traditionally made its home in the GOP. From mutual-fund managers and some big-business types to small entrepreneurs and anti-tax activists, these folks believe in the bottom line. "If GDP increases, all is well," is their credo. They write checks to campaign coffers, and they vacation out of state.

Net worth is the key to their hearts and minds.

There have been substantial defections from this group to the Democrats in recent years, especially from the higher income brackets, where laissez-faire lifestyle politics holds sway. Unfamiliar with the redistributionist zealotry of the old Left (or so rich they don't much care what slice the government takes), these newly wealthy technocrats tend to discount the importance of politics. Their discomfort with the Party of Faith propels them into the arms of their natural enemies.

The irony, of course, is that the Democratic party's middle tier, the Party of Government, would love nothing more than to empty the pockets of its counterparts in the GOP. The Party of Government comprises the labor unions, especially the newly dominant public-employee unions like teachers; the environmentalists, both nonprofit and bureaucratic; the consumer advocates; and all others who need government to keep them employed and powerful. This is the most rapidly growing sector of American politics today, as the administrative state continues to expand, especially at the local level. This sector demands new tax revenues, without which it cannot grow.

Just below the national leadership of both parties are two further groupings—the Party of Patriotism and the Party of License. Both carry influence disproportionate to their numbers.

The patriots are nationalists, or American exceptionalists, and include professional foreign-policy wonks, the remnants of the anti-Communists, and nearly every member of the armed forces. They are secular defenders of the American ideal, and Reagan was their embodiment. As Thomas Ricks points out in *Making the Corps*, the military is increasingly Republican even though its own unique culture breeds contempt for the wealthy and it remains at arm's length from the Party of Faith.

Across the divide is the Party of License—the academic Left, the feminist cadre, and the gay community. They are everything the patriotic party is not, and they will never cross over.

The elites of both parties thus see below them groupings whose

defining qualities will not shift over the next few election cycles,
but whose interest in politics will wax and wane. Because political
energy now resides in the components of the Democratic pyramid,
the near term looks rosy for Al Gore. And given the disgust of the
Party of Faith with Republican leadership, the prospects for Democratic gains in 1998 and 2000 are high.

Since 1980 the GOP leadership has held captive the Party of
Faith with a threat: Imagine if the Democrats won everything. For
a long while, this worked. But a sea change has occurred. The
leadership of the people for whom God matters most is now asking,
How could things get worse? The culture is completely eroticized,
drug-drenched, and crude. Religious practice is marginalized. And
kids routinely kill other kids. The country, in the eyes of the faithful,
may be irretrievably diseased.

So James Dobson served up a warning in March, much as
Jesse Jackson did back in 1987. The Party of Faith will not be
lectured to any longer on the need for tolerance and compromise.
It will bolt if it has to in order to demonstrate what it means to be
the party's base. Gary Bauer may launch an explicitly faith-based
protest campaign that could lead to an independent candidacy for
president in 2000.

Speaker Newt Gingrich, Senate majority leader Trent Lott,
and a half-dozen presidential candidates need to stop trying to persuade the Party of Faith to pipe down for the good of the country.
Rather, Republican leaders need to defend that group's interests
and proclaim its legitimacy over and over again. California's
Republican candidate for governor, attorney general Dan Lungren,
has begun this process.

Lungren, a practicing Catholic, is firmly pro-life, pro-faith, and
pro-church. It's a powerful message, especially when combined
with the promises Republican candidates must make to the Party
of Wealth concerning taxes. Oklahoma governor Frank Keating
is another politician who has managed to energize all the groupings within the Republican party. So it can be done. The question
is whether anyone in Washington has sufficient credibility with

the Party of Faith to give it assurances that won't be dismissed as posturing."

Though written in May of 1998, this basic cartography of American politics is still in place, but the risk of fracture on the GOP side has shifted.

As you know, as I know, as everyone knows, the "Party of Faith" within the GOP has nowhere to go. They lost the "culture war" over marriage and are barely holding on to religious-liberty tenets that were thought to be so deeply ingrained in the American civic religion as to be assumed in every debate, even in the radical reaches of the sexual frontier. They know that their only hope for defensible lines around their right to believe and practice their beliefs regarding traditional Christian norms of sexuality lies with restocking the federal bench, and especially the Supreme Court, with originalists who are especially strong on Free Exercise Clause issues and the First Amendment's other provisions protecting the broad "right of conscience."

Harry Reid's trashing of the filibuster makes this restocking a possibility. Expect the GOP nominee to push the issue of the courts to the center of the campaign. The religious conservatives aren't leaving the GOP, and they won't be staying home in 2016. They are in the life raft, paddling furiously, even if Mitt Romney re-emerges from a dead-lock as the nominee as you fear.

No, the key crack in the GOP's core constituencies is deep within the critical group delineated above as the "Party of Patriotism," the national security conservatives, described above as "the nationalists, or American exceptionalists, and [they] include professional foreign-policy wonks, the remnants of anti-Communists, and nearly every member of the armed forces. They are secular defenders of the American ideal, and Reagan was their embodiment."

Almost all of them believe you to have been a disaster at State, your national security skills *de minimus*, and your husband to have been only marginally better while residing at 1600 Pennsylvania. Neither of you seem to understand or care much about grand strategy or military matters.

Those who want to be president have to do more than fly around the globe, or the Kardashians would be senators or more, and FDR would have been a failure as Commander-in-Chief.

BUT—the biggest BUT of all—you aren't Rand Paul, or more specifically anything remotely like what both his GOP opponents and his most ardent supporters believe him to be. I will discuss below the challenge Paul presents should the-hard-to-imagine-but-nevertheless-possible happen and he lands on the GOP ticket. But even if he is dispatched in the primaries fairly quickly, his brand is wider than his father's, and his followers much more numerous and for the most part much better at message discipline than the "PaulBots" who roamed the nominating process of 2012, like wasps stirred daily from a nest under attack.

Paul the Younger is a thousand times more sophisticated than his amiable if idiosyncratic father and he represents a very old, pedigreed isolationism that had been banished from the GOP by Ike. But like the Shadow of Mordor I have often accused you in print of representing, it has returned to live again in the Party of Lincoln. "It isn't evil," you must say if you take up this analogy, "but it enables evil." (LOTR junkies can employ a Saruman analogy here.)

"America cannot retreat from the world," has become a favorite saying of yours. Good. So too was your declaration, during your book tour, on CSPAN on June 27, 2014:

> "We have to learn to be agile and ready for the unexpected, while we try to build the world we want, especially for our children and now my future grandchild. We have got to be aware of the fact that all these other countries, all these billions of people, they are making hard choices every single day. We have to be ready for that. Because I am absolutely convinced we have to continue to lead the world into the kind of future we want. We can't sit on the sidelines. We can't retreat. We're going to have setbacks. We are going to have disappointments. But over time, our story has become the dominant story. It represents the hopes and aspirations of people

everywhere. That is what I want Americans to understand. And
the main reason about why I wrote this book — I know there is
a big debate going on about our role in the world, and there are
some real unfortunate consequences still to deal with from prior
decisions and the like. But we can't abdicate our responsibility.
How we decided, how we execute it will be the stuff of political
debate. But the world needs us. America matters to the world, and
yes, the world matters to America for our prosperity and our security and our democracy."

This phrasing is almost wholly without content, but it serves notice
that if push comes to shove, you would use American military forces to
defend important American interests abroad, and that those occasions
would be far more numerous than those which would trigger a President Rand Paul to ask, "Where are the carriers?"

Senator Paul is working hard to change his brand from "neo-isola-
tionist" to "non-interventionist," but that conservative influencers even
claim Rand is an isolationist presents you with an enormous opening.
The fear of the return of the isolationists is deep within most of the
GOP, like the fear of the return of the White Walkers in the *Game of
Thrones* fantasy epic, and its HBO series. (NOTE: You will have to be
current with television pop culture hits such as *Game of Thrones, House of
Cards, Breaking Bad, Homeland, True Detective* etc.) Getting caught clueless
about some cultural campfire will reinforce the idea of your age being a
huge obstacle to effective governance. Your pratfall about being "broke
when you left the White House" reflected an out-of-touch moment, but
not with popular culture but with the middle class, and that is to be
expected of wealthy people, even wealthy Alinskyites. But you cannot
be clueless about culture. Besides, Bill will love *Game of Thrones*, just as
he did *House of Cards*, and for all the reasons we all know.

Many national security Republicans fear—really, really fear—a
genuine inward turning, an exhaustion from the burdens and costs of
the empire of reason and classical liberalism. They know the seeds are
there and they know some of them will flower, first in a distancing of

America from Israel, even as your own party's anti-Israel fringe forced the 2012 convention into a deeply embarrassing charade about Jerusalem. The fringe in both parties amplifies anti-Israel rhetoric far beyond its actual reach, but the party that can be most trusted on Israel picks up some loosely attached partisans, who are nevertheless strong supporters of Israel. Even a mainstream GOP national security conservative must hammer again and again on President Obama's open hostility towards the Jewish state and your complicity in it. So you must continually restate your strong, unswerving support for Israel while hinting that the isolationists have already won within the GOP.

A few sample paragraphs for your stump speech can accomplish both goals. You have never been this explicit before, but allow me to replace your (obviously) less-than-talented scribbler again and offer you this draft:

"Many of you already know of my unwavering support for Israel. You know how hard, first Bill as president and then I as Secretary of State, worked for a comprehensive peace accord that would provide Israel with borders that reflect adjustments necessary to its defense, with an undivided Jerusalem that is recognized by the entire international community and not just America and a handful of democracies, and with a supply of the weaponry that allows Israel to stand against the existential threat of a near-nuclear Iran and its terrorist ally Hezbollah.

"Many of you know we cannot allow Iran to acquire nuclear weapons. Thus did President Obama and I work to impose sanctions on the regime and for the same reason did Secretary Kerry and President Obama work to impose a veriable set of inspections and restraints on the regime in Tehran. But how many Republicans believe that keeping Iran a non-nuclear state is in the nation's interest, really? Does Senator Paul really believe it is in America's deepest national interest to deny the radical mullahs access to the most fearsome of weapons. If so, why did he sign Senator Cotton's 'open letter' understood to be a sabotage of our efforts then and now? Why did Senator Cruz sign it? And Senator Rubio?

"Or, as I fear, do Senators Paul and Cruz and other Tea Party isolationists not really care if Iran goes its own way on nuclear weapons provided they get some headlines along the way and the contributions that come with those headlines? I don't doubt Senator Paul's sincerity on many issues, but I do doubt his wisdom and certainly his commitment to the defense of Israel. I think many in the Republican Party do as well. That's why I am asking them to join with me in a bipartisan administration committed to the non-partisan ideals that drove every president during the Cold War, from Truman to George H.W. Bush, who, by the way, despite being my husband's opponent was also his friend from the start. That's as it should be in politics, and as it can be again.

"I pledge to you tonight, as I have from the very beginning of this campaign, to reclaim national security and national defense from the endless partisan trench warfare of Washington. I pledge a non-partisan or Republican leader for the Department of Defense. I pledge a budget, wherein every year 5% of our GDP goes to national security. I pledge not 11, not 12, not even 13 but 14 fully built-out carrier strike groups, which is what this world needs for stability. I pledge to you a budget that will put us back on a path to 350 ships in the world's finest navy, and to do so by the end of my second term. I pledge a Marine Corps of at least 200,000 and a rebuilt if leaner army and air force.

"We know that some Republicans will make similar pledges—though none have yet—but we also know that the alliance among the libertarians, deficit hawks and isolationists within the GOP will never make such pledges or support them. We know their number is growing. We know they opposed the use of drones to kill terrorists even after the nation's finest legal scholars approved of the necessity of such applications of lethal force. I wonder would Rand Paul have sent our special forces to kill bin Laden in 2011? I was in that room. I knew the risks we were taking with an ally. I approved of not notifying Pakistan in advance. I am a realist about our national security.

"Who in the GOP is not? And who in the GOP is willing to

join me in the remaking of an old coalition that commits to ending politics at the water's edge. My 5% of GDP proposal actually needs to go into the Constitution, as a floor that no future Congress can hold hostage as the Republicans did when they refused to negotiate on the sequester. That was the real GOP, the party of austerity, beginning with defense. We proposed modest hikes in both defense and social spending, but the ideologues would have none of it.

"Now they would like you to forget the sequester, forget the defense cuts, blame it all on President Obama, try to hypnotize you into forgetting who would not lift the caps imposed by the sequester.

"I think we can rebuild and renew our military. I have spent more time with our men and women in uniform than any other candidate and I have been, believe it or not, a military spouse, though not of the sort that make the so-very difficult sacrifices of watching their husbands or wives go off in deployment. No, my time as First Lady—when my husband was ordering troops into combat to stop the killing in Kosovo—impressed upon me deeply what it means to families to have their loved ones sent off to war. As Senator, as Secretary of State, all those years in the White House as well brought me again and again into the company of America's finest and their families. I have glimpsed, but not shared those sacrifices of spouses at home, caring for the kids, fixing the blown water heater, worrying over every report of a terrible event. I have not shared that suffering, but I have seen it, and I will be a reliable commander-in-chief as well as a First Friend to the military spouse.

"The soldiers, sailors, airmen and Marines and their spouses, children and parents deserve more and the country requires more for its defense, more than the Republicans with their isolationist caucus strong and growing, will give them. Whenever you hear a Republican say, 'The deficit is a national security threat,' mark that man or woman as a threat to a fully funded Pentagon. They are. That's code for 'more cuts to the Defense budget,' cuts that would be ruinous beyond reasoning. I did not agree with Defense budgets submitted by President Obama in his second term, and I did my best as a private citizen to urge their reconsideration, but I also know he was working against this ideological zeal deeply embedded in the Tea Party Republicans for a tiny American military force, and his spending plans had to meet them halfway. "Enough. Of. That. Until the Republicans rid themselves of their extremists and isolationists, the internationalists among them must come and join us, even if that means hanging out with people who believe in global warming and the EPA. If, that is, they truly believe what they have been saying all these years."

That way, Madame Secretary, lies victory. That speech would, to paraphrase Henry Kissinger's famous quip, have the added benefit of being "almost true," yet close enough to peel a few percent of the national security Republicans off of their party.

Think about it. Post-nomination, your people have nowhere to go, but the *Commentary* crowd, the Petraeus people, the career military: they pay attention. They are "high information voters," and some of them can be flipped. Truth be told, they are desperate.

Call their thought leader, *The Weekly Standard*'s Bill Kristol. Invite him to a private lunch. Or two. Or five. Bring your Bill and have him "jaw, jaw" rather than "war war" with Bill. Plant the seed now. The neocons can come home, can have a role, can hope to influence you and your team.

But that won't be possible if you won't pick up the check on a refunding of the Pentagon. It has been gutted, and you know it. The Navy is scandalously low on ships, and worse, the industrial base to service those that still float. And you know it.

The Marines—our best hope for a quick reaction in strength to an incident that cannot be handled by Special Forces—are breathing hard and need fiscal oxygen. Give it to them and earn their trust. Convert a Marine to your cause and you have brought home a platoon. They talk and stay in touch like no other branch. Play on that loyalty. Use them for more than the Band at Christmas and Marine One. Identify with the Marines, rebuild the Marines, and the country will think you are preparing not for withdrawal, but for highly lethal applications of force and not only very precise and deadly raids by Navy SEALs.

The popular imagination has been shaped, Madame Secretary. Take it as it is. Don't try and persuade it. Ride it.

No memorable president has been shy about using American arms. The greatest presidents were the ones who employed the greatest force. You already suspect the resurrection of W's reputation, and the recalibration of Bill's to account for his awful disinterest in bin Laden. You know Obama will be ranked the worst president by the best historians, and that these calculations will not be long in coming.

Resolve then to be the lion and not the fox, at least in the eyes of the world. Find your Grenada early in your tenure and build from that.

Above all, make the Islamic State your mortal enemy, and pursue them in reality to the rhetorical "gates of Hell" that the addled Joe Biden mused about. (He really is off his rocker, and the American people must be winked at in such a way as to tell them you know and that everyone can breathe much easier when he is not "a heartbeat away.")

You do not have to pick a fight with IS. They are coming for you. You know this now, perhaps in a way no other president has ever known. You have seen their message boards, and you have received their messages sent specifically to you.

Go Thatcher on them. They are your Argentinians, and the region of the now-erased border between Iraq and Syria is your Falklands. Say it. Out loud. As soon as the nomination is yours—and that will be quickly—before the GOP frontrunner can paint you in the indelible ink of Benghazi and the failure to reach a deal with Iraq's then-Prime Minister Maliki on a Status of Forces Agreement.

You must be a hawk now, even though you have never been a hawk before. The new enemy wasn't anticipated by Alinsky or any of your professors, or even by dear departed Holbrooke. No, these are the barbarians at the gate. Put on your fiercest Queen of the Picts and you will carry all before you. Dissemble as you have done to date, and you will be dismissed. America has awoken again to 9/12, and the holiday for history is over as surely as the last frolic ended on 9/11. Understand that, or lose.

CHAPTER 10

"Energy is Freedom": Talk Like a Conservative, Tax Like a Liberal, Build a Patronage Machine of Unprecedented Reach and Effectiveness

In Chapter 1, I laid out the trio of Amendments to the Constitution that you should propose, and in the first chapter I also outlined the two sets of policies you ought to pledge to pursue.

As only Congress, not you, can propose Amendments to the states, your rhetorical pushing of the three Amendments is the perfect framing of a political campaign that then requires little in the way of effort and time from the White House Office of Legislative Affairs as follow up when you win.

But they do provide the twin benefits of a powerful, framing narrative for your campaign, and an inevitably damning indictment of Congress to deploy in the 2018, 2020, and 2022 elections and beyond.

To hammer down the narrative, an early and full campaign day or perhaps even a weekend retreat to places connected to America's founding—Philadelphia, Williamsburg, Annapolis—should be devoted to a conference on each of your Amendment proposals. At each meeting, you will sit and listen carefully to scholars and public intellectuals—and a handful of the highest campaign donors whose egos will be massively massaged and their wallets even more widely opened by inclusion in the "substance" of what you should refer to as a "Second Founding"—debate exactly how these "amending proposals" should be worded, thus showcasing your "listening tour" skills again, and reminding the older journalists of how Bill expertly used such day long "summits" to establish his reputation for an engaged, amiable—and smart—wonk. He kept working on this image through the White House years with his long, rambling Roosevelt Room gabfests. That reputation for "smarts" helped him rebound from national disgrace. You very much need to refurbish your "whip smart" credentials that were badly damaged first by the mess of Hillarycare, then by your terrible record at State, and of course by your awful second memoir and the bungled book tour. People are talking in whispers, attributing your bumbling and stumbling to age, so you will need to demonstrate mental acuity and physical energy and capacity. "Early Gore," not "Late Reagan" must be the genuine conclusion of onlookers.

The thinness of your actual record at State, in the Senate and as First Lady will not bear close scrutiny. You must divert attention from the facts of your record to the "received wisdom" of the Manhattan-Beltway media elite, the vast Mainstream Media or MSM, for whom the general assumption of intellectual capacity and actual achievement is far preferred over a real record of accomplishment that they neither know about nor understand in much detail, even when it exists. Thus, this appearance of studiousness and curiosity must be substituted for look-backs, allowing especially the younger scribblers to simply assume that what they think they know about your time in various jobs and positions is true. You can count on a great deal of ignorance and indifference from the press, but they need props on which to lean. Give them this parade of scholars and roundtables, and they won't look back at your record too closely or for too long.

(Aside: Obama's youth and alleged "law professor" credentials accomplished the same result for him on the issue of "intellect," as did his "presidency" of the *Harvard Law Review*. We both know the real score on both of these accounts, and you and Bill already suspect an unflattering truth as well: that his academic performances at Occidental, Columbia and Harvard Law have never surfaced for a reason, nor has the question ever been asked how, in an era of affirmative action over-reach, the young Obama—filling out his applications from the prestigious Punahou School—could not find a college in the mainland with more cred than Occi, which he knew to be third-string then, and from which he had to transfer if he was going to ride the train of preferential admissions and ideological zeal? The MSM is estopped from even asking the questions now, so vast was the failure to investigate these basic questions in 2008, and so significant the consequences of that failure. But you may find it very useful to employ the team to distribute the real data and the real explanation early in your term, an explanation of the comprehensiveness of your failure being found in the revelation of his lack of intellectual abilities, curiosity and depth. "I tried, Lord how I tried, as did others. But Valerie fed his insecurity about his own abilities...it was how she controlled him, of course..." Better still if friends would risk all and put the details out now that have been so carefully packaged and stored at the four schools, but that would be a huge risk to them, as you are not a sure thing and won't be until the day after you win. If even one thread in that large tapestry of "achievement" was well and truly revealed, exposing fraud in the first selling...)

At the conclusion of each weekend conference in your package of "Second Founding" amendments, you can task a smaller working group from among those assembled to come up with the final and exact draft of the amendments, which will create excitement about the subject and the exact language to be used. That drafting process will not culminate until your inauguration and your first State of the Union address, but publicly task them to work in utter and complete secrecy as the Framers did in Philadelphia in the summer of 1787, thus inviting parallels and a subtext that you really are reaching for a legacy as bold as Reagan's. In so doing, you will distance yourself from the failed small ball with a price of trillions pursued by Obama. Have members of the working groups swear an oath of secrecy, which will allow you to leak a draft here or there, and denounce leakers as Washington famously did in 1787, when he presided over the penultimate act at the First Founding.

If you take on the role, you have to play the role. No half measures. And thus the utility of your leaking some of the secret work product of your working groups.

It is a very good thing to early on establish that you will ruthlessly hunt down and exile leakers. Thus among the academics, intellectuals and hangers-on you will have assembled into the three working groups, you will have to exile a half-dozen innocent individuals to get this point across.

"I know at least a few of you are wholly innocent," you should declare when exiling suspected offenders, "and even the leaker may have acted out of negligence, but when I say no leaks, I mean it." The point must be made, so you must make it. Notice will be served, and the press will not only love it, but frenzy about the draft language itself will grow.

In your Inaugural Address, you can pledge that the proposed drafts will appear in your first State of the Union address. And on that occasion, you should indeed deliver your proposed exact texts of the three amendments, as well as "notes of the proceedings," which hammered out the language, thus giving the law professoriate and the pundits enough material to fill their (unread) academic journals and more broadly consumed columns. You will urge the new Congress to act with the speed of the First Congress in referring the three amendments to the states, again linking your tenure in the public's imagination to a "Second Founding."

If Congress acts, you have already secured your place in history. If it does not, this demand for action is a demand you will repeat every year, piling up in the public's mind your long record of demanding action and Congress' adamant refusal to do so.

President Obama's charge of a do-nothing Congress never grew roots in the public's imagination, because he was himself a do-nothing, golfing president—a "lead-from-behind" president.

And because he never framed exactly what it was the Congress "didn't do."

He changed demands on Congress almost quarterly—sometimes monthly in fact—and ended up sounding petulant, rather than determined to lead. Your "Amendment Trio" will be the report card for the

Congress they will almost certainly fail at first, perhaps even for a few years, and every year you will remind the American people in the State of the Union that you campaigned on these Amendments, received a mandate for them, and Congress turned deaf ears to that appeal for the 'Big Three.' Every day that Congress does not move forward on the Amendments is a political victory for you.

But in addition to these huge goals, these keystones of the "Second Founding," you of course must submit a budget, and you must also provide a legislative package. The outline of the latter is particularly crucial for the campaign, as it will again demonstrate your capacity to fix the mess which Obama has gotten us into. For the legislative agenda, I suggest two broad categories.

The first of the two sets of proposals I lay out for you taps into your need for revenue and provides a political advantage of appealing to consumers of gasoline and heating oil. The second seeks to bridge—to great political advantage—the immigration debate divide. Republicans cannot be counted on to forever cede control of the details of this legislative arena to John McCain, and thus guarantee stalemate, so take no time in introducing both packages of bills. (More on immigration in the next chapter.)

Now on energy, the summary from Chapter 1:

> "An ironclad commitment to massive development of our own energy resources, via fracking onshore and development of select new offshore, out-of-sight platform drilling. Campaign on authorizing the Keystone XL Pipeline, once you have the nomination. What is Mr. Steyer going to do, disown you? The left will think you're posturing. Some in the center will be seduced. Cite the statistic that for every energy job created, four are generated downstream. Sell the true statement that "energy is freedom," and cite the knowledge you gained as secretary of state of the Third World's desperate need for energy to alleviate poverty and power growth."

We can admit to each other, and increasingly to the world, that whatever comes of global warming—whether disaster or new and even more productive weather patterns—will come no matter what you do, say or even accomplish legislatively. You and I both know that the U.S. could turn off all its cars and finances tomorrow, shutter its factories, return to subsistence living and not change the game of overall emissions significantly. China and India are driving that bus, and they are stepping on the gas, not easing off it, as they must to avoid domestic insurrection and famine.

Explain this to voters. Once nominated, where will your environmentalist supporters go? A new bid by ancient Ralph Nader? A third-party, vanity race by Tom Steyer? Of course not. Once nominated, you are all they have, and the Clinton machine is all they will ever have for a generation. They will get over it.

Give them a bone, as defined below, but be blunt: "We are going to develop our own energy, and we will do it massively, and safely, and towards the end of destroying the Islamists' income flow and our dependence on their energy policy. We will drill and we will frack and we will be an energy exporter."

Pause.

"And this way lies not just energy independence, but also fiscal renewal and a new federalism of robust strength, for I will insist that Congress impose a robust national severance tax on our vast reserves of oil and natural gas. Henceforth, the common inheritance of all Americans will not go into the bank accounts of Big Oil alone, but will be shared with the American people. Henceforth, the same kind of severance tax employed by states as diverse as Alaska and Ohio will have a federal counterpart. With that tax will come not just gushes of revenue, but a remedy for our massive national debt as well as the fuel for a renewed federalism.

"I propose a significant tax on every barrel of oil produced from US land and water and on every BTU drawn from within US borders. I will leave it to Congress to calculate the initial level of the tax. It must come with an escalator clause that not only keeps up with inflation, but also with the need to guide production towards a price consistent with all environmental concerns. An 'energy tax' has long been a goal of climate activists as a means of discouraging unnecessary energy consumption, and they will have their tax."

"But half of all that revenue will go into one of Al Gore's most favorite devices, the good old 'lockbox.' And Lord knows we could have used one from 2000 to today. Sixteen years of Mount Everest-sized deficits from both Republican and Democratic presidents and Republican and Democratic congresses need liquidation. The debt must actually shrink. Fifty cents of every dollar of severance tax will go to buying back the debt the Chinese hold over our head. This is like the 'sinking fund' used by the great English statesman, Pitt the Younger, to dig Great Britain out of a huge hole. It worked then and it will work now. Vast energy development will bring vast new fiscal discipline and security."

With these paragraphs you will have stunned and splintered the deficit hawks who will hear a melody they have hummed for years. They won't like the tax, but coupled with your commitment to production and your direction of the revenues to retiring the debt, they will find common ground. You will have again split the GOP as you did with your defense amendment.

Now, the *coup de grace*. You will have pledged half of the new severance tax revenues to the cause of debt reduction. The other half? You will call it a "renewed commitment to federalism as crucial to the 'Second Founding' as it was to the First." But it is actually the framework of a vast new network of patronage, a network your dynasty will need to endure.

Patronage got a bad name when the progressives came to power. Imagine what you and Bill might have accomplished from 1993 through 2000, if you could have made not just the tiny number of 3,000 appointments to your administration, which you were allotted, but two or three times that number or even more instead. Here is how you do that very thing this time around.

Every state in the Union has counties or their equivalents. There are a total of 3,144 counties in the U.S. Declare that half of the revenues from the severance tax will go to new boards established in every county, free of strings that are available for whatever purpose that county's leadership desires. Honor in word and deed the cherished American ideal of "local control."

But in doing so, create a vast network of new appointees for your own political benefit. Here's the part of the speech, in which you set in motion the making of half of this patronage machine.

"What of the other half of the massive revenues from a severance tax? That will not be for Washington, DC to squander. We have enough money as it is, and must cut, not grow, our budget.

"Rather we will send half of that money back to the states, but not to the often corrupt and always special-interest-dominated state capitols, but rather to each and every county in the U.S., dividing the revenue by population, and establishing in each county a new board charged with spending that money—or saving it—as that local board sees fit. I propose that each board number nine citizens, and that I, as president, will appoint six of the members and the governor of each state appoint three members to terms that are co-extensive with our own, so that agendas are genuinely advanced at the local level by people seeking to make a difference, not a name for themselves. My appointees will be women and men who have deep roots in the communities they serve—in a part-time, slightly compensated but hugely important role. They will have discretion over a large pot of money and they must do what their communities need doing, without the oppressive burden of faraway bureaucrats, clueless about conditions in the ground.

"Does Boise, Idaho need a new community college? Does Reno need to expand its airport? Does St. Louis need a massive injection of school funding? Does the Upper Peninsula in Michigan need the latest in technology to expedite cross-border trade with Canada? Do the Keys in Florida need money to assist in protection of its fragile ecosystem?

"Local boards with local membership served by local staff will set these priorities. I and the governors will have it in our political best interests to appoint the best and the brightest—young or old, black, white, brown or red, male or female, gay or straight—but all of them will be men and women of the local community, not of this city's bloated and entitled permanent class.

"These county boards will work a profound revolution in how our country works, but it will be a very old revolution, a Jeffersonian renewal of the ideal of local control of local matters.

"A severance tax will solve our debt problem and it will help solve our national crisis of declining civic engagement. These new boards, let's call them what they are, County Community Corps—the new CCCs, building on FDR's CCC legacy—will energize, inspire, renew and build, build, build a new foundation for the Second Founding."

They will also, Madame Secretary, empower you to select the guardians of a vast public wealth, free of congressional oversight and wholly empowered to reward friends and punish enemies. You know how this will work. They will be vast engines of patronage, but without the stumblebum mistakes of Solyndra-like pratfalls that come with faraway people making big bets instead of local folks making local "investments" in pools, parks and clinics.

And, again, you will have split the GOP, which has long flown flags demanding what you will propose to give them. Another slice of the Republican pie will be served to you, and the voters of that slice will never leave.

Talk like a conservative, tax like a liberal. And construct an enormous network of indebted appointees. If you appoint wisely, the empty husk of the GOP will truly be a sad thing to behold for you will be able to co-opt their next generation by allocating one or two of these seats to their best and brightest, cutting off talent from their body. More on appointments later. Now to the second sweeping set of legislative proposals.

CHAPTER II

The New Americans (and the Permanent Realignment)

Here is the summary I provided in Chapter 1 of your fifth overarching general election platform:

> "A near compete amnesty for all illegal immigrants coupled with
> an iron commitment to the immediate construction of a long,
> double-sided, high fence covering at least half the length of the
> 2,000-mile, Mexican-American border. The GOP has long failed
> to understand how to make this dual commitment work, to find the
> easiest way to hit the sweet spot. To your supporters on the left, as-
> sure them that the gate in the fence will be wide. Open it soon after
> construction is complete. Then close it prior to 2020. Then open
> it again thereafter. With the majorities you build in your demo-
> graphic surge, you can put forward the constitutional amendment
> removing term-limits on the presidency."

Your abysmal record at State has left you vulnerable on national
security, and every outrage by the Islamic State reminds the voters of
this, as will the GOP's continual harping on Benghazi and Ukraine.
President Obama's horrific lassitude and then overreach on immigration has left your party exposed on the entire issue, defenseless to the
charge of a simple, complete open-border collapse. The issue threatens
to submerge the 2016 race in a frenzy of accusations and charges, all of
which are volatile and many of which could sink you. Only your phan-
tom server and the threat of suddenly reappearing emails captured and
stored against October 2016 is a greater threat to your campaign than

a repeat of the border chaos that marked the children's march north of 2014.

You need to sail between immigration's Scylla and Charybdis, and you can do so, by simply appropriating the policy that ought to have been the GOP's all along, but wasn't because of the ineptitude of some and the egos of a few—principally Senator McCain, who while a great American and still a force for great good on national security matters generally, is for the most part a lousy senator, a horrible Republican and perhaps the worst legislation writer of the past quarter century between his unconstitutional campaign finance reform and detainee laws and his two failed attempts at immigration "reform."

The right policy—both as pure policy and as pure politics—is simple: A long, tall, double-sided fence with a road running between the two sides, stretching along every passable mile of the border and even some that aren't. Essentially, this means building a mini-interstate o along the border, open only to law enforcement. If this country can build the I-0 and all the other interstates, it can build one along the Mexican-American border, with a fence that is high, double-sided and tightly patrolled. It can do so quickly. It can do so, by the way, by spending on public works and actually creating a shovel-ready project that will employ thousands.

The long, strong, high fence should have a lot of gates, and a lot of legal immigrants coming through them, along with trucks and trains. Push border trade as much as Arizona's new governor Doug Ducey did in his 2014 campaign. Push large numbers of temporary work permits for agricultural workers as well. Farmers from California's Central Valley to Ohio's tomato fields will applaud this and most Americans get it.

What they don't get—what they are afraid of—are the cartels' gangs and the prospect of wide open borders and streams of children and their coyote handlers pouring over the border as they did throughout 2014. Or terrorists. One terrorist attack—one!—originating from a border-crossing jihadist sinks your campaign, if you do not come out strong for a long, high fence.

The US-Mexican border is 2000 miles long. Simply assert that half is widely regarded as unpassable, but half yields to the determined border jumps so a 1,000-mile fence/road will have to be built, and will be built in year one of the new Clinton era.

Announce as well that as it is being constructed, you will have been given—by the same law appropriating the funds for and mandating the fence construction "notwithstanding any other law," thus overriding the crazy environmentalist objections to the project—the authority necessary to prepare for the issuance of "purple cards" to the tens of millions of illegals, who already live in the United States. These cards that will allow them to remain here if their conduct remains in good standing, cards that can become "green cards" in ten years—permanent residency—and citizenship in 20 years, if indeed they are deserving.

Here is where the vast, vast majority of American hearts rest: humane, compassionate, careful regularization of immigration, and all of the other hocus pocus—fines, self-deportation, fears of diseases, etc.— vanish when met with calm, reasonable propositions. Frenzied cries of "amnesty" and the shrieks of the dead-enders like Tom Tancredo will help you provided you hit the mean. That means acknowledging that some small percent of the illegal population—5 or 10 percent—are bad people, dangerous people, or simply helpless, expensive people who have to go back to their home countries. How to separate this group, from the hardcore gang members, to the simply-incapable-of-caring-for-themselves-except-via-costly-government subsidies?

Not by a rules-based, quasi-court system as we have now, but by using the county-board model discussed in the previous chapter. Only, you will be appointing full-time, new employees of the federal government to this second set of county-based boards—more patronage— and limiting the applicant pool to former officers of the US military —men and women, who for the most part have experience evaluating people, having spent years writing and processing "fitness reports" on their troops. They are practiced appraisers of men and women. There must be in every county in America, at least a score of retired Army,

Air Force or Marine Corps colonels or Navy captains, for whom evaluations of character are second nature. Hire boards of five—one for sparsely populated counties, many for the densely populated urban areas—and give them one task and one general rule: Issue purple cards to good folks, who want to work and want to stay; deny them to people who are sketchy. Period. End of edict.

There will be some mistakes made, even as draft boards of the '60s and '70s made mistakes when it came to classifying draft-eligible, young men. But for the most part, the drywall contractor who has been at it for seven years or the maid who has been cleaning rooms at the Ramada Inn for ten, and all their children and elderly parents will be able to tell their stories to such boards and quickly get the purple card that allows them to enter the above-ground economy and start paying taxes. They should not be eligible to receive benefits other than primary and secondary education—this is the hard part, eligibility for benefits is reserved for US citizens and green-card holders—except for public schooling, of course.

If a bad guy gets a purple card, his or her first brush with police will mean forfeiture of it. If a good guy is denied a purple card, provide for an appeals process.

Establish a national database and hit employers, who hire people without their cards, with devastating fines. Simple. End of the regularization process. Why the GOP did not do this years ago. . .well, it did not do so because of the ambition of John McCain, who thought himself an expert on the border and the laws governing immigration because he lived in a state bordering Mexico, when in fact, any first year lawyer could have written better legislation than his two epic fails.

So your old pal—and he might even support you if the GOP doesn't court him, again, if you dangle SecDef in front of him—left the door open to you. Mitch McConnell might be smart enough to slam it shut before the campaign gets going, but the screamers are loud in my party, and there is money to be made and books to sell and ratings to gain in stepping on this broken leg, but you can be the fixer.

Propose the fence, the cards and the boards. Scold the opponents. Play to the big hearts of most Americans even as you address their legitimate fears. Talk like a grandmother, but also talk as a mom worried about her school-aged children and unvaccinated immigrants, as well as the most notorious and violent cartel-backed gangs.

Here, the best politics is also the best policy. And the men to help you—and they are all men—are the Roman Catholic archbishops. Some are already cardinals, a few more of whom will soon be, such as Archbishop Chaput in Philadelphia, Archbishop Gomez in Los Angeles and Archbishop Cupich in Chicago. Soon after your nomination is secure, reach out to these men along with Cardinals Dolan of New York, O'Malley of Boston, and Wuerl of DC, and invite them to an all-day discussion of the plight of immigrants. Although they disagree with you on the rights of the not-yet-born, they will all back comprehensive and humane immigration reform, even the most conservative among them.

In your meeting with them you will have to endure some lecturing on religious liberty. Listen closely, for there is another area of campaigning on which you will have to thread a needle between people of faith and your LGBT supporters—and of course, an appeal to join in promoting a new culture of respect for life and family. The photo op will be magnificent and the political impact of their support for your proposals—though couched in a policy endorsement, not a political one—will be a meteor strike on the GOP. That is worth a few hours with these men, at least some of whom you loathe, isn't it?

Of course it is. Your concern for the illegal population is of course a quarter-inch deep—really, hope that no one looks too carefully at your long silences on the subject when in power and especially as First Lady—but you can fake a deep, longstanding compassion for these millions and thus earn the Latino vote with one decent policy proposal and one day spent with the collars.

Your campaign pros cannot count on a replay of the GOP's fumble of the Spanish-speaking media in 2012. Jonathan Alter's book on that campaign has an astonishing assertion in it: Obama ran seven spots on Spanish language media to every one put forward by the Romney media wizards. The rotten core of the GOP consulting class was out-maneuvered, but the massive fail of 2012 won't be followed by a replay in 2016. Still, you can carry the Latino vote—even against a Marco Rubio–including ticket—if you get the policy right. To paraphrase Kissinger again, the proposals have the added advantage of being good policy as well as terrific politics. Take them away from the GOP, before someone with vision kicks McCain from the room and puts forward the same plan with an elephant logo on top.

The political effect of this proposal if passed and implemented will be real border security that, while not a guarantee against cross-border attacks, will at least be insurance from political damage in the after-math of such a blow, and an enduring political realignment, a genera-tional grip on Latino voters every bit as strong as your party had on Irish-Americans for a half-century or more after the great migrations. African Americans have nowhere else to go, but Latinos do. Put up signposts and markers and pay off the promise that President Obama made and broke, made and broke, made and broke.

Asian Americans will of course be watching and to them must go the promise of vast numbers of high-tech visas and continued expan-sion of visas-for-cash, which has made for quite the under-the-radar legal trade in people and money. Not many Americans know of the fast growth in the U.S. visa program that traded permanent residence to any foreigner who invested $500,000 in a US project that created at least ten jobs, but the EB-5 visa is well known among the voting groups whose extended families and communities have benefitted from it. Since the EB-5 program was created in 1992, around 30,000 immigrants have used it. While the government is quick to point to the alleged 500,000 jobs created, the annual limit of 10,000 such visas per year chafes at some, especially the new technocrats of China and India and all those voters, who see in their ethnicity a common bond if not actually common blood.

This is a sophisticated demographic, or actually many demographics, and driven primarily by economics and foreign policy, not racial identity except in a nationalist attachment to their various homelands, not in appeals to their racial classification and circumstances within the U.S. Voters whose families came from the Philippines, Japan, South Korea, Vietnam, Indonesia, Malaysia—they will want to know where you stand on the security of their country of origin—in other words, where you stand on China. On China, you will have to bluntly state that it must be contained, and that the United States Navy, rebuilt and robust, will do the containing. Of course, you cozied up with the PRC throughout your tenure at Foggy Bottom. So terrible was your tenure at State, vis-à-vis the ChiComs, you will simply have to make up a new narrative of your time there, and count on the surpassing ignorance of the MSM to facilitate it. That narrative will bring along the Asian-American voters, even as your policy on neo-amnesty (or "regularization" as I have vainly tried for years to encourage sensible Republicans to call it) will cement Latinos to you and your family's cause for decades to come.

PART II

YOUR OPPONENTS, NUMEROUS AND FEW, LARGE AND SMALL, IMMEDIATE AND LONG-TERM

CHAPTER 12

The Virtual Hive

Everybody "knows" that the rise of new media "changes everything" when it comes to electoral politics, but they don't know how it has changed, or how fast the change will continue, or what to do about it except scramble to recruit to their campaigns "new leadership in the digital era."

Those who profess to understand it are lying or at least fools. Even the president's "A-Team" of techies barely understands the speed with which the billions of online interactions are bending politics and government here and around the globe. Admittedly, they were ahead of the curve in using the new tools to identify and bank data on millions of Americans who had been only crudely counted and categorized before 2008 and 2012, but a decade from now the president's best will seem like three-year olds. There is no privacy anymore, and everyone's behavior can be predicted with increasing accuracy, an accuracy that improves with every exponential expansion in the amount of data banked on them.

Your people will hire Obama's people and try and supervise them, and you will try as well to understand what is going on but it is actually beyond your ability to do so. You will have to trust some people on the data side, and figuring out whom to trust with regards to the data will be an enormous challenge, one that only your most-trusted, longest-serving aides can be asked to advise upon. And their long service all but guarantees that they too will be babes-in-the-techno-woods they are exploring.

You can control what you can control, however, and one of those things is the input machine into level one of the buzz machine that is the modern social media giant noise machine.

If you think about when Bill first ran in 1991 and 1992, it was a relatively simple time in media. There were the big networks, a handful of papers led by *The New York Times, The Washington Post, The Wall Street Journal* and the newsweeklies. Sure AP and UPI were in the mix, and a few key opinion outlets like *The New Republic*, but not much else concerned a Democratic campaign for the presidency. The nets and the key reporters and editors at the key publications—those were the gatekeepers.

In opposition were Rush Limbaugh and his very early stage colleagues on the radio. I was a young weekend radio host in LA in those days while also doing the television news for PBS each night as cohost of a precursor to the nightly gab-fests held round-the-clock now on a half dozen channels. Sean Hannity was laboring in Huntsville, Alabama about to head out to Atlanta, and The Fox News Channel would not even launch until October 7, 1996. Laura Ingraham was clerking for Justice Thomas and Mark Levin was leading the Landmark Legal Center. There was the editorial page of *The Wall Street Journal* and *National Review*, but not much else on the right. *The Weekly Standard* would not launch until 1995. A much simpler time, even if you occasionally had to worry about *The Economist* or *Le Monde* or *Der Speigel*.

Then along came Drudge. Hard to believe it started up only in 1996, but that's the date. Just in time for the second term. Just in time to change everything.

When I wrote *Blog: Understanding The Information Reformation That's Changing Your World* eight years later, the world had indeed changed. That's an ancient book now, a decade later, though you'd do well to read the chapter on the death of the gatekeepers like Dan Rather and to review the key sentence in the entire book: "The byline is the brand now."

And that is the secret to the "buzz machine" of level one of the social media giant noise machine: The bylines that matter. Who feeds the beast now? Really feeds it. Who and how?

Ask your staff this day—recall Churchill would scrawl on his memos "Action This Day!" and you'd be well advised to emulate that, if only so people saw you emulating the great man—to prepare a list of the 200 most influential commentators when it comes to spreading political messages via social media including Facebook, Twitter, Vine, Instagram, Meerkat—the lot. When you get those 200, ask for 200 more, and then 200 more, then 200 more, then 200 more. You will end up with a thousand names, and every one of them will have a Twitter account that you should be following every day, all day. Yourself. With your own eyes.

Watching the buzz river run, on and on and on. That is step one. (Dress them down by the way if they neglect the "Mike and Mike" shows of the ESPN and Fox Sports world. Here are the vast audiences of younger men with whom you must simply connect via some bridge.)

Step two, ask for a binder with background on each of these 1,000, and insist on knowing their ages. Many of the youngest ones—like *Bloomberg*'s Dave Weigel, *Townhall*'s Guy Benson, *Hot Air*'s Mary Katharine Ham, Tommy Vietor, *Politico*'s James Hohmann, the *Arizona Republic*'s Yvonne Wingett Sanchez—will be strangers to you unless you have worked with them like you have Vietor. But they are out there, in the new virtual hive which replaced the old one of Mark Halperin's imagination, which he labeled the "Gang of 500" for ABC News' *The Note* back in the day. If the "Gang of 500" ever existed, it is disbanded now, routed actually, by the virtual mob of thousands. Halperin imagined a world where only the Manhattan-Beltway chattering class mattered, and of course it still does, but far from exclusively. Joe Scarborough is on in the background when most East Coast people are shaving, and Jake Tapper while they have a tipple in their offices before heading home that night. Of course, the Manhattan-Beltway media elite matter, but they do not matter one-tenth or even one one-hundredth of what they used to, because every day in every way the barbarians are climbing the virtual walls, and every day in some places they are getting in.

This new virtual hive buzzes 24/7, 365 days a year. You cannot hope to control it, or even move it much. But you can curry favor with its most important members until such time as you can in fact control it via the Federal Communications Commission and your own data collection operations. Only now, at the beginning of the dynasty's second rise, do you need to pretend other than contempt for its members.

There are less than 500 days until the election. You need to personally reach out to three of these 1000 every day, beginning with the very youngest. Your staff must bring them to you. You must know their stories and give them a story. You must be the first major candidate every to figure out that press secretaries and communications directors are a relic, just like spin rooms after debates. Oh, someone will have those titles, but everyone on your campaign with an iPhone and a Twitter account is a press secretary, just as everyone you meet in every room is a reporter looking for a career-making moment like Joe the Plumber or the bartender who taped Mitt Romney's 47% moment.

The web of connectedness is beyond this small book's capacity to describe, but I hardly need to. You cannot hope to become president if you don't already know about it, sense it, and understand its speed and dizzying ability to move from story to story. Level one feeds every other level, and sometimes level two and three push material up to it.

You can do your best to take as many of the pieces off the board as possible, or at least have them think twice before charging at you. Start now. Work earnestly at the effort. You will never see the payoff because it will be in posts not posted and tweets not tweeted. Pull on that invisible arc of news ever so gently and every day. Until they don't matter anymore.

CHAPTER 13

The "Not Serious" Republican Candidates and the Serious Ones

Unless you intend to gum up the GOP's internal deliberations, do not ever, ever respond to a candidate's attack if that candidate cannot possibly face you in the general election.

The goal in life of such "second tier" candidates is to bait you into noticing them, seize upon that response and amplify it via their own social media networks, and thus help them elevate their own standing among the Republican primary voters of Iowa and New Hampshire.

Now, you may want to, say, refer to Carly Fiorina in a positive way and note again and again that "out of all America all the GOP could find to use as a token woman on their debate stage was a failed-Senate candidate, who had previously failed at running a big corporation." Fiorina has incredibly sharp instincts though, so such an attack could boomerang. And if delivered against the former Hewlett-Packard CEO with the deeply compelling personal story, better to use the thick-as-a-brick Barbara Boxer to deliver it. Because Boxer beat Fiorina —not hard to do in deep blue California—Boxer can throw a few verbal darts at Fiorina without dragging you into the fray, but be careful of Carly.

And be very careful of Dr. Ben Carson, unless you mean to seriously try and get him onto the ticket or increase the attention paid to him as a means of setting a few time-bombs down the road for the GOP. Dr. Carson is much, much more than a man of color; he is also a fundamentally different sort of figure on the American political stage—a genuine achievement from the worst part of the long urban nightmare that is Detroit, and his accomplishments cannot be derided without risk to you.

But do recall the famous July 5, 2003 story in the *Washington Post* by Juliet Eilperin, entitled "Rove Spends the Fourth Rousing Support for Dean," which began:

> "Talk about lining up the competition. President Bush's chief political adviser has seen the possible presidential candidates among the Democrats and has found one he apparently thinks his man can beat: former Vermont governor Howard Dean.
>
> Karl Rove tried to stir up enthusiasm for Dean marchers yesterday at the 37th annual Palisades Citizens' Association Fourth of July parade along the District's MacArthur Boulevard, which always attracts plenty of politicians.
>
> As a dozen people marched toward Dana Place wearing Dean for President T-shirts and carrying Dean for America signs, Rove told a companion, "'Heh, heh, heh. Yeah, that's the one we want,'" according to Daniel J. Weiss, an environmental consultant, who was standing nearby. "'How come no one is cheering for Dean?'"
>
> Then, Weiss said, Rove exhorted the marchers and the parade audience: "'Come on, everybody! Go, Howard Dean!'"

The truth is Rove would have loved to have run W against Dean in 2004, just as you would love to run against the untested, wholly-unready-for-a-massive-management-task-like-overseeing-the-conduct-of-a-presidential-campaign guy like Dr. Ben Carson, but forays into the other side's politics are at best wickedly sharp, double-edged swords. Rove was just having fun there, hoping to get a pass from the anti-war crazed left in 2004. No such pass developed, but Rove may have helped nominate the ultimately very formidable Kerry by signaling to mainstream Democrats just how crazy Dean was. Don't play that game.

You don't need to take any risks you don't have to take, give any interviews you don't want to give, respond to any inconvenient questions. The advantage of being an inevitable nominee is that you alone decide what you will do and when. You might even refuse all but a handful of debates with Webb, Bernie and Yoda (if Jerry Brown runs). You saw what the two dozen clashes did to Romney in 2012, and you recall what the debate marathon of 2008 did to you. You can make your own rules until the fall and maybe beyond (depending of course on whether Senator Warren stays on the sidelines and the server stays hidden, the emails "disappeared").

So stay far, far above the fray. Raise money and wait. Study. Do a few interviews with Friedman, Rose and other aging reliables. If you are offended by a slur from the "never-going-to-be-nominated" crowd, ignore it. Or, if your temper is truly up, dispatch a suitably low-level functionary like Barbara Boxer to deliver the message. The aging Boxer, for example, will be eager to imagine herself doing you a favor and will scuttle out to do your bidding, expecting a job in your new regime, even though she is even older than you and dumb as a desk. (Perhaps Ambassador to Finland, to keep her out of sight and far away, and thus minimize the risk of her damaging your first crucial years at 1600?)

In this category of extremely unlikely nominees are Fiorina and Carson, but also Ambassador John Bolton—be very careful of that extremely smart fellow Yale Law grad—the voluble and amusing Congressman Peter King, the gifted Barnum of our age, Donald Trump. The only congressman you have to at least think about running against is Paul Ryan, and that is extremely, extremely unlikely, one of two acceptable candidates a deadlock in Cleveland could produce. Other than that, you need only direct your staff to begin opposition research projects on your own potential vice presidents and on the GOP 12 plus one: Jeb Bush, Chris Christie, Ted Cruz, Mike Huckabee, Bobby Jindal, John Kasich, Rand Paul, Rick Perry, Marco Rubio, Paul Ryan, Rick Santorum, Scott Walker—and of course Mitt Romney, who though he is out again after being briefly back in, may yet return if the GOP's Cleveland Convention freezes as noted above, and who in any event will surface on VP lists if one of the Republican's "next generation" of would-be nominees rises and wins, and then needs some Cheney-like gravitas on their ticket.

Your team should also begin opposition research projects on the likely vice presidential short list for the GOP which will include all of the above plus Senator Kelly Ayotte of New Hampshire, Senator Joni Ernst of Iowa, Governor Susanna Martinez of New Mexico and Governor Nikki Haley of South Carolina—and perhaps young Senator Cotton should the war being going truly badly and a mass casualty attack upon the United States a reality again and not just a nightmare in the offing. Many Republicans will believe they simply have to nominate a woman, and one that brings a second plus such as new ethnicity and thus appeal to MSM—Haley is an Indian-American—or a swing stater like Ayotte and Ernst, or both ethnic novelty and a swing state, like Martinez. The overwhelming likelihood is that Senator Rubio or Governor Martinez will be the choice, so start now to retrace their every step and dispatch the video cams to film her every appearance and word. Store up the nuggets, like they have them stored up for Governor Patrick, your likely running mate, or Senator Booker, your much less likely running mate.

But most of your thinking must be about the men you are likely to face, and every day you ought to spend some time thinking through that baker's dozen, especially Bush, Cruz, Rubio and Walker, who are your top-tier possible opponents. Such different challenges. Kick them all around, every day, with Bill and Chelsea. Envision them on the stage with you in October. Prepare now.

The Dalai Lama once told me —really, he did, and you can watch the interview in the archives of PBS—that he envisioned his own death every day so as to be prepared for it when it arrived. Such discipline. It is mirrored in the old Roman Catholic admonition to think every day about four things: death, judgment, Heaven and Hell.

Anyone your age should probably contemplate how little time you have left on this earth, but not for long and not to the exclusion of thinking through the key understandings and the character of each of the candidates listed, one of which will be opposite you in the fall of 2016. Don't make the mistake of the German general staff preparing for Patton to lead D-Day at Pas de Calais, only to be surprised to find Bradley and Montgomery on the beaches of Normandy. They couldn't imagine not fighting Patton, so Patton became the great diversion. Ike was always a step ahead, and not just of the Germans, but later of MacArthur, Taft, McCarthy. The only one who stayed a step ahead of Ike was of course Nixon, who outmaneuvered the general twice, with his "Checkers" speech which kept him on the ticket in 1952 and again in 1956 when RN clung to the ticket by a thread.

You and RN have much more in common than you'd like the press to know, but this part of Nixon's political operation you simply have to copy: He never stopped thinking about his opponents and his enemies, and neither can you. Even when you win, most of them will still be around and readying immediately for 2020. You cannot spend too much time just thinking about these 13 men, and the chapters that follow will give you some starting points.

Don't presume you know whom will the nominee will be. Don't expect Patton. Prepare for them all. Every day. Study them and their speeches. Task a staffer to bring you a daily report on where they went and what they said and did. Think on them.

CHAPTER 14

The Heir and Future Rival: Paul Ryan

Paul Ryan is not going to run against you—this time. But he is certain to be back, somewhere, somehow, as the leading man in your opposition. Like Senator Marco Rubio, well known and loved on the right, acceptable to the center, possessing the "it," piling up accomplishment and practice in the particulars of the old politics. When you unveil your platform, he will be the one to respond in detail even as the announced candidates stick to their primary battle plans. And as future Speaker — on his timing, when he wants it, probably in January, 2017—he will be "negotiating" with you should you prevail on your demands for budgets, bills and of course the amendments. John Boehner and Kevin McCarthy have the titles now, but Paul Ryan has the love of his caucus and the admiration of great deal of his party including me.

But, but, but...he is vulnerable if only for a little while. You should move before an opponent of this stature moves to repair the breach in his own walls. Delay and he can mend his fence. So don't delay.

Ryan made an enormous mistake in 2013, and who knows, you may have talked your friend Patty Murray into tricking him into it. The Ryan-Murray budget deal of 2013 included cuts to the earned retirement benefits of the men and women who have fought the long war. Ryan thought it a down payment on entitlement reform and badly misjudged just how far off course his calculations were. I argued with him about it on air then, but displaying a somewhat noble if deeply compromising stubborn attachment to his own principles, Ryan would not budge even as the swelling chorus of criticism crescendoed.

He got rolled. And branded. As "anti-military." Astonishing to have let that happen, but no error by a key opponent can be allowed to go unexploited. He set the fire. Throw on the gasoline.

First, when you campaign, wherever you campaign, remind people that Paul Ryan not only wants to privatize Social Security and replace Medicaid with vouchers redeemable at crowded clinics full of the unwashed and undeserving. ("You have worked hard your whole life to earn these benefits, and now Paul Ryan wants to hand out coupons the equivalent of drive-through restaurants dispensing aspirin instead of medical care of the highest quality.") Be sure to add with studied emphasis that Ryan even wanted to cut the earned pensions of military veterans with at least 20 years of service and who knows how many tours logged, miles traveled, bullets and IEDs dodged, anniversaries and birthdays spent away from their families.

This was the line of attack that forced nearly every member of Congress to retreat in 2014, but not Ryan. He built his own cross. Crucify him on it.

This is where your 5% plank will help you most, against every member of the Senate and House that took up legislative arms against those who bore the real arms and the burdens of the nation's defense from 9/11 forward. You voted for the Afghan and Iraq invasions, but you did not vote to punish the men and women who fought those and other wars. Many of your opponents did. Make them pay.

Starting with Ryan. Every speech on national security, every debate on defense, every editorial board meeting when you start to speak of rebuilding America's hollowed out military, be sure to make the future Speaker pay the price for his short sighted deal of 2013. You will never beat him in Janesville, and you cannot remove him from House leadership for as long as he stays in office, but you can rebrand him permanently via repetition of his mortal sin against the uniformed military.

Chairman Ryan will shrug this off, and pretend not to care. But he will eventually snap back in a memorable outburst. Or he will recant and admit an error of judgment.

This latter move would be to his inestimable benefit long term, but most American politicians have never learned the art of the apology followed by "now I have to get back to doing the work of the American people" flash of indignation invented by Bill. They double and triple their sunk costs, always digging, digging, digging deeper into their holes, never remembering the "first rule of holes," which is that when find yourself in a hole, first stop digging.

Chairman Ryan could recognize this and work to defuse the issue. Could assign it to the desperation brought about by your and President Obama's unprecedented fiscal recklessness, could admit error and move on, adopting or even anticipating the 5% standard and using the ongoing erosion of America's position in the world to justify the pivot.

But he hasn't yet. Before he does, put down the markers to make sure everyone knows who made him turn—or dig even deeper—and why.

CHAPTER 15

Your Brother-in-law Jeb

I don't need a last name, and you don't need a last name. The other dynasty candidate, with just as much muscle and instant name recognition.

And even more of an exhaustion factor than your burden of tiredness.

All you need to know about Jeb came from an interview Candy Crowley did with his older brother, your husband Bill's pal W, on December 7, 2014. The complete text is online and it is full of 41's obvious love, esteem and affection for whom he hopes turns out to be 45. Then there is this exchange:

CROWLEY: You've often referred to Bill Clinton and you talk about his relationship with your father and how it developed, and your mother as well, and he's your brother from another mother.

(LAUGHTER)

CROWLEY: What does that make Hillary Clinton to the Bush family?

BUSH: My sister-in-law!

CROWLEY: Interesting. And do you think that your brother could run against your sister-in-law?

BUSH: Yeh, and I think he'd beat her.

CROWLEY: Do you?

BUSH: I do. I do.

CROWLEY: She's formidable.

BUSH: Very much so. No question. So is he though.

CROWLEY: So you'll take that bet.

BUSH: Absolutely.

CROWLEY: Do you think she'll run?

BUSH: Of course, you're not going to make it because you're an objective newscaster.

CROWLEY: That's why I'm asking you.

BUSH: Do I think she'll run? I have no clue. I have no clue. But I know this—that like Jeb, she knows what it's like, and she's taking her time. She's got a new complicating factor, and that is she's a grandmother and, like you, and like me from the grandfather side, she's going to understand the joys of what it's like.

CROWLEY: Just being available.

BUSH: Absolutely. And it'll enrich their lives like no other event has. And, but both folks will make—yes, she'd be a formidable candidate, no question. And both folks, Jeb and Hillary, are going to make very considered judgments.

Your decision is made, and so is Jeb's. He would be your most formidable opponent for the same reason Romney threatened you, albeit briefly: simply because Bush and Romney have both been to the circus a few times and know, as you know, what is coming.

But former Governor Bush seems not to know, nor does his brother, that a torpedo has struck the Good Ship Jeb amidships, a torpedo named "Common Core." In the end, I suspect this will sink his campaign unless he finds a way to persuade people of his fundamental and passionate opposition to what Common Core has become. Common Core is a slow motion disaster, and one metastasizing as you read this, reaching out to every dining room table in the land, throwing parents into fury and teachers into confusion. It has Jeb's trademark on it, and he seems not to understand the need to repudiate the Frankenstein monster he brought to life.

So he will probably not be opposite you. But just in case he does manage to be against Common Core after he was for it and somehow survives the conservative gantlet, prepare for that early on by denouncing Common Core, and more emphatically than he eventually will.

The late Lee Atwater famously remarked once that if your opponent is on the ground with a broken arm...step on it. Atwater was the first President Bush's political guru and you must appropriate his advice. Jeb has everything necessary to beat you, so early on give a speech to either the National Education Association or the American Federation of Teachers denouncing the chaos and confusion caused by Common Core. Mix it in with all the appropriate bows and nods to the enthusiasts in the room, but make no mistake that you think Common Core poorly planned and terribly rolled out, that much work needs to be done, especially on the Math curriculum that is confounding moms and dads, and that perhaps America's educators ought not to have trusted a tight-fisted Bush to design their curriculum overhaul.

Your "brothers-in-law" won't be amused. But you don't beat Achilles by carefully avoiding his heel. You aim for it with every arrow you let fly and every stroke of your sword.

Then there is the prospect of a "third Bush war in Iraq," and this rhetorical gut-punch needs to be among the ones you throw most often. I myself questioned the former Florida governor about this on air on February 15 of this year, and I did so because it is the toughest question he can face and he needs the practice in answering it as you will be throwing it his way often if he escapes the Common Core trap and becomes the nominee:

HH: *Now Governor Bush, what interests me about that is when you look forward into a possible third Bush presidency, not how the Iraq wars went or your opinion of your father's order to invade Iraq, or your brother's order to invade Iraq, but whether or not you'd be overly cautious about using force for fear of having a "third Bush war" occur?*

JB: No, that's an interesting question, and I'm glad you asked it. It wouldn't, if I was, if I decide to go forward with a race and I'm fortunate enough to go through that whole process, and God willing, win, then I would have a duty to protect the United States. And there are circumstances where a commander-in-chief, the president of the United States has to make tough decisions. And history's full of examples of that. I wouldn't be conflicted by any legacy issues of my family. I actually, Hugh, am quite comfortable being George Bush's son and George Bush's brother. It's something that gives me a lot of comfort on a personal level, and it certainly wouldn't compel me to act one way or the other based on the strategies that we would be implementing and the conditions that our country would be facing.

HH: *So a conservative who is a strong Defense conservative would not have to be hesitant to worry that you would be reluctant to use force anywhere, but especially in the Muslim world?*

JB: I don't think there's anything that relates to what my dad did or what my brother did that would compel me to think one way or the other. I think that history's a good guide for our country. And the simple fact is you start with the premise that America's role in the world is a force for good, not for bad things to happen, you'll have, lessen the likelihood of having to use military force around the world. America's foreign policy is more successful when we're clear about who we're supporting in terms of our allies, and that our enemies fear us a little bit rather than take advantage of us, to create insecurity that then compels the world and the United States to react. I think a better solution is to have a forceful foreign policy where we're supportive of our friends, where there's no light between our closest allies, like Israel, like our neighborhood, like NATO. These are the alliances that have kept us safe. And the more that people are assured of that, the more likely it is that we'll live in a peaceful world.

A fine couple of answers, those, but will they wear? They might.

Jeb Bush—without warning of what was coming, for I do not

telegraph my questions to friends or foes—instinctively knew that he had to answer that he would do what was in the best interests of the country whatever history had said about past wars or what talking heads would say about future ones as they unfolded. He knew he couldn't be chained to the past in any way, and he declared as much on the spot. Great instincts on the part of that very experienced fellow. Not that you shouldn't try again to get under his skin. But his skin is thick, and his experience is as deep as yours. Remember that. Cheap tricks won't work as they might on a rookie.

Our interview on February 25, 2015 ended this way. Note how he closes it:

HH: *Well then, let's look at, assume you are the nominee and you'd be up against former Secretary of State Clinton. That would be a 69 year old Clinton versus a 64 year old Bush. Now...*

JB: Hey, hey, buddy, hang on now. Sorry, I'm 62. 62.

HH: *(laughing) 62, sorry. Is that a little bit like Magic versus Bird playing one on one now? I mean, isn't that...*

JB: I'm in the best shape of my life. I'm an idea-driven guy. I think campaigns need to be about the future, and they need to be hopeful and optimistic. And they need to embrace technologies in ways that allows you to have two-way communication with potential voters. And a campaign that's going to be successful for conservatives is to campaign outside of one's comfort zone.

HH: *And then the last question, Governor, what's the message to the newly-emerging democracies, that the world's oldest democracy keeps recycling Bushes and Clintons and Clintons and Bushes? Does it send the wrong message to the Nigerias and the Indias of the world about dynasty?*

JB: If the campaigns are about, if the campaign's about a dynasty, I'm not sure that that's going to work. If it's about how you advance ideas that will help people rise up, then it will be an inspiration for others. And that's what we need to do. We need to be talking about the future by fixing a few really big, complicated things, to allow the middle to rise, and for people stuck at the bottom to rise up as well. And we can do it. That's the good news, is the inspiration of America is going to be when we start growing at 4% per year rather than 2% per year. We will inspire the world to emulate us.

Jeb Bush knows you will want the dynasty card played because he's a third and very different Bush, and you are the same old Bill-and-Hillary act. He's also suggesting, ever so slightly, that while he is in "the best shape of his life," well, perhaps not all of his opponents are. They know this game, Madame Secretary. Specifically, Governor Bush knows this game, very, very well.

You will be working overtime to blend three Bushes into one. You should talk about "Bush wars" and "Bush economics" and "Bush appointees" and "recycled Bush rhetoric." This will work only in the GOP primaries, so deploy it before those primaries begin. As in tomorrow and every day thereafter.

You should know as well that Jeb Bush plays to win. Just as I went to press on March 30, 2015 with this manuscript, the former Florida governor came by my California studios. You were in the news again for your, well, unusual arrangement with Sidney Blumenthal, and of course for your legacy in the Middle East. Note this exchange:

HH: Will it be fair, if you're the nominee and campaigning against Hillary Clinton, to argue "You broke it, you bought it" with regards to Libya and all the other chaos that swirls around the region?

JB: Yeah, no, I think she can't do the Heisman on the first four years of the Obama foreign policy. She'll try. I mean, she's going to, look, this is very Clintonian, I think, to figure out a way to get out of a mess. But she was Secretary of State of the first administration. And while some of this disruption and then all the stuff playing out right now didn't exist in the first four years, its roots were there. The pullback began then. The reset with Russia, the discussions with Syria, the red line, all these things created the beginnings of what we're now seeing. And so…

HH: We've got one minute left, and I promised your people a half hour, so I'll let you go. What about her server and wiping it clean? Or you can stay around if you want to talk about that longer. But what about that?

JB: I don't know. I don't know. I put my money on Trey Gowdy, for start-
ers. That guy is a superstar. He respects the rule of law. He'll be a gentleman
about it, but he's not going to give up on this notion that she needs to come
clean with what she knows about that information and other things for sure.

"And other things," Madame Secretary. "Coming clean," Madame Secretary.

These are problems. The time to hang Sid out to dry and call on
him to take the ultimate fall is upon you. If you want to be president,
he will be pushed under the bus by the end of the year, and in such a
spectacular fashion that no one will ever have any worry that Sidney
Blumenthal will be around to make Chuck Colson in Nixon's first term
seem like an amateur.

CHAPTER 16

The Big Guy

I introduced Meg Whitman before the California delegation at the Tampa Bay Republican convention in 2012, and she in turn introduced New Jersey Governor Chris Christie to a breakfast gathering memorably captured by the *New York Times'* Mark Leibovich in one of his essays in the paper, subsequently collected in *Citizens of the Green Room.* What Leibovich could not have seen that morning was the scene in that particular green room, a holding room off the stage where Whitman, Christie retainers, contributors and I gathered.

These are the moments that tell. If you let them. It is has been my habit to stand back from the scrum and observe. As I worked hard for the ill-fated Meg campaign, I had been in a few such rooms with her, and the eBay billionaire turned HP CEO is as wonderful with a small crowd as Christie is with a large one, but their personas invert in the opposite settings. Christie in a crowded room: terrific. In a small room, not so much. He expects to be approached and he expects to be praised. He is the proverbial "big guy," with all the strengths and weaknesses of that "big guy," the blocking tackle, the heavyweight champ, the tough-talking, straight-ahead, union-busting, Springsteen-loving Jersey prosecutor.

No Rick Fazio here. He would make no mistakes with you that way, no untoward approaches across the debate stage. If you get into the ring with him, your glass jaw will shatter. He will ask the question: "Why did you flee the State Department at 1 a.m. the night of Benghazi with your ambassador dead and your second–in-command left hanging? Why didn't you at least call Mr. Hicks back? How can you expect to lead the country in the future when you flunked that crisis so obviously and thoroughly?"

So best not to get into the ring to begin with. Take him out early. The GOP primary voters will finish off Jeb, but they may in fact be drawn to the combativeness of Christie, a long sought after genuine brawler. (The same deep desire will give Cruz a huge lift.)

"Take him out" means planting the same doubt about his electability that Rove so artfully planted about your health. It will take only one appearance, one "joke," one mention that you'd enjoy facing an opponent that could be indicted the weekend before the election.

Oh, that will travel. It would endure. You can distance yourself immediately, fluff it off as a joke, but in giving voice to the collective fear of media-orchestrated sabotage that every GOP primary voter harbors, you will have pulled the pin on the grenade. Most serious Republican activists and voters over 30 recall the Bush DUI, and many even remember the Lawrence Walsh indictment issued days before your husband beat the first Bush, a blast that destroyed 41's then-growing momentum. Remind my people that the MSM loves to at least try to sink GOP nominees in the last week (now month with early voting), and your work here will be done. There is a federal investigation underway into Christie' dealings. There is almost certainly "no there there." But oh, the risk of an unprincipled indictment. Rick Perry was indicted in Texas, but with enough time to fight it off. If Christie is indicted as the nominee in October of 2016...

Just to be sure, put a second torpedo in the water, just before Iowa and New Hampshire and the two Super Tuesdays in March. Remind everyone of the hug Christie gave President Obama just before the 2012 vote. Another joke will do. "Chris Christie looks like he is surging. Perhaps President Obama will return the favor the governor did the president in late October in 2012 by finding a reason to go to New Jersey for a visit to the towns destroyed by Sandy?" That's enough. The memories will flood back.

Not fair, of course, but effective. Effective is all that counts. You really can't risk Christie in the general. Much better to retire him early, and with the lightest of touches in 2015.

CHAPTER 17

Ted Cruz

Ted Cruz can beat you. You can also thrash him and take 43 or 44 states. It could go either way.

His ambition matches yours, which makes him so formidable. He is much, much smarter than you, though, which of course rankles, but which you must overcome. If you underestimate him, it will be to your peril.

Cruz is hated by your friends in the MSM for the same reason you intuitively dislike him: That blistering intelligence and the verbal ability accompanying it. They —and you— are jealous. This is a sad failing in many politicians and you should work to overcome it. In this you have no guide as Bill clearly has never thought himself the second to anyone in ability or intelligence, and perhaps he is correct in that, as his failings in other areas are also second-to-none.

But whether Bill is Cruz's equal, you most definitely are not. He will slice you up in debates, so begin to consider now the possibility of refusing to debate him. There would be some bad press for breaking precedent, but a flat statement of "his unpreparedness despite the GOP's madness in nominating him does not compel me or the voters to endure his antics," will do. He really would take you apart, muscle and joint.

Do not believe the echo chamber on this one. As Cruz himself likes to say to people, MSM has for years labeled any Republican president or nominee as either stupid or evil. Cruz tells small groups that MSM has created a third category for him: "crazy."

Cruz often neglects to note that the MSM has used that category before—on Barry Goldwater and briefly, during the 1980 campaign, on Ronald Reagan. You will have to work hard to resurrect the memory of Goldwater and attach it to Cruz. If you could arrange for a Cow Palace-like howling at center-right Republicans during the Cleveland Convention in July 2016 when Cruz could be nominated, that will help you, just as Pat Buchanan's rant in 1992 in Houston helped your husband by driving some key voters out of the GOP and into Perot's or Bill's waiting arms. Cruz needs every Republican and is working hard to cement over the cracks in the broad GOP coalition. Get out your jackhammer. Summon the prospect of a "3 a.m. phone call" that you used effectively, though too late, against then Senator Obama in 2008.

But not in a debate, because Cruz will strike you down and do so with a smile and a very light touch —the quickest of reminders that you went home on the night of Benghazi, and were not at State at 3 a.m. to make or receive calls that terrible night.

Cruz will crush you one-on-one, so attack him via your surrogates in the MSM. Let them do the work.

As I write he may be the favorite to be the nominee, with Scott Walker and Marco Rubio tied in a distant second, Kasich a struggling third, trying to get traction, deterred by Jeb until Jeb withdraws. Walker could take the nomination from Cruz, and Rubio is your biggest worry as a wild card catching fire, but Cruz is your likeliest opponent given the mechanics of the GOP calendar and rules, so begin now to plan on a long march from his nomination in July, 2016 through the election where every day you mention "temperament" at least ten times. Bill will do the heaviest lifting here, comparing Cruz unfavorably to "my Texas friends W and 41," whom Bill will archly hint share his views that Cruz is simply not in the mainstream and not qualified to steward the globe. Your veep nominee will hammer this every day. But you must be regal—not hard, that. You must just refuse to walk on to the stage. Cruz, like Rubio and Walker, can make people believe. Don't give him that chance.

Your "brain trust"—the same folks who gave you the wrongly translated "reset" button to give to Russian Foreign Minister Sergei Lavrov—they will mock Cruz. Shut that down today. Underestimating an opponent has been the death of many a presidential campaign. Ask President Dewey. Ask President Gore.

Actually ask Jimmy Carter, and appear with him for an obligatory consultation at the conclusion of which he could helpfully say "I knew Ronald Reagan. Ronald Reagan beat me. Ted Cruz is no Ronald Reagan. He is Barry Goldwater, and Hillary is going to beat him soundly, and to the great relief of the country that cannot afford adventures as poorly thought out as many of Senator Cruz's remarks."

But don't doubt the power of the age gap. I conducted a dozen mock Iowa caucuses for young conservatives on the campus of Colorado Christian College in the summer of 2014. There were six groups of between 20 and 40 students, and I polled each group twice, Iowa-style, first after just listing the candidates on a board and allowing the various supporter groups to organize and speak out, and then again after teaching them advocacy and argument in a studiously neutral fashion. (I have remained neutral throughout the 2016 run-up and will until the nominee raises his hands with his veep selection in Cleveland.)

Cruz won all twelve pseudo-caucus votes. Crucially, he won simple majorities in all six of the re-votes. This shocked me then and was inexplicable until I saw *Politico*'s research into online engagement by Cruz and his team, which is massively more than any of his GOP opponents. He has been living where the young voters live, and they will like him much, much more than a candidate their grandmother's age. You will be able to scare them a bit, but not much. They are young.

You will have to scare the old folks, and thoroughly. They are the GOP's bedrock, but Cruz can be made to frighten them. So do so.

And. Do. Not. Debate. Him.

CHAPTER 18

Mike Huckabee

"Will he or won't he?" was a question that filled some airtime in 2014, with the "he" being Mike Huckabee. But early this year he left Fox News Channel, a lucrative, ego-boosting gig, and most accounts say it was his choice. Huck is in. Huck is back.

It doesn't much matter to you, Madame Secretary. The former Governor of Arkansas, winner of the 2008 Iowa caucus, enabler of Senator McCain's nomination, destroyer of the first Romney run, may or may not end up entering the lists in 2016. It already cost him his great gig at Fox for a season, and aging white males don't give up television spots easily for fear they won't be coming back, but he cannot win the GOP nomination. He might just love the trail for a bit to renew and rework his populist chops, and have a handshake deal with Roger Ailes to return.

So be very generous to him, and find an opportunity to talk in public of your shared Arkansas roots. He is a gentleman and a Baptist preacher. You can handle 30 minutes with Mike. Remind him and the audience—it has been so long that people forget—of all your time on the back roads of Arkansas, traveling on behalf of children's health (and your then young husband's career). You can chew through 30 minutes or an hour with Mike and bank the b-roll.

It is important, by the way, to have a sit down with each Fox host in the fall of '15. Go one-on-one with O'Reilly, Sean, Greta and of course Megyn but be very careful of the last. O'Reilly and Van Susteren will be aware that the windup of their careers will coincide with yours, and will be eager to preserve their access through the next Clinton era. Hannity will go for blood, but even if he draws it, you will benefit from having battled television's most consistent conservative. Only Megyn, not really believing the succession theory of this book, will see she has decades beyond you in which to dominate news, and if getting to the network anchor means creating "a moment" with you, well, she will.

So would Bret Baier. So too will any younger cable anchor eager to put the "question" to you as Bernard Shaw did to Jimmy Carter in 1980. All media want to put that "question" to all nominees and you are the nominee even though not yet designated formally, so everyone is gunning for you as surely as every NFL team shoots for the Super Bowl champion from last year.

The trick will be to be comfortable and anticipate those moments and turn them back on the host, as George H.W. Bush so memorably did on Dan Rather, to the latter's embarrassment and as Newt did so often in the debates of 2012, and as you can do.

Do it once, and hosts will be gun shy. Not with Gov. H though. Find a joint appearance opportunity and play memory lane, emphasizing how you were once a young mom in Arkansas, sympathizing with the young moms in near poverty. "You recall these folks, Mike, you cared for them too," and he will be yours.

The governor is very much against same-sex marriage, and on this you ought to be on the offensive when you join him on air. Bring it up. Encourage him to repeat his declarations on abortion and gay marriage.

"I am utterly exasperated with Republicans and the so-called leadership of the Republicans, who have abdicated on this issue," Huckabee told the Family Research Council's "Values Voters Summit" annual gathering in 2014. "If the Republicans want to lose guys like me and a whole bunch of still God-fearing and Bible-believing people just go ahead and abdicate on this issue. And while you are at it, go ahead and say abortion doesn't matter either because at that point you lose me." He continued:

"If they continue this direction, they guarantee they are going to lose every election in the future. Guarantee it. And, I don't understand why they want to lose because a lot of Republicans, particularly those that live on the left coast or those who live up in the bubbles of New York and Washington are convinced that if we don't capitulate on the same-sex marriage issue, and if we don't raise the white flag of surrender and just except the inevitable, then we are going to be losers. I tell you, it is the absolute opposite of that."

It isn't the "absolute opposite of that" of course, but that is what the governor's audience that day wanted to hear and he let them it hear it, believing it sincerely to be right of course, but also confident that he had no general election campaign to run.

Your calculation should be very different. You should want to encourage Mike to split the party down these lines, to fan the fire within the base of religious conservatives upset by court-imposed decrees on same sex marriage and to bring up abortion again and again. He is a most useful wedge. Hit the road with him, once, in the late summer of 2015 and follow quickly with sit-downs with the rest of the Fox line up. Then rest and point to them through the entirety of 2016 as evidence of your willingness to go anywhere and debate anyone in right wing media.

This "illusion of availabilty" created by a round of Fox News interviews will be transparently thin, but it will also become a talking point among your MSM fans eager to diminish the Fox brand and immunize you into being a reliable guest on their reliably safe venues. After you have appeared on each Fox headliner's show once—one and done— you are home free.

Three other media people to worry about: Neil Cavuto, Jake Tapper, and Chuck Todd. Be very, very careful around these pros. They won't blink before putting in a shiv. The best laid media plans....

CHAPTER 19

Bobby Jindal

I have watched the Louisiana governor work and from different perspectives. From the audience, from behind him at a Mitch McConnell event in late October 2015, beside him asking questions of him and Carly Fiorina at the same event, and via the phone on the radio again and again over the past many years.

Such an intellect, and he would be a very formidable general election candidate except that he will be a vice presidential nominee before he is a general election nominee, so not a concern of yours—yet.

But have the oppo done and track him everywhere. And begin to define him by his most exotic episode—the exorcism.

I asked him—twice—about this much-written-about event in his life (very few presidential candidates have been present at an exorcism, and when Governor Jindal was on the short list of candidates for Romney's VP, I didn't miss my turn at bat on that question). He simply bypassed it the first time I asked. The second time was another deflection:

HH: *Now Governor, unlike President Obama, though, your autobiographical writings are accurate. You didn't make up people or events, or any composite characters. And you're standing by it. Are you prepared to defend that exorcism article, because that's what they'll come for on day one that you're nominated for vice president?*

BJ: Yeah, look, like I said, all the VP stuff, I defer to the Romney folks. I'm absolutely prepared to defend my faith, who I am, and what I believe in....

And then he proceeded not to defend it. Such deflections are like red arrows pointing at vulnerabilities understood to be vulnerabilities by the candidate. Your job is to pass off a few references to exorcism and Governor Jindal when you can, or better yet, have Bill do it. Playfully, of course, perhaps in a joint appearance. Your husband is so skilled at such maneuvers.

The long game requires a long-game, and Jindal will be in the Senate before you know it, and is very young, a future Chelsea obstacle. Wound him while you can, and when hardly anyone will think twice about it.

CHAPTER 20

John Kasich

The governor from Ohio should concern you, somewhat. Jeb has frozen him for the time being. Kasich is *very* good at connecting with people. His religious faith is deep and sincere. He is ebullient and comfortable on television, a skill set honed during his years as a Fox News host, anchor and analyst. He is a key to unlocking the GOP's Electoral College map via Ohio. He turned his state around after terrible mismanagement by Democrats and adjusted after early missteps. He won re-election by 30-plus points! In Ohio!

In many respects Kasich is everything you are not, especially likable. You look worn-out, stale, and bored. He is always full of life and good humor, an endless energy machine. You will have to kill him with kindness. You will have to begin now to praise "his support for Obamacare" as a "model of successful governance" and the key to his re-election.

Talk early and often about his expansion of Medicaid in the Buckeye State. Focusing your attention and thus the MSM's on Kasich's Achilles' heel with the conservative GOP electorate is like talking about Common Core when you discuss Jeb. Hammer the nails into the primary coffins of those you do not wish to face, or whom you want off the GOP's veep list.

Your advisors will want you to focus on the collapse of Lehman Brothers when Kasich was a partner there, but any journalist with a brain knows Kasich didn't have anything to do with the panic of 2008, but Freddie and Fannie did, and throttling a genuine look back at that set of events is what you need to do. Keeping Freddie and Fannie off the front pages, or any pages, is more important than trying to get a dig in at Kasich over a non-role in an unforeseeable event.

No, your opponents' greatest weaknesses are where you need to focus your attention. Kasich expanded Medicaid in Ohio as hoped for by Obamacare supporters and he used an "end around" the state legislature to do so. This was a two-strike count on the governor for some GOP primary voters before he even uttered his now famous explanation for the expansion of Medicaid:

> "I had a conversation with one of the members of the legislature the other day. I said, 'I respect the fact that you believe in small government. I do, too. I also know that you're a person of faith. Now, when you die and get to the meeting with St. Peter, he's probably not going to ask you much about what you did about keeping government small. But he is going to ask you what you did for the poor. You better have a good answer.'"

Such answers suggest moral superiority on the part of the action taken, and a sort of all-purpose trump card against arguing the case. It isn't that Kasich expanded Medicaid that drives conservatives crazy, but that he did so while at the same time suggesting moral failure on the part of his opponents.

Conservatives have grown very weary of being told they are either bigots (the same sex marriage debate), racists (for not overreacting to the deaths of Michael Brown and Eric Gardner), or indifferent to the poor (as implied by Kasich and countless others). This "moral superiority" argument—Rick Perry's "I don't think you have a heart" comment regarding opponents of immigration reform in the 2012 race is of the same family tree—is certain to offend those who believe themselves at least as moral as any elected official.

Third strike for Kasich? Perhaps. He is also a Common Core defender of sorts telling the *Columbus Dispatch* editorial board last year "What do I care about Common Core? I just want kids to learn. I don't have any ideological, personal or emotional commitment to anything other than: Let's make sure our kids do well."

This is as good a response as can be had and leaves the Ohio governor room to maneuver around Jeb Bush when the going gets tough. You need to stick to the Medicaid issue for Kasich and the Common Core issue for Jeb. Don't confuse the MSM with multiple lines of attack on each would-be November opponent. If you want to sideline Kasich, and you should, aim for his rather-on-his-sleeve heart: The Medicaid expansion and the approximately 300,000 people he brought willingly into Obamacare.

"I really don't know how the GOP nominates an Obamacare enthusiast," is how you begin. "Sure, he will disavow and trim and distinguish when the going gets tough in New Hampshire and elsewhere, but that didn't help Romney and it won't help him."

Done and done. Kasich's only real option will be to defend the Medicaid expansion vocally and volubly, making an argument that—if it does succeed in surviving the primaries—will make him very, very formidable in the fall. You need a Goldwater to beat, not a Reagan with an even cheerier disposition.

Medicaid expansion and St. Peter. Rinse and repeat. Always go for the soft spot. Always.

CHAPTER 21

Rand Paul

Your advisors will tell you that Senator Rand Paul, unlike Ted Cruz, does not have a path to the GOP nomination, that he will peak at 25% in a handful of states and be given a key slot at the convention, that he cannot be on the ticket. "The highest floor and the lowest ceiling" they will say. They are probably right. If they are wrong you will win in a landslide of Reagan-like proportions.

But, unlike the case for you praying for a Ted Cruz nomination, you cannot waste even your occasional prayers on Senator Paul. The non-interventionist moment died many deaths in 2014 and early 2015, most spectacularly in Anbar province but also in Syria, Ukraine, Nigeria, Pakistan, Australia—even in Hollywood at the offices of Sony Pictures. The world will not allow America to withdraw. Rule or be ruled.

He could, in some circumstances, be the GOP veep. This is small possibility that increases as the GOP race becomes more jumbled. In an open, "brokered" convention in Cleveland next July, Senator Paul will have a lot of delegates. Not enough for a nomination, but more than enough to drive a very hard bargain for whoever does become the nominee.

You know this, and so does Senator Paul, a very, very smart pol buoyed by his father's 5% and a command of modern communications second only to Senator Cruz's. He can try and pivot from his legacy and his first filibuster by arguing for robust defense spending and a new cyber fortress America, and his edges are much softer than his father's, shaved down by his genuine commitment to Christian service on medical missions.

Senator Paul is a good man and a better foil. You will need him for years to come. He can be your Arthur Vandenberg as you go about transitioning the country to your long-term vision of a fortress America without the messy allies. Chelsea will need him too, and with proper encouragement, he could form the "third way" party of the GOP's nightmares, the permanent Ralph Nader of 2000, playing again and again and again the role of Ross Perot in 1992 and Mike Huckabee in 2008. Third party Paulistas could easily destroy not just presidential campaigns, but Senate campaigns like Republican Ed Gillespie's in Virginia in 2014. It is a project worth investing in, but only at a distance.

It would be wonderful if one of your closest friends could form a Super PAC devoted to all things Rand, and especially to running him against his will wherever possible. Certainly he will object in 2016, but cannot those legislatures under total Democratic control tinker with the laws now to allow non-consenting nominations of candidates to new parties later?

The Paulistas are the bone spur in the heel of the GOP. Make it worse. Make it gangrenous. A long-term transition needs a long term cover. Senator Paul is your best bridge to Chelsea's tomorrow. Don't waste it.

CHAPTER 22

Rick Perry

Do not underestimate this man, who did so much in 2012 to lower his own expectations and thus increase his odds of facing off with you in 2016. He does run with a gun, and he kills coyotes with abandon. This is his last race unless he wins. There will be no "next times" for the four-term governor of the Lone Star State and his financial backers know it. And they will fight Jeb as Reagan fought Ford, and they will fight Ted Cruz with the intensity of a second front in a civil war. Jeb-Ted-Rick is a "Texas Death Cage Match" and the governor took down Kay Bailey Hutchison in 2010 like Ted Cruz took down David Dewhurst in 2012. Like they both intend to take you down. Methodically.

Perry could rally the W base even against W's brother. He could pull Tea Party and national defense conservatives together because he is imminently believable. He will joke and joke and joke again about his brain freeze in front of the country, and it won't get old because Rick Perry doesn't get old. He gets funnier. When I asked *Time* Magazine's Zeke Miller who was the best pure communicator in the GOP field, he said first Rubio, then Walker, then...Perry. A million events and speeches is practice. So he had a mighty strike out once. That just tempts you to mispitch him the next time.

So better to end it quickly and with big dollar allocations from your friends to Ted Cruz and Rick Santorum in Iowa, New Hampshire, South Carolina. (Enduring support for Rick Santorum is the other internal bleeding that Perry cannot afford.) If Perry doesn't carry one of the first three contests, the loss in 2012 will haunt him and he will crumble.

Perry is one of the candidates you cannot afford to face: an authentic, tested conservative governor with a record of managing things successfully from start to finish. Think of his 2012 campaign as a giant and early head fake to draw your attention elsewhere. Don't be drawn into that. Invest early and heavily against him.

CHAPTER 23

Marco Rubio

Meet your worst nightmare, speaking in fluent Spanish, reminding everyone, every day of: Just. How. Old. And. Tired. You. Are.

Like Rick Perry, Rubio is believable on national defense because he genuinely, authentically believes in it. Like Ted Cruz, he is the son of refugees from the tyranny you applauded and helped whitewash when President Obama "recognized" Cuba. Unlike anyone else in the field, the young senator will make young single moms and single women swoon. Cruz will come close to possessing "it," but not accomplish "it." And Ryan—while he has "it"—isn't running, though he will be in the future.

Like Ryan, and to a lesser extent Cruz, you need to retire Rubio from the field in his cycle before he can complicate your future. He may try to not allow that, by avoiding the confrontation for now. Jeb Bush's early entry complicated things for Rubio, as did his declaration of refusing to run for both reelection to the Senate even as he seeks the presidency, but in fact, it appears as he settled on his course long ago and is fully, forcefully and skillfully pursuing it. He may lose the March 15, 2016 battle for Florida with Jeb, and have to settle for the Veep slot, or run as governor to succeed Rick Scott in 2018, waiting you out—not unaware of, but not fully crediting the scope of your ambitions. What is eight years to anyone in their early 40s?

Events in the world of chaos you helped create are changing so dramatically as to propel him forward though, dragged by a party desperate for youth, fluency in Spanish, credibility on national security and above all: "it." Indeed, as I write this, he looks and sounds like a young man in a hurry, a young man with exceptional good looks and energy, who has built a record of solid positions on national security. He has even earned the over-amplified enmity of the anti-immigrant sliver of his party's base, which is actually an assist to him in the general election, not a handicap. He will not have the money that Jeb Bush can amass, but by running he all but assures himself a place on the national ticket. If he faces you or your running mate, you are in deep trouble. Unless you can wound him, early and deeply.

Assume though that Rubio does not in the end win, and that by losing it to Jeb cannot be the veep nominee, and somehow pivots back to the Senate seat he holds or on to the Florida statehouse. Even then he is the number one bystander, waiting. Anybody but Jeb Bush will put him on the ticket, and even Jeb might find a way around the 12th Amendment's technical prohibition of electors voting for a president and vice president from their own state as Dick Cheney did by re-registering in Wyoming in 2000.

So Rubio will be a huge electoral force in 2016 and beyond, and thus you must allocate the dollars to beat him in the primaries in a humiliating fashion. Now. Your advisors will want you to ignore the effort to destroy a GOP nominee until that nominee is all but certain, afraid of wasting resources. but you can still attack Rubio by investing heavily in a Democratic senate candidate whose job will not only be winning the seat for the Democrats against Rubio's successor in interest —probably Congressman Ron DeSantis but there are many would-be replacements in the Sunshine State's GOP. Their second job will be to launch attack after attack on Rubio's six years in the United States Senate and his long years in the Florida legislature. If he or she wants your help, they have to help you bleed the young superstar. Of course you need Florida's electoral votes anyway, and by hand-picking a candidate to take Rubio on now, you can invest in that key turnout machine. Beating him in humiliating fashion ends him, and beating him removes the GOP's only immediate threat aside from Jeb to the "new Americans" vote, and the votes of their families.

You will need a Puerto Rican Floridian to beat a Cuban-Floridian, one rhetorically as fluent in Spanish and as telegenic as is Rubio. You must deny him his natural Telemundo and Univision advantage as well as his Spanish radio edge. How Mitt Romney did not pick him remains the great unexplained question of 2012, so probe as well every detail of his story and his family's story.

Recall season two of *House of Cards* when the opposition research team found the vulnerability even Kevin Spacey and Robin Wright had not imagined could be unearthed from Princess Buttercup's past? That is the level digging we are talking about. There is no whisper among GOP circles of any impropriety except some charges on his GOP credit card, but dig away anyway.

The right has long suspected you have capabilities in this area of opposition research, which you could not actually have. How else could you have missed obvious things on President Obama that I and others found, like his audio book recording of *Dreams from My Father*, or Reverend Wright's sermons, on sale in his church's gift store?

In this respect, you are like the wizard in Oz, but only in this regard: the "pay no attention to the man behind the curtain" line. Your opposition research team is horrible and has been since Bill ran in 1992. You have never trusted anyone to be your Murray Chotiner, Nixon's most effective operative. But you need one, especially with regard to Rubio. But really for everyone in and out of your party.

This sort of sleuthing isn't hard to buy, so buy it. And not just from one source. Bounty it and—see Part III—be transparent about it. Speak out loud about the need to be vetted and to vet. Revel in what you should call "the new scrutiny." Go full Gary Hart, but when you challenge the press to follow you, be specific about those beside you "they" should be trailing:

> I welcome scrutiny. As one of my predecessors said famously and
> to his misfortune, go ahead and follow me around. But do not put

just me under that microscope as has so often been the case these past eight years, and even before my run for the Senate or Bill's 1992 campaign. Follow us all. Follow Senator Rubio and Governor Walker. They won't mind any more than I do. The *Washington Free Beacon* wants to plumb the depths of my two letters to Saul Alinsky in search of a secret code, or desires to send sleuths to the Clinton Library or the University of Virginia oral history project? Fine.

But let us have one standard for all candidates, one rule of thoroughness. Find all of Senator Rubio's legislative correspondence from his decade of deal-making in the Florida state house. Dig into Governor Kasich's Lehman Brothers tenure or Jeb Bush's Barclay bank buddies' best bets. Find out what the John Doe investigations in Wisconsin were really about and the extent of Governor Walker's dark money ops.

One standard. One rule. We have heard so long about so-called MSM bias that we have begun to believe it while the media really looks only for dirty laundry in the pile marked 'D'. Bill and I have lived so long under the kleig lights that we expect nothing less, are surprised by anything other than the lurid and the laughable.

But we will not accept a double standard and we will insist that one not be practiced. When we think there is a story worth pursuing, we will point to it and ask 'Why is that dartboard not covered in feathered missiles?' We won't be patsies. I won't be a victim of the vast right wing conspiracy which indeed does exist, has always existed, has grown stronger and stronger in the dark as this avalanche of dark money was called down by the Supreme Court on our politics.

There. Done. Pointers in bright red, hidden in broad sight.

Research and recruitment. Hand your hand-picked Senate candidate in Florida the weapons with which to bleed Rubio even though Rubio is not running for re-election, and build the best turnout machine of all your state operations in Florida. You are not playing for just one election but many, and you have to plan that way. If Rubio does indeed come straight at you, speaking Spanish and pointing to the chaos in the world you helped birth, he could easily carry the GOP with him and every dollar you spend now in prepping to beat him in Florida will be repaid with interest.

This recruitment-of-candidates-in-Florida-and-elsewhere process must advance instantly by the way, and not just in Florida, but across the country if the larger project is to succeed. You will need to age out the relics in the Senate and recruit more young and loyal—and compliant—friends and allies of Rome. As you remake the Senate, look for candidates with military experience, keeping in mind how effective the GOP was in recruiting Tom Cotton, Joni Ernst and Dan Sullivan in Arkansas, Iowa and Alaska respectively in 2014. You cannot overestimate how important it will be to clothe your tenure in the approval of veterans of the wars you were for before you were against them, and of those that you helped launch as Secretary of State, in Libya and Syria, or re-launch in Iraq. You need these people. Chelsea will need these people. Go and find them. Befriend them. Make them indebted to you. The officer class is 90% against you, but the 10% is all you need to co-opt and display to accomplish your goals.

And as you do, make it your business to discredit and ultimately defeat these three senators and every other "fast burner" on the GOP's bench in the Senate, like Colorado's Cory Gardner, or in the House, like Kansas' Mike Pompeo or Florida's Ron DeSantis.

It is never too early to thin the ranks of your opponents and build the numbers of your allies.

Start with Rubio. Soon. The likeliest tickets you will face are Bush/Cruz or some combination of Rubio and Walker. The first ticket combines establishment and grassroots in a traditional marriage of the power and the passion. Either Walker/Rubio or Rubio/Walker presents two candidates that have straddled the establishment-grassroots divide artfully and could bring enormous energy to the campaign. More on Walker later, but you look at Rubio and you see a man the world would respect in the Oval Office, and whom some would instantly fear. So should you.

I proposed a "Putin Primary" a few months back, asking in a column whom the Russian tough guy would most fear as a replacement for President Obama. Goodness knows that's a primary your and your "Reset Button" gang wouldn't win. But Rubio might—indeed probably would. Think about that as you get ready for 2016.

CHAPTER 24
Rick Santorum

I know, I know. Why bother to read this chapter at all? You and all the other really smart people who couldn't win Iowa in 2008 are saying that even though Santorum won Iowa in 2012 he really never had a chance then, and doesn't have a chance now.

Roll your eyes if you must because everyone else in the room rolls their eyes when Santorum comes up. The sweater vest. The dog-man thing. "Discount the Bella effect and he wouldn't even have finished third" you are all thinking. He is still the social warrior of old. He is so Jerry Falwell. So Pittsburgh. So last century.

Except he did win Iowa and you didn't, and he does draw crowds and he does know his own mind and the minds of those "Blue Collar Conservatives" for whom he titled his generally well written book of 2014. Santorum knows a few things, and but for the epic undertow of the 2006 anti-Bush election and a legacy candidate with the famous last name, he'd still be in the Senate and very much a contender understood as legitimate even by the Beltway cognoscenti that despise him for his arch-Catholic values.

And those "arch-Catholic" values are widespread if not widely reported on, a semi-Silent Majority that slumbers but has not died, and which Cruz, Rubio, Ryan and Walker are all comfortable crooning to, though not nearly with as perfect a pitch as Santorum can summon. All those people kneeling in all those churches, crossing themselves, saying the Rosary. The Pope still has no divisions, but there are millions of "arch-Catholic voters."

No, study Santorum not because he is a lightning strike about to happen, but because of the light he supplies when he doesn't hit you but strikes other Republicans instead. Watch his speeches and listen closely. Ask for delivery of the links to videos of his appearances taped by your legion of trackers. His indictment of the current GOP is detailed and nuanced, and much of it will travel to you and with you in the general if you have the ears to listen.

If was long ago when the first Bush damned President Reagan for his "voodoo economics," and the phrase that is still attached to 41 and will forever be, a classic "admission against interest" if ever there was one, the killer condemnation from within the party's own tent. You saddled yourself with such a Thor's hammer of a phrase against President Obama when you warned the primary electorate in 2008 of a "phone ringing at 3 AM" that then-Senator Obama wouldn't know how to handle. That line will never be forgotten. (And certainly not by Barack and Michelle. Whenever the president doesn't help as you had hoped, or delivers a half or a third of what you need, recall you uttered that phrase that has stuck to him as surely as "voodoo economics" stuck to Reagan.)

Rick Santorum will be a fountain of such material in the months ahead, if you will only pay attention. He understands himself to be in competition with Cruz, Perry, Rubio and Walker for the same voters, but unlike them, he was there in DC in the Senate from 1993 through 2001, fighting for the legacy of the Reagan Revolution through your husband's false "peace dividend" and extended holiday from history. He knows where all the GOP bodies are buried, and who was there and who genuinely fought through and who stood on the sidelines of the lost battles on marriage and the Supreme Court. His every speech is a code-breaker's handbook to the GOP.

When 2008 came down to Romney and McCain, Santorum was for Romney because McCain hadn't been there on the Senate floor fighting for Reagan's legacy. Santorum was outspoken, detailed, precise in his blasts at McCain. He will be the same candidate in 2016 as he was in 2012, and as specific in his critiques of the others in the GOP field as he was of McCain in 2008. Follow him and you will find much and more to use against whomever is the last man standing on the Republican side in 2016.

CHAPTER 25

Scott Walker

While the GOP faithful call him courageous, a "man of steel," and the smiling assassin of public sector unions, you should brand Wisconsin Governor Scott Walker as the "Republican Rasputin." Like the mad Russian monk who survived countless plots and assassination attempts —the last one only successful after he was shot three times after being poisoned, then thrown into the river only to be found 140 feet from it—the amiable, likable, innovative and soft-spoken Cheesehead cannot be put down by your labor union allies, in Wisconsin of all places! On three different occasions! You and your team want to think "Walker is Pawlenty," as flawed by good humor and good grace as the former Minnesota governor was in 2012; but unlike T-Paw, Walker has won not twice, but three times in progressive paradise, and he did so without the help of a third party spoiler on the ballot which Pawlenty had in both of his successful governor contests.

And Pawlenty might have gone the distance in '12, but for Congresswoman Michele Bachmann's kamikaze run and the mistaken trust in consultants who spent all his money early. Pawlenty had the best staff except on budgeting. Walker will study the Pawlenty campaign as he studies everything and learn the lessons. He won't spend his money early. He won't rely on Beltway sharpies. He will play a longer game and understand that he need only hang around through the carnage, smiling and amiable, reminding people that he is, Thatcher-like, "not for turning." He won the first big cattle call of Iowa,

Congressman Steve King's Iowa Freedom Summit on January 24, 2015, with a straight-from-the-heart recounting of the battles of Wisconisn that raged over four years, a narrative that included threats to "gut your wife like a deer" and creeps stalking his kids to their schools. He laughed off the attempt to turn his CPAC speech into a gaffe. He has hired a superb Comms Team and some deeply experienced operatives, and his foreign policy bench is as deep—and very different—from Jeb Bush's and Marco Rubio's, the trio of top tier candidates on matters foreign and not just domestic. (Cruz is working hard to catch up here but hasn't yet.) The GOP base knows it needs a strong man to stand up to your machine, rusty as it is, as old and worn down as you are, as desperate for Air Force One again as Bill sometimes lets on. Walker looks like that guy. He has already run the gantlet—three times!

Walker will use that enormous list of supporters generated during his reputation-making solo performance against organized labor and the left that, though not often brought up by conservatives, is remembered by them all.

And he will use that Harley-riding, pastor's-kid innocence and ready smile to press on and on.

So, you have but one card to play. Play it early and often and use Bill:

> "I don't have anything against anyone who couldn't finish college. I almost didn't make it to Georgetown, Oxford or Yale Law School, and but for some saints along the way I wouldn't have. Hillary of course had her mom and dad, and though they were, shucks, Goldwater people—Hillary was one of those kids running around as Goldwater girls ya'll know—she wouldn't have made it to Wellesley or Yale Law either. It took breaks in those days, great parents and teachers and a lot of luck, so I think the college degree thing leveled at Palin and Walker is just rubbish and unfair."

See, a three-fer. Not only do you play to America's love of credentials without exciting jealousy, you also cut Walker deep by noting his resume gap and, presto, by linking him to the most radioactive of names in centrist America, Sarah Palin. No one divides a room as quickly or with as much clarity as Sarah Palin, and her negatives are as enormous as the state she governed. You can use her only against one target, so match her up with Walker and stand back. The atom is spilt.

Walker might survive this, and his lack of a B.A. which the *Washington Post* trotted out in early February might even get traction in whispers during the GOP primaries, though Walker would be smart to plant question after question about it, and answer it every day and to his advantage in joining his own story to that of every American who either didn't finish or didn't start college. He can bring up Lincoln even as he talks again and at length about the costs of college and how he knows better than everyone how the system works against kids from middle-America's middle class. Powerful stuff that.

I asked Walker the question about credentials in the course of a January 6, 2015, interview that gives you a glimpse of his skills set. I began by asking whether his wife, Tonette, was on board for a 2016 race after having run in 2010, 2012 and 2014—the first and last races being brass-knuckled state house races, and the middle contest being the nastiest recall election in the country's modern history—by a lot:

HH: *What, is she okay with it?*

SW: Absolutely. I mean, she is a trouper. Tonette was a widow before we were married. She lost her husband and her only sibling within a year. She is a tough and remarkable woman in her own right. And she and now our 19- and 20-year-old sons, who themselves, not just me, over the last four years, were targets of protests and attacks, and all sorts of other things. They weathered this. It made us, sometimes a family goes through traumatic things like that, and they grow apart. We grew closer together. And I think they've realized after not just two years ago in the recall, but even this last November's election, I was the number one target in America, you know, for AFSCME, for the AFL-CIO, for the teachers union nationally, the NEA. I was their number one target. Washington-based special-interest groups spent just about everything they could. They brought the president in. They brought in Clinton. They brought in Elizabeth Warren. And we prevailed, because we took the power away from those big government special interests, and we put it in the hands of the taxpayers. And in the end, the taxpayers wanted someone who was going to stand up for them.

HH: Now, I, because of the nature of my business, I talk to everyone about this, and you are almost everybody's second choice to be the Republican nominee, and many people's first choice. But I hear the same two questions again and again, so I want to pose them to you first in 2015.

SW: Sure.

HH: First of all, you're too nice to beat Hillary. Can you beat Hillary?

SW: Anybody who watched me over the last four years knows that you know, I ran against the mayor of Milwaukee twice, who was former member of Congress, had all the backing in the world behind him, and I ran against a very strong businesswoman this last time who have had, like I said, all the Washington base behind her. And we had no problem. Yeah, I'm nice. I'm Midwestern nice. There's no doubt about it. But I don't think anyone's ever wondered if I was able to stand up and fight the big issues. And we've done that, I think, both on the campaign trail, and equally, if not more importantly, in the capital.

HH: The second thing I always hear, in a field full of lawyers and even one doctor, Rand Paul and a couple of businessmen, you're the only guy without a college degree.

SW: Yeah.

HH: What do you say to that?

SW: I say I'm like the majority of people in America. I'm someone who went to college, had the opportunity in my senior year to go and take a job full-time, which was not the only reason I went to college, but one of the biggest reasons was to get a job. And the American Red Cross offered me a job my senior year and I took it, thinking someday, maybe, I'd go back. But a few years later, I met my wonderful wife, Tonette, a year after that, we had Matthew, the year after that, we had Alex. And now, like a lot of folks in America, you know, your family and your job take the time away from you from finishing it up. But I don't think anybody, and I've got a master's degree in taking on the big government special interests, and I think that is worth more than anything else that anybody can point to.

This sort of facility with tough, pointed questions and his brilliant back-story is why you will need to launch the Palin missile early. Opponents with controversy and especially controversial people about whom few opinions will ever change is the wrecking ball of politics, second only to personal scandals, and there won't be any of those with Walker. Every bit of oppo that can be done, has been done to Walker. It is a dry hole. He is the only preacher's kid in America who never raised any Hell. Accept it, and try the Palin dart.

Quickly, and through Bill. Pretend-admiration has no better practitioner. You would blow it. Don't try.

If it doesn't work, you are in serious trouble, especially if Walker as the GOP nominee in Cleveland and summons Marco Rubio to join him on the stage, even as Rubio would stun you by picking Mitt Romney as his Veep. Either combo is a killer for you. So don't spend the next year raising money and waiting to spend it until August. The GOP has done the rarest of things, by accident. It has presented you with a political MIRV, and like these missiles with multiple warheads, the GOP's legion of good candidates makes it very hard for you to attack them all simultaneously. But you must. Just spend most of your time and money on Bush, Cruz, Rubio and Walker.

The biggest rap on Walker is that he isn't read for the national security issues, that his "Eagle Scout" demeanor and his backstory about taking on the public sector unions gets jumbled into the mix of complicated foreign policy narratives and makes him sound naive. That's what your MSM buddies tried to do with his PATCO quotes at CPAC and what the lefty trackers tried to do when, in response to a question I posed on whether he had thought about being Commander-in-Chief, they posted a video arguing he had tried to compare the achievement of becoming an Eagle Scout with preparation for being atop the U.S. military. Neither attack impressed anyone outside of Team Hillary because they were both absurd over-reaches and Walker didn't over-react. He never does. That is what scares you most—his unflappability when your machine is designed primarily to destroy opponents by occasioning their meltdowns.

So you will go after him on the names and places around the globe you have been, suggesting that perhaps the lack of a degree is a signifier of larger gaps. Beware. He is a learning machine. On the same day of the "Eagle Scout" comment, Walker sat down with me for a wide ranging chat about all things foreign and domestic. Again, no telegraphed questions, no notes in front of him, just us, two mics and an audience of millions:

HH: *Sitting across from me, the Governor of Wisconsin, who's not in the very cold far north. Scott Walker and I had a little Q&A in front of the Chamber of Commerce [earlier today]. Governor Walker, thanks for coming over to KKNT and continuing the conversation.*

SW: Thanks for having me on, and thanks for a great interview over there at the Chamber. It was outstanding.

HH: *Well, it was pretty easy after about a thousand people gave you a standing ovation. You're kind of getting used to that, I think. And we'll come back to some of that. But I sat down here, and there's breaking news everywhere.*

SW: Yeah.

HH: *Sgt. Bowe Bergdahl's been charged with desertion, the Saudis are massing troops on the Yemen border. This is what you're going to have if you decide to run for president – headlines breaking. So how do you prepare for walking into an interview when Bowe Bergdahl all of a sudden is charged with desertion?*

SW: Well, every day, I've started with Mike Gallagher, I was going to say a "former" Marine, but you're never a "former" Marine.

HH: *Captain, two tours, Anbar Province, right?*

SW: Right, a great, great guy. He's now our national security advisor, and used to work for Senator Corker on the Foreign Affairs Committee, really super guy. Every day, he gives us great information, great briefings, and I obviously reach out to a lot of others. But there's things happening all over the place. And as we talked about at lunch, and we'll talk about even more here, you've got to be ready on multiple fronts. When I think about this desertion charge, the thing that gets me the most frustrated is this administration gave up five Taliban, five Taliban for this guy, and I can't, I mean, logic tells you all this information that they're bringing against the sergeant now isn't something that just happened since then. This is stuff they knew about when they put American soldiers' lives at risk to try and rescue him. And they gave up five Taliban leaders in return for a guy who now is going to be charged.

*HH: It goes to the question of judgment, Governor Walker. And earlier today, Eliana Johnson said of your campaign in **National Review**, "the best of times, the worst of times." And yesterday on this program, Dave Weigel said Walker's going to be haunted by the speech where he compared public employee unions to ISIS, and I said "He actually didn't do that." But nevertheless, the small becomes large, and the large becomes small. What do you think of the President's judgment, not your judgment, but the President's judgment as it's evolving and unfolding?*

SW: Well, the unfortunate reality is this is what happens when you put someone in office who's never led before. He's not listening. When you're a governor, you're a mayor, you're a county executive wherever you're at, and when you have a cabinet and you have to act on behalf of not just the people who elected you, but the whole group, the whole constituency as we talked about a little bit at lunch. You've got to lead, and you've got to listen to people who hopefully are smart or smarter than you are on any given topic. You ultimately have to make the decision. This president, unfortunately, having been a senator, a state senate, and community organizer, never led anything. And so he's never been in a position to make those sorts of judgments. And so we've seen time and time again, they're just faulty decisions, which would be one thing if it was something off on the side. But this is affecting not only American policy and American lives, but people around the world.

HH: You mentioned today, you called it "the safety issue," not the "national security issue," that sort of brings, explain to people why you use that terminology.

SW: I do, because I think it's come to the forefront not so much because "national security," that, to me, as I said [at lunch], is on page 6A of the newspaper where only a handful of us read into that. But when people see the videos, when they see the Jordanian burned alive in a cage, when they see the Egyptian Christians who were beheaded, when they see some of these other folks from around the world, including James Foley, who went to Marquette University where my son's a junior, and suddenly, that becomes very real to everyday Americans.

HH: One of the beheaded Islamic State videos.

SW: Absolutely, whose parents are actually from New Hampshire, not far from where I was at a weekend ago, and you just realize, you can see it on your phone, you can see it on your iPad. You don't need the filter of the network news or the daily newspaper to tell you how bad this is. It suddenly becomes an issue of safety, because that's not something, national security, foreign policy is something over there. Safety is something you feel inside your chest, you feel in your heart. And I think increasingly, Americans feel a sense of concern that particularly if they have family members or loved ones that ever want to travel again, they see France, they see Canada, they see other places around the world, not just the Middle East, and it's a safety issue. And they, and then I would just add to this, as they look at this more closely, they see a president whose drawn a line in the sand and crossed it, who called ISIS just a year ago the "jayvee squad," who called Yemen last fall a success story, who calls Iran now a place where we can do business. Think about how screwed up that is. I remember the movie in the '80s, *Trading Places...*

HH: Right.

SW: ...you know, with Dan Aykroyd and Eddie Murphy, it's like Iran and Israel are trading places in the sequel. In the eyes of this president, our ally is supposed to be Israel. Our adversary has been historically Iran. And yet this administration completely does it the other way around. We need to call radical Islamic terrorism for what it is, and a commander-in-chief who's willing to act.

HH: Now I asked maybe one of your potential competitors yesterday, Senator Marco Rubio, who I know is a friend of yours.

SW: Good guy, yeah.

HH: I asked him yesterday would you disown any agreement that this president signs with Iran that leaves Iran uranium enrichment. What's Scott Walker think about the deal, because that's the outline, it appears?

SW: Absolutely.

HH: *Would you reject that deal if you took the Oval Office?*

SW: Absolutely, on Day One. I mean, to me, it is, the concept of a nuclear Iran is not only problematic for Iran, and certainly for Israel, but it opens the doors. I mean, the Saudis are next. You're going to have plenty of others in the region. People forget that even amongst the Islamic world, there is no love lost between the Saudis and the Iranians. And so they're going to want to have a nuclear weapon if the Iranians have a nuclear weapon. This is something that just escalates right before our eyes. And the fact that this administration began these discussions essentially conceding that they're going to allow enrichment to go forward with the Iranians just shows you that they don't have the same level of concern that I think I and Senator Rubio and many others out there have, that a nuclear Iran is a problem for the entire world, not just for Israel.

HH: *Does the rising of these headlines, Saudi Arabia may be going to war with Yemen before this broadcast is over, if some of these Reuters reports are true.*

SW: Right.

HH: *And the Quds Force general is in Tikrit, right? So the world's on fire. Does this hurt a governor's claim to the presidency and elevate perhaps senators who have been there or other people who have been abroad and done that sort of thing? Or does it help you?*

SW: Well, I think leadership is the fundamental ingredient that's important in anything, particularly when it comes to foreign policy. And I won't belittle any of the other would-be candidates. I would say, though, that my lifetime, the most significant president when it comes to foreign policy was a former governor, Ronald Reagan. The most faulty president, I would argue, when it comes to foreign policy and national security is a first term senator by the name of Barack Obama, who was on the Foreign Affairs Committee. And so, just those qualifications alone aren't enough. Now again, I think Senator Rubio and I are very much aligned on these issues. I agree with a number of my other colleagues who might be prospective candidates should I and others get into the race in the future. What people need to look at is what do you bring to the table, who do you surround yourself with, what kind of leadership style do you have, and people, I think in this case in particularly, not just in the travels and the studies, need to know how you think. In this case, I think Americans more than anything want a commander-in-chief of the future who does a couple of things—1) calls out radical Islamic terrorism for what it is, and says we will do whatever it takes to take the fight to them before they bring the fight to us, because unlike the Cold War, when containment was enough, when the Soviet Union and the United States could have leaders like Gorbachev and Reagan talking about containment, that's not enough. When you have, not only with ISIS and al Qaeda, but you have an Iran, you have other places around the world groups that that want to not only annihilate Israel, but annihilate us in America, it's like a virus. You've got to eradicate it. You can't take out part of it, or it will come back.

HH: You also have people like Putin, Governor Walker...

SW: Absolutely.

HH: ...who are pushing everywhere, and we've got Baltic allies. And people are wondering whether or not we'd actually come to their defense if Putin pushes into Estonia or Latvia or Lithuania. What do you think?

SW: We absolutely have to. I mean, NATO is the strongest military alliance we've had in history. It was part of, through Reagan's leadership, but certainly part of the ingredient that allowed us to win the Cold War without firing a shot. If we don't defend NATO members in a scenario like that, now I think we preempt that by showing strength in even dealing with Ukraine, which is not a NATO member, but is very much geographically aligned with what we're talking about. Remember, Putin isn't just aggressive for the sake of being aggressive. He's a nationalist. He believes in the history of Russia and the old Soviet Union. Part of what you see here is the old Lenin adage that you probe with bayonets. If you find mush, you proceed. If you find steel, you withdraw. Well, in Ukraine, he's found mush, and he's found mush not only from the United States, but from others like, others and NATO partners out there. If it were to extend, and my belief is we need a president who's going to act aggressively by giving lethal force to the Ukrainians and others to try to preempt that from happening. But a couple of weeks ago, I met with the president of Estonia. Certainly, we saw a week ago the Lithuanian leadership is literally giving out literature telling their own citizens what to do if Russians invade. Latvia, I just talked to someone the other day whose mother immigrated here from Latvia, and in each of those Baltic states, there are real serious concerns about what happens if we don't deal with this in

Ukraine. We need American leadership not just for America's sake, but for the world.

HH: We'll come back after break, but very quickly, they're finding mush everywhere. I love your line. The bayonets are finding mush everywhere. To replace that, we need Defense spending.

SW: Absolutely.

HH: And there is an effort being led. Ron Johnson, your colleague from Wisconsin was on yesterday. Are you fully supportive of the effort to get back to the [DoD] baseline 2012…

SW: You look at the Gates proposed budget in 2012 to get to where we need to go going into 2016. I'm for limited government. I think the federal government's too big, too expansive, too much a part of our life, and I'd like to send a big chunk of it back to the states, and ultimately to the people. But in the end, Defense is something that we should be doing, and we should be doing well. You can't do it if you've cut beyond muscle into bone. And that's why we need to go back to where the Gates budget it. And that's what I would support going for.

HH: I'll be right back with Governor Scott Walker. We'll talk domestic policy, particularly the reform efforts, the right to work in Wisconsin, congratulations, another win.

SW: Thank you.

HH: You're not resting on your laurels, huh? The second term is not for…and what he said today about education. Don't go anywhere, America. It's KKNT 960. You can follow Scott Walker, @ScottWalker on Twitter. It's the easiest Twitter account to do so. I'll be back to talk about as well his timing, if and when he's going to make a decision. And by the way, Tonette Walker is a star.

SW: She's awesome.

HH: I've been married a decade longer than you, but she is a lot like the Fetching Mrs. Hewitt. She's a star.

HH: *During the break, we were talking New Hampshire politics. So I've got to go back and say, so New Hampshire's like Wisconsin?*

SW: It is. I mean, if you look at the upper two-thirds of Wisconsin, Milwaukee and Madison are the bottom third. That's the big population base. But the upper two-thirds, the geography's a lot alike, the size is a lot alike. If you look at Green Bay, Wisconsin, of course, the home of the Green Bay Packers, about 100,000 people, it's about the size of Manchester. Concord's about 45,000, so that's like a number of our cities in the northern two-thirds of the state. There's a lot of similarities.

HH: *So what in New Hampshire is like Madison, because that's kind of like your left wing university…*

SW: Yeah, there's nothing in the state of New Hampshire. Concord's the capital city. But it's nothing like…Madison's more like Berkeley.

HH: *Now you got a jab in at lunch. I happened to bring up the fact that Ohio State, The Ohio State University, won the first ever national championship in college football on the backs of the Badgers….*

SW: Hat tip to that, yeah.

HH: *But then you came right back, your Badgers are still fighting for the…*

SW: I said last time I checked, I didn't see Ohio State in the Tournament. So Wisconsin Badgers well on their way to hopefully a repeat in the Final Four, and this time I think we'll beat Kentucky.

HH: *All right, on a more serious subject, one of the things you've done that impressed people the most is your education reform in the public sector. Tenure is gone.*

SW: Yeah.

HH: *Merit pay is there. How has that worked out in the classroom? And then I'm going to transition to Common Core, obviously, so you can cover them both at the same time. But how's it worked out actually on the ground in Wisconsin?*

SW: Well, it's great. I mean, we can hire and fire based on merit, pay based on performance, put the best and the brightest in the classroom. When you look at the statistics, the data doesn't lie. Graduation rates are up since I took office, third grade reading scores are higher, ACT scores are now second-best in the country. And what's great for teachers, for really quality, excellent teachers, they could be rewarded. They don't have to deal with the union steward. They can talk right to their principals. They can interact. And for the handful, and there aren't many, but the handful of teachers at schools, at least in our state, who weren't cutting it, and most good teachers knew who those bad ones were, they're gone. They don't have the tenure protection, or they don't have the shield that principals say they couldn't get rid of them. And so when I go around our state and I talk at schools, usually they kind of look both ways and whisper, because there's still a few union activists there, but the bottom line is people know that it's worked, and it's working better. And I'm glad, because I had two kids in public schools. I've got two nieces in public schools. I want great public schools, just like I want choices in the private schools and charter schools and home school environments out there.

HH: I had three kids who all went through public school all 1 2 years, and 13 years in kindergarten, and they had great teachers. And teachers are of two minds.

SW: Yeah.

HH: Conservative teachers are afraid that if you take tenure away, they'll get lopped off by liberals, and vice versa.

SW: Yeah.

HH: What do you tell them about that?

SW: I say in the end, in practice, if you've got good principals, and you have good people who are willing…a lot of people in the past weren't willing to run for school boards, because they knew they couldn't really do anything. Well, in our state, because of all the reforms we did with collective bargaining, the taxpayers are in charge, and the people they duly elect are the ones running the schools now. And so if you have good school board members, and good superintendents and principals, good teachers are always going to do well, and the same that in the private sector outside of government, if you work hard and you do well and you perform, most times, it's not 100% guaranteed, but most times, people who do well in their businesses with their employers are going to do well.

HH: Two years ago, I would have said Obamacare would have been the defining issue of the primaries.

SW: Yes.

HH: *Now, I say it's Common Core. And I know the pros and I know the cons. What's your position on it, and what do you, I'm sure you've seen it erupt at the grassroots.*

SW: Absolutely. Over the last couple of years, that's what really got my attention back in 2013 in particularly, actually, even late after the recall election of '12, but particularly in '13, where it wasn't even on our radar screen. And we just literally got it from listening to parents, and even from many teachers who were frustrated at this saying what is this, this comes from outside our state, they're making us do all these things, it doesn't make any sense. And so we started looking at it, worked with our legislature to try and repeal it, because it, in our state, had been put in long before I was governor. And I don't have a cabinet position for education. I'm one of those few states that has an independently-elected superintendent of public instruction. So if I want to make a change, I actually have to make it in the statutes. And that's what we've done with our budget proposal. We took out any funding for the Smarter Balanced tests, which is based on Common Core, and we put in place language that says that no school district has to use it, because I'm all for high standards. I just mentioned a moment ago the second-highest ACT scores in the country for states where more than half the kids take the ACT. I'm proud of that. But I want those standards set not by people from outside of my state or any other state, I want them set by parents and teachers, school board members and business community leaders at the local level, because that's where it's going to make all the difference in the world.

HH: *Now Scott Walker, I've got to ask you about, Dave Weigel is a good reporter...*

SW: Yeah.

HH: *We disagree, but yesterday he said on this program, talking to me about you, you're going to be dogged by that CPAC comment. Now I was on **Meet the Press** that day, and I said that was not a gaffe...*

SW: Yeah.

HH: *...he did not say that. But if you're going to be dogged by it, what are you going to do about it?*

SW: Well, I said, I mean, I did that Sunday as well, I did *Fox News Sunday*, and I clearly spelled it out. I don't think any of the people that were there at CPAC took it that way. They took it as hey, it's a sign of leadership, and I immediately said after that, I said let's be clear. I'm not comparing the union protesters with ISIS or anything else. I'm talking, my point was it's about leadership. The closest thing that I can compare to the type of pressure the next president's going to be under is what I went through four years ago with not just the protest, but the death threats, with the intimidation, with all the interruptions, with the recall and all the things that happened. And we didn't back down. We won without caving not just when it came to the ballot box. We won without caving when it came to policy. And I think that's when Americans want, whether it's taking on radical Islamic terrorism, or whether it's taking on the size and scope of the federal government, or whether it's pushing to put the power back in the hands of the hardworking taxpayers. They want someone who's going to fight and win every single day.

HH: *Now today was "off the record," at lunch with a thousand people, which doesn't really work.*

SW: Age of Twitter, right.

HH: *But as I listened, yeah, you made a comment and I'm going to put it on the record. You said when we were talking about drug legalization...*

SW: Yeah.

HH: *You're against it. You said "my friend, John Hickenlooper, Democrat..."*

SW: Yeah.

HH: *...and you said it casually. It wasn't a point. I just picked up on it that you have friends who are Democrats. This is going to shock a lot of the public employee union activists out there.*

SW: Yeah, it doesn't fit their narrative.

HH: *That's it. do you think you could go to D.C. as Reagan did and get the Democrats to reform the public sector?*

SW: Well, I think we'd certainly try. I mean, you mentioned Hickenlooper, Jack Markell, there's others out there I've worked with, and you know, to me, I used to tell new lawmakers when I was first in the state assembly in state government at the most local levels in state government. I used to say for new members don't personalize your differences, because your opponent today may be your ally tomorrow. And so that doesn't mean you should back away from policy. Obviously, if people watch me, I didn't back away from the big challenges. I took on the big issues not just on public employee unions, but right to work, you name it. And voter ID just got upheld the other day. We've done all the big issues. But we don't personalize it. The other side might, at least some of the activists might. But I still meet every week with the Democratic leadership in the state assembly and state senate.

HH: *Something you pointed out the President has not made a habit of doing.*

SW: Yeah, just like I do with Republicans out there. And I don't get why you wouldn't. I mean, to me, that's just a fundamental thing. If you're talking every week, it's hard to be nasty. You can have your disagreements, you can speak out. It doesn't mean, sometimes I think there's a mistake that it's one extreme or the other. Working with people on the other side doesn't mean caving. And that sometimes in the media it means, bipartisanship means just do what the Democrats want. On the other side of it, working, talking, actually communicating with the other party doesn't mean you're caving in, so that people who are strong conservatives think well, you can't ever talk to them. Sure, there's a lot of things you can do that when it comes to, for example, Iran, there's a lot of Democrats out there, that like us, have some real serious concerns about a nuclear Iran, and we need to pull them into the mix.

HH: *Back to defense, because I always ask everyone the same thing about the Ohio Class submarine and carrier groups. You've got one minute, Scott Walker, what do you think about our Navy?*

SW: Well, I think it's dangerously low right now. Not only do we need to make sure that we invest in the Ohio Class submarines, nuclear, that gives us, that's you know, one part of our nuclear triad, and it's probably the most important part. We've got bombers that are getting old, we've got intercontinental ballistic missiles. But in the larger context, we've got a Navy that's about, headed towards about half the size as it was under Reagan. We need to reinvest in that. And that's why I push and support going forward the Gates level funding as a minimum, and we need to make sure that instead of heading down to 250 vessels, we probably need to be at 325 to maybe 340,

346 at some point in the future, under a new commander-in-chief.

HH: *Governor Scott Walker, great to be with you twice today. Thanks for coming to KKNT.*

SW: Thank you, Hugh.

So be forewarned, Madame Secretary, even if your private intelligence service shenanigans stay as secret as your email and server, and even if Sid Blumenthal doesn't unintentionally blow you up—Chuck Todd told me two days after I spoke with Walker when the "wiped clean" server story was breaking that nothing involving Sydney Blumenthal would surprise him. (See the transcript of this exchange later in the book.) Nothing will surprise Scott Walker either. Not about Sid. Not about your team's dirtiest tricks. Not about the world and its bad actors. Nothing at all.

Scary, that, isn't it? So unlike the people around you. So unlike you and your people the night the terrorists attacked in Benghazi.

CHAPTER 26

The Truth about Mitt

When I wrote *A Mormon In The White House?* in 2007, I wanted a different title, one using something along the lines of "Reagan's Heir"? The publisher insisted on using "Mormon" in the title for selling purposes and I conceded the point, trusting as I did then, but no longer do, to the occult powers of publishers when it comes to titles. (My biggest bestseller came with the title of my own invention—*If It's Not Close, They Can't Cheat*—and I am now more convinced than ever that authors are as capable of choosing a title as publishers, though not publication dates. There is art, and there is science.)

My book was then and remains now the best guide to Romney, better than even his own memoir *Turnaround* or his 2010 campaign book, which I edited for him. I know him well enough, though not well, and know he could have beaten you soundly if he had entered the race, using mostly your many and obvious foreign policy failures as his frontal attack, and the picture of Ann and him and his family the silent rebuke to everything Clinton. He is also, as John McCain's campaign manager said in 2008, a "scary learning machine," and 2016 would have been his third round even as it is your fifth or sixth, depending on whether you count your stand-by role in the hapless Gore debacle as another lap around the track of presidential politics.

The 2008 primaries and internal GOP politics beat Romney then, but he studied and learned and beat them in turn in 2012. The general election peculiarities—plus Sandy, Candy and Orca—beat Romney in

2012, but he has been studying and learning and I have no doubt he would beat them or their surrogates, and you, in 2016 if he had run. (Or yet again, changes his mind after the field shatters itself, though the filing deadlines complicate late entries.)

There is simply nothing you can do about Mitt, either as a late entrant or as a vice presidential nominee should Cruz, Rubio, Walker or Jindal want to add heft and Establishment credibility to their first term. Romney is much smarter, much more able, much younger-looking, and more energetic in fact than you. He is healthier and smarter than you, has accomplished much more than you and is as scandal-free as you are scandal-plagued. He has studied his defeat thoroughly, and you should note that Romney has already stated he lost that race in Spanish-language media in 2012. This guy never repeats a mistake. No, a Rubio-Romney ticket (and an explicit promise of Speaker Ryan) teaming to restore America would be very formidable. A Romney-Patrick or Romney-Castro vice presidential debate would be a fun evening for the GOP, though such clashes mean little in the end game. What would matter is Romney on the stump every day, reminding the country that while he was warning the world about Putin and the Islamic State, you handed the former's front man a reset button and fled Foggy Bottom at 1 a.m., when the Islamists stormed the Benghazi compound on 9/11. Romney as Veep nominee would be a huge problem for you. Pray that ego gets in the way, or ethnicity, as an Anglo nominee for the GOP cannot—simply cannot—select an Anglo running mate.

You are helpless against even Romney's second-place position, because he is immunized, even as you are immunized against Bill's many and well-known failings. Even as you are hoping you are immunized against Benghazi. There are no second acts in American politics because they bore the public, but that doesn't mean no second chances. Or third. It just means no recycled storylines that fatigue a public that hates reruns but will watch many seasons of a well-written sitcom or drama. You can't make the 47% barb stick a second time any more than the GOP can resurrect Monica.

"What have you scandalized me with lately?" is the murmur among the cable-channel-shocked-and-awed masses. Romney's alleged plutocratic tendencies? Meh. The 47% spanner? Old news. "Severe conservative" and "self-deportation"? MSNBC fevers and tremors.

He was right about Putin, you see. You, by contrast, gave the dictator's henchman a funny red button that didn't even translate "reset" correctly.

He rushed out to speak to the press on the morning after Benghazi, yes. You fled the scene at State in the middle of the disaster. Which is worse? If the public gets to decide, you will lose.

He will, as the Looney Tunes characters say, *murderlize* your running mate in any debates.

He did not want to get down and dirty in the GOP primaries a third time. If he enters late, executing what his opponents will quickly call "his latest flip flop," he ought to declare, "Been there and done that. The voters know me, so I let them see the new guys," and await the primary results. Maybe mount a late-arriving front-porch campaign, above the fray, with no frayed nerves. Romney will truly not be sidelined until the filing deadlines for the March primaries come and go and he hasn't entered. Like I said, no sweat for Romney who has seen it all at close range. No frayed nerves.

Except yours. Your greatest advantages all come from having been around five of these things at close range—1992, 1996, 2000, 2008 and 2012. Now your sixth run for the roses would make Romney's third seem relatively fresh by comparison. You will both have that rarest of experiences, this time around the track won't be your first. No surprises. No learning curve.

You know all this, but someone with as grand an ambition as yours also knows that there is nothing you can do except hope Romney doesn't change his mind—so close to saying yes in January—and get in because Ann doesn't want to go through it again. He genuinely loves her and genuinely will be guided by her wishes here. As people of genuine faith, they will pray and decide and that will be it. That's what they did early this year, and they may yet feel the call to do it again.

There isn't any dirt holding them back, only weariness of the absurdity of the media and the game even as the world burns.

Given the lessons he learned, there would be no more "47% moments," either as a very late entrant to the lists or as a Veep nominee. Romney will assume every bartender is a tracker. Live and learn, and he does. This time I will suggest myself as the lead writer. No one will hold back their talents or their money. The country's responsible people are more than a little desperate at the condition in which you and President Obama have left us.

Truth is, there would be no major mistakes from Romney this time, no "I'd like a lifeline" moments for Candy Crowley to act upon.

He won't forget the military in his acceptance speech as Veep or in the keynote he will deliver flawlessly if he isn't on the ticket, the keynote that skins your record as thoroughly as anyone in America can. He wouldn't again allow any campaign of which he is a part to be outspent on Spanish media 7-to-1, and he won't allow this nominee to be so outflanked either, even if he has to start his own SuperPac to accomplish that end. He won't ease off the attack, even if he isn't on the ticket. He is a patriot, and sees you and Bill as a genuine menace to the country's survival. Perhaps alone among the GOP elites. he senses the scale of your ambitions.

Neither Romney nor any GOP nominee can control for the weather in '16 any more than Romney did in '12, and even as hurricanes hurt him in Tampa Bay and in the closing days, so they might hurt any GOP nominee this time.

But storms won't help you as they did President Obama in 2012, and your Benghazi cover-up is as threadbare now as it was fully knitted together then. Indeed, it is as full of holes as an Oscar night's winner for most revealing dress, and the server scandal and the maybe-possibly-might-actually surface emails you deleted are an anchor around your party's enthusiasm. The whole Clinton act is old and tired, and your new platform—if anticipated and answered—is as frail as Bill sometimes looks and you feel.

You just have to hope Romney isn't on the ticket. And that's the truth.

CHAPTER 27

The Truth About Transparency

The following section, Part IV, collects all the key excerpts of all the key interviews I have done about you for the last two years. It is a transparent laying out of my project, just as this book is a transparent attempt to hurt your chance of winning by appearing to help you design a winning strategy which, truth be told, could do either or both. That's just the way it is as Uncle Walter used to say, transparently so. No sense in denying the obvious. It seems to me there just isn't any margin left for spinning in America in 2015 and beyond. Every American is in on the joke. They all get it. They all get everything if they get anything at all.

But you are so buttoned up inside the Beltway in which you have lived so long, so weary and worn out, so out of touch with how the culture has changed, you are unlikely to read much less understand what all these people are saying about you. Has anyone even told you Harry Reid quit because he knew he couldn't win in Nevada with you at the top of the ticket? Telling you true, hard things isn't your inner circle's gift, thus their decision to advise you first to get a private server for your emails and then to destroy them.

Apparently you live in a candor-free zone when it comes to staff. Thus these transcripts are gifts to the GOP which if you don't ignore them completely—like you ignored Reverend Wright's sermons until it was too late—you will discount as so much noise from the chattering class, and thus unaware of their potency to your GOP adversaries.

You of course will primarily be selling yourself to the 30% of the electorate that genuinely "gets" little if anything but lottery tickets, and those aren't called a "tax on stupidity" for no reason. You have zero chance of moving the 45% locked into the GOP's corner either.

You—and the eventual GOP nominee—are playing for the 25% of voters who are genuinely up for grabs, the center and the center-right, and you have to win them through a very intentional "transparency" play as they know all of your many acts very well. You have to wink at them, let them know you know, and let them in on the big plan.

The Amendments, the amnesty, the defense spending, the tactics against the field forming up against you, indeed every hour of every day is an old, old play and the folks who write the reviews are weary to death of it. Another Clinton "revival" is like taking *Camelot* on the road to Pittsburgh and selling the Steelers fans on the idea that the 1960 Lerner and Loewe smash hit is as fresh and new as it was 55 years ago with Julie Andrews, Richard Burton, Roddy McDowall and Robert Goulet. The 25% isn't easily fooled but it can be soothed and charmed and above all calmed and made to see self-interest since they won't be feeling any passion.

"I'm all you have got," is your basic pitch, and you have to promise them you will continue their deals and secure their fortunes and their children's fortunes. We are all "security moms" now. We want the '90s back. So promise the 25% that and more. Promise them the end of gridlock and the end of the drama. Give them an 18 game NFL schedule and the promise of a "Follow" on Twitter and a shout out at a presser. Promise to make 'em rich and make them forget their fears and the facts.

There have been no new discoveries in the art of governing since the man who wrote *The Prince* made his deadline 500 years ago. Now there are new tools, of course, lots more of those, and of wealth. But power is the same now as then, and theology hasn't changed much in more than a millennium either. We are who we are, and the barbarians are very much at the gates both virtual and real. This is the truth about which you must be most transparent. The only truth really, and the means to that end, the language of communicating the real danger, is left for last.

First though, you need to study what people have been saying *about you*. You can win this against anyone except Romney and he isn't running, and more than win, you can change the rules forever. But not if you are indifferent to what the "known knowns" are, to quote Donald Rumsfeld's most famous and prophetic line. If you are the same Hillary as 2007-2008 or from Benghazi to the present, you could lose to Bush, Rubio or Walker and maybe even Cruz, Kasich or Perry.

You will be tempted to skip Part IV. Nixon used to tell me — this was in '78-'80, after I had just graduated from college and was scribbling away for him at America's Elba in San Clemente, after you helped force him from power, before his return— that he had never watched himself on television or read what people wrote about him. He insisted this was true. Often.

If it was true—he intended me to believe it certainly, and intended me to tell people that he said it just as certainly, and I have—it was a grievous fault, and grievously did he pay for it. Had he read—had he studied—what his enemies, opponents and especially his friends had said about his weaknesses, had he acted on those critiques, he might have avoided their culmination. "Had he" being the key phrase there. By his own admission he didn't. His flaws grew and crippled him then killed his presidency though not his legacy.

Study what they say about you, Madame Secretary, if you want to have what you want to have.

My conservative friends who have read this say I am helping you too much with this project. They underestimate your vanity and the vanity of your husband, and the jealous infighting within your machine. Those who read the transcripts will dismiss their sources, or think they have double meanings, or waive away critiques as outdated, and problems noted as already fixed.

Mostly though, like everyone on the left, your and their arrogance will be your undoing. How could you and Reset Button gang get anything this important so wrong?

PART IV

WHAT YOUR FRIENDS, OPPONENTS
AND ENEMIES ARE SAYING ABOUT YOU

You might be inclined to think it is just I, the GOP partisan and talk show host, who holds the concerns I have tried to help you address via this book. I assure you, it isn't.

Many of your advisors will say they have "talked" with so-and-so who said thus-and-such, but I began talking to "opinion influencers" about your campaign way back in October of 2013, certain even then that you were going to run, and eager to use my platform to put as many small pebbles in your path as I could. I thought of a plan, and executed it, wherein I would ask key Beltway elites—and a couple of other folks—about you and your campaign, and especially about the themes of this book: your glass jaw, your age and obvious weariness, your evident fatigue, Bill, and especially your dismal record at State and all your other failures.

I began with one of your inner circle's favorite reporters, Maggie Haberman (then of *Politico*, now of *The New York Times*), on October 28, 2013, and kept at it, finishing up on President's Day, February 15, 2015, with a conversation with Karl Rove exclusively devoted to you, eventually doing interviews about these themes with operatives and MSMers, especially those among the latter group whose publications and platforms will certainly move to try and put Humpty Dumpty together again a fifth time—Hillarycare, Monica, 2008 and Benghazi being the first four—should you smash up early in the campaign.

Among my guests on the "Hillary" beat were **TheVox.com**'s Jon Allen and *The Hill*'s Amie Parnes (your biographers in *HRC*), *The Daily Beast*'s Jonathan Alter, Haberman, *The New York Times'* Nicholas Kristof and Mark Leibovich, *The New Yorker*'s Ryan Lizza, *The Washington Post*'s Dana Milbank, MSNBC's Joy-Ann Reid and NBC's *Meet the Press* host Chuck Todd. These are ten MSM "voices" very representative of what the Manhattan-Beltway media elite are collectively thinking and murmuring about you.

Of course, I posed similar questions to folks like Senator Marco Rubio who, as I wrote in the main part of the book, would be your toughest opponent other than Romney, and even a "Bill question" for former President George W. Bush. Asking potential opponents about you allowed me to see if the critique I knew would be coming your way had begun to form among the right's standard bearers.

Three revolutionary political operatives—Rove, David Axelrod and former House Speaker Newt Gingrich also stepped up to the plate for their swings against your candidacy. I begin these transcripts with them, because they have won big battles. They know winning, and of course they know losing as well, as do you.

My plan, hatched back in the fall of 2013, was to lay up acorns via interviews for this very book. I didn't want anyone to notice what I was about for fear that guests from the MSM would stop agreeing to come on the show and talk about you—not behind your back, really, but right in front of your face—though perhaps they counted on the left's general disdain for conservative media to cover their sins against you and yours.

Doggone it if then *Slate*'s and now *Bloomberg*'s Dave Weigel didn't notice right away what I was up to. (He is a sharp one, young Mr. Weigel, and attentive to everything being said everywhere, and no ally of my party, or obviously of yours either, though, of course, he must be a man of the left working for *Slate* for a bit, or either the deepest of MSM moles.)

Weigel picked up on what I was doing immediately, and in a column titled, "The Hillary Clinton Knockout Game," on December 10, 2013, Weigel referred to my Haberman interview of six weeks earlier and wrote, "I don't see evidence that many reporters saw this interview, but Hewitt did beat the trend and shape the narrative."

"Damn," I thought, "Weigel is going to ruin this plan." Especially since he pointed out that I wouldn't politely skip over the fact that Haberman didn't have any answers for the hardest questions about you. "Hewitt wouldn't let go," Weigel wrote. (This is an indictment not of me but of most Beltway journalists, of course, who always "let go" when one of their lefty elected friends is on a particularly hot seat and facing an uncomfortable line of questioning.)

I didn't see any evidence that many reporters read Weigel's piece though they all ought to be reading everything that scamp writes as he and the "new breed" I wrote about earlier will be around for decades unless you take my advice. The MSMers thank goodness kept coming on the show throughout 2014, like the *Babes in Toyland* toy soldiers. (See, you got that reference to the 1961 Tommy Sands and Annette Funicello movie and most every other reader did not, another proof of just how many years have piled up since your freshman year in high school when that movie came out. Anyone born in 1947 and making their wonder-struck way through their first year in the hallways at Main East High School in Park Ridge would have loved that flick. But you cannot allow such trick questions and references to remind young voters of your actual age.)

So the MSMers kept coming, and I kept piling up the acorns, like Mark Leibovich's interview in November of last year in which we pointed everyone—again!—to your college era letters to Professor Peavoy. Mark of course had a book to sell, *Citizens of the Green Room*, so of course he was going to come on to flog his book and once on, I could turn the focus wherever I wanted, which eventually, in the middle of the conversation, was to you and those letters, which reveal so very much.

"I read but few lives of great men because biographies do not, as a rule, tell enough about the formative period of life," wrote Ulysses S. Grant. "What I want to know is what a man did as a boy."

How 19th century, when boys and girls had to grow up quick. In the middle of the 20th century they began "to grow up" in the college years. Nowadays they "grow up" in their early-to-mid 20s, if by "growing up" we mean to put on the identity they will wear their entire lives unless tragedy, addiction or religious conversion changes them completely and roughly.

Those Peavoy letters show you as you made that choice, show you in a very bright light, becoming the ambitious, oh so ambitious Hillary Clinton we see now. Comfort yourself with a bit of Alexander Hamilton who wrote that the "love of fame" is "the ruling passion of the noblest minds." You can see in those letters that passion taking hold, and you were testing out themes on Professor Peavoy.

But how could he give all those letters—your letters!—to Mark Leibovich, whose scalpel is sharpest of all? Of course you know. You dropped him, didn't you? Put him away like an old coat long out of fashion. Gave him to the thrift store where all your old friends pre-Bill went. Not even one or two invites to a White House event, one mention of "my old friend, now a professor..."? Had you really forgotten you poured your soul out to him?

So he got his revenge, just as you will get yours on all these folks who talked and talked and talked about you when they thought you were done, done, done or worse, not paying attention.

And all of these things were said about you just on my own show! When the speakers knew that they were talking to a center-right audience, aware that their words would carry farther because they were spoken outside of the sealed dome of the Beltway.

They didn't care that they were trashing your record and your abilities. Careful in how they limned your failures and your political vulnerabilities, but certainly not rising to your defense. They couldn't be bothered to.

This is, collectively, a foreshadowing. In many of their eyes, your DC "sell-by" date had passed and they figured you for finished. Or they just could not come up with answers to the obvious questions about you and your candidacy. There is an old saying: "Forewarned is forearmed."

There is another old saying, this one Irish: "If everyone says you're drunk, you'd better sit down." Note the themes that emerge from all these conversations, and then consider sitting down. Consider getting out.

Because it is going to be brutal. Truth be told, you did fail at State, you are worn out and getting wearier and older by the day, there are abundant joys in being a grandmother and a revered, if somewhat dusty, elder statesman. (How often do we hear from Madeleine Albright after all? Out of the game is out of the game. Can you stand it? That's the problem, isn't it? Read *When The Cheering Stopped: The Last Years of Woodrow Wilson* by Gene Smith, but don't worry that the same silent days of the still-stroke impacted Wilson living out his days on S Street would be similar to your last decades. There are many more past times, many more joys. You just have to give up the need for power...)

Of course you won't sit down. There is the dynasty. There is the legacy. There is that "first of firsts," and the first woman in the Oval Office is actually going to seem far more remarkable after a century or two than the first African American because it had to be earned without an economic collapse wafting you up, and two wars weighing down your opponent. You will have to do what George H. W. Bush did, win a third term for a tired, talent-depleted party. Only you aren't following the Gipper. You are following the worst president in American history,

So you will go forward and try to start the new age, a second "Clinton Era," and if you go about it the right way, as advised above, you may pull it off. But read these interviews or snippets of interviews carefully. They are the best debate prep ever but also a window into the world of Manhattan-Beltway media elites in the post-modern era when the byline is the brand and the true believers of the left not credible enough to carry a campaign. The MSM are, God love them, vampires of a sort and they need people like you to feed on.

Unless, of course, you turn out to be a combination of Caesar Augustus and Abraham Van Helsing. A few will suspect the former, but only those who take this book seriously will anticipate the former.

If you get to 1600, I hope my assistance won't be as forgotten as

Professor Peavoy. I don't need much, just an exclusive sit-down or two early each year, a token display of your willingness to engage with the center-right even as you are laying out the plan and putting it in motion. No one will believe any of it until the first Supreme Court vacancy comes along and Justice Kirsten Gillibrand is replaced in the United States Senate by Chelsea. Then they will begin to wonder....

CHAPTER 28

Interviews about you with Three Political Svengalis:
Karl Rove on February 16, 2015;
David Axelrod on February 11, 2015;
and Former Speaker of the United States House of
Representatives Newt Gingrich on January 6, 2015

With Karl Rove:

HH: I want to begin, five days ago. I talked to David Axelrod, your counterpart, in many respects, as a person who successfully advised a candidate for and then the reelection of a president, about Hillary. And I wanted to ask you where you think the former Secretary of State stands vis-à-vis the possibility of her winning in 2016 as of today in early 2015.

KR: Look, I think it's very early. The early polls that are out there show her ahead. What's interesting to me is that rarely is she above 50% against Republican candidates. I think this is one of the things that is going to, this election is going to depend upon the quality of the candidates and the quality of their campaigns. And if you look at the arc of the last two years, if you're inside the Clinton campaign apparatus, you can't be happy. Her favorables, when she was leaving the office of Secretary of State, much higher than they were than they are today, her likability was much higher, she has had a bad year and a half, nearly two years since leaving the Secretary of State's office, and particularly since she launched her book last summer. I thought it was probably one of the most ill-timed and ill-prepared and ill-executed sort of strolls on to the national stage. "We were dead broke." You know, she takes apart a National Public Radio personality who attempts to give her a chance to talk her way out of her previous opposition to gay marriage. She goes out on the campaign trail and says it's businesses that don't create jobs. She does virtually no good for any Democratic candidate on the campaign trail, and then she ends just before Christmas by saying insofar as it's possible, we ought to have "empathy for our adversaries." I mean, come on, she's getting worse, not better as a candidate.

HH: Do you think Elizabeth Warren could beat her if Elizabeth Warren got into the race?

KR: I think she might. She would certainly give her a scare. Remember, this contest opens up in some places that are not particularly friendly to Hillary Clinton. She came in third, as you may recall, in Iowa eight years ago. And so you know, I think this, Elizabeth Warren's hard left prescriptions on the economy sing to the heart of Democratic primary voters. So yeah, I think she could give her a run for her money. I don't know at the end of the day if she could beat her. I mean, Clinton is going to have a lot of money. She does have an expert political advisor in the form of her husband, and she's about ready to get a mastermind of her presidential campaign in the form of John Podesta, who's tough enough to probably, I think, keep the warring factions that always make up a Clinton campaign together.

HH: What David Axelrod told me last week, Karl Rove, was, "My strong feeling is that if she, Hillary, is a candidate, she can do well. If she's the first candidate, if she retreats back into the cocoon of inevitability and is cautious, then she'll have a much harder time." Do you agree with that?

KR: I agree with it totally. And in fact, that's my point. Her instinct is to say...what's her message? She went out and tried to borrow Barack Obama and Elizabeth Warren by saying corporations and businesses don't create jobs, and it was so transparently sort of unnatural to her that she didn't get any applause from anybody. So yeah, I think the problem with Hillary Clinton is what is it that she wants to do as president that gives the American people a sense that she'd be up to the job? What is it that she has done? She can't point to the success as Secretary of State. That's going to be a huge problem for her. Does anybody think that in a year or eighteen months that the world is going to look a lot safer and a lot more peaceful and a lot more calm than it is today? I don't think so.

HH: Does she carry any of the burdens, Karl Rove, of the nightmare we see, the 21 beheadings over the weekend in Libya by the Islamists of Christian Copts, or of the attack in Denmark, or the attack in Paris, or just general chaos as the Islamic State metastasizes? Is any of that burden on Hillary's back?

KR: Look, the burden of that is Barack Obama's foreign policy. President Obama, when he came into office, admitted that Iraq was relatively stable, relatively peaceful, and moving in a democratic way. And what did he do? He withdrew all US forces from Iraq. He initially said he wanted to have a stay-behind force. His vice president talked about how a stay-behind force was necessary in order to combat, you know, conduct targeted counterterrorism efforts. But then he screwed it all up by demanding of the Iraqis that they give parliamentary approval of any status of forces agreement. We've never required that from other governments. But he required parliamentary approval at a point where he knew Maliki could not get that, because of the nature of the parties in the parliament, and the moment right then that he was trying to form a new government. So what we've seen with the explosion of ISIS across Syria and Iraq is I think a direct result of the lack of an American presence in Iraq. Can you imagine what would happen if we had 15 or 16, or 19, or 20,000 American troops in Iraq when ISIS, if ISIS began to move across the border of Syria into Iraq like it did last year? I mean, they would have been quickly, the United States and the Iraqis would have quickly moved. We would have stiffened the Iraqis' spine. We would have had sufficient forces on the ground between them and us in order to stop this from happening. And instead, what they have sensed is weakness of the United States in the region, and they've seized upon it.

HH: *Now, but that's the President's foreign policy. How much of that sticks to Secretary of State Clinton?*

KR: She was his Secretary of State during those critical years. 2009 through 2013, early 2013, she was there. She was the one who was there as he made these critical decisions to precipitously withdraw from Iraq, and precipitously draw down in Afghanistan. Now to her credit, there is evidence that she argued against the precipitous decline of forces in Afghanistan, and encouraged him to keep US forces there longer. She clearly agreed with and supported the decision to conduct the surge in Afghanistan in 2009. Having said that, though, she was his Secretary of State, and when all of these chickens come home to roost in a very ugly way, how does she differentiate herself? Does she say all the good decisions that have paid off at the State Department and in our foreign policy I was part of, and I opposed him on all the bad decisions? She can't do that.

HH: *What does she have to say about Russia, Karl Rove, because she gave the Putin reset button, not to Putin, but to Sergei...*

KR: Lavrov.

HH: *Lavrov. She gave him the reset button, and now the reset button's being reset again and again and again in Ukraine with every new round of talks. Does she own that one as well?*

KR: Well, absolutely. In fact, and she bears an even bigger responsibility, because you had the sense in the early months of the Obama administration that this was how she was going to make her mark. She was going to remake the relationship that we had with Russia, and her mere presence there was going to remove any of the difficulties that had emerged during her predecessor's time in office. And it was clearly, you know, the sense was this was all our doing to screw up the relationship, and it could be my leadership in order to solve the problems in this relationship. And instead, she got taken to the cleaners. Look, this guy, Putin, Bush knew this early on, that this was a guy you had to endeavor to have a relationship with so that he could see your resolve. And what happened is Hillary Clinton took half of that lesson. He needed to get to know her. And his people needed to get to know her. But they didn't see resolve. They saw somebody who was desperate to win their accommodation and their approval, and shows up with a toy. As you may recall, it, they had the reset button that they got from I guess at Staples, but they had a mistranslation on the document they gave with it so that it didn't even say reset the relationship. It had something even, that didn't make any sense.

HH: *Well, given all these handicaps, and we could catalog her failures at State, and they go on for a very long series, Karl Rove, if you're Elizabeth Warren, how could you not take advantage of the opportunity that what may be a glass jaw is sitting right out there waiting for a hard punch?*

KR: Well, Elizabeth Warren can't attack her on foreign policy. I mean, Elizabeth Warren is to the left of Hillary Clinton. Hillary Clinton did argue for we don't need to withdraw US troops from Afghanistan as fast as that. In fact, we ought to add to them temporarily. She was in favor of that policy. Elizabeth Warren, I don't know where she was on this, but I find it hard to believe that she was in favor of it. Elizabeth Warren is to the left of Hillary Clinton on many of these questions. Hillary Clinton's vulnerability is on the domestic side where Elizabeth Warren can come at her and say you're the person who's taking hundreds of thousands of dollars from Wall Street firms for speeches. You're the, the Clintons are the people who are in bed with Wall Street in the 1990s when we had deregulation. Remember, this is one of the interesting thing to me, President Obama and Elizabeth Warren share something in common. They blame the collapse of 2008 not on Fannie and Freddie's misdeeds, but upon the deregulation of the Clinton years in office, of getting rid of Glass-Steagall and other changes that President Clinton made. They don't blame it on Fannie and Freddie, as I think you and I do. You and I, I think, share the view that you know, when you've got the good credit of the United States taxpayer being leveraged by organizations like Fannie and Freddie to where they were holding mortgage instruments, they were leveraged 70 to 1, which means a 1.2% decline in the value of their assets bankrupts them, that's exactly what happened with Fannie and Freddie. They don't blame, Obama and Warren don't blame Fannie and Freddie for that. What they blame is…

HH: *I…*

KR: …what Clinton did.

HH: *I agree with that analysis, and what I want to go to, though, is can Elizabeth Warren borrow from President Obama his playbook in 2008?*

KR: Sure.

HH: *In other words, can she do to Hillary what Obama did to Hillary?*

KR: Yes. She can enter late, because Hillary's entering late. And if she comes with a focused message that says the Democratic Party has to cut its links to Wall Street and the financial excesses of deregulation that we saw under the Clinton regime, she's got a chance to really do some damage to Hillary Clinton. Whether she's ultimately successful in that, I don't know. But my personal view is that I don't think Elizabeth, I think Elizabeth Warren has a sense of time. I think she feels that she can be emboldened by serving in the Democratic Party, in a Democratic caucus in the Senate, and pulling them to the left, and that she's got time and a future if she wants to exploit it. But you know, who knows? If she's willing to go out there and say I'm 1/64h Indian in order to get law school appointments, she's certainly capable of saying for months and months and months I'm not running, and then change her mind at the last minute.

HH: Will the money keep her off? Earlier today, or actually, two days ago, Tracy Sefl tweeted out the news that they had raised $1.2 million dollars for Ready For Hillary from 13,000 supporters in January. In other words, trying to portray that the Clinton money machine is so vast and so deeply net-rooted that no one need apply for the position of taking on Hillary. Is that a false bravado?

KR: Well, it certainly is a sign that they are a little bit nervous about this. But look, they will have plenty of money. The money is not going to be the problem. It's going to be properly spending the money, because they wasted a lot of it last time around, and more importantly, having a proper message, spending the money to share a message. And that's where, look, the Clintons may have a big bank account, but when it comes to Hillary Clinton's intellectual treasure, that's bare. I mean, we've had every chance...when she, she, in my opinion, made a mistake by putting the book out in 2014. If I were her, I would have taken 2014 and avoided the campaign trail, and avoided getting the book out and instead said you know what? I'm working hard on my book, and I hope to get it out in early 2015. And I would have spent 2014 figuring out what it is that I wanted to make the campaign about, and get rested, and getting prepared, and thinking through these things, and practicing them so that when you emerge in 2015 with the book, you not only had a good book and a good book tour because you were ready and prepared and rested, but you also could flow naturally into the message that you wanted to lay out in 2016. But having, you know, that was my view last year. She obviously had a different view. Having done what she did last year, and by getting out in the world with the book and the book tour and the campaigning and the campaign stops, she's given us a preview of what her mindset is. And right now, it is I'm entitled to this, I'll be the first woman, I had to put up with Bill for eight years, it's my turn, I'm the person. And that's not a very substantive message.

HH: All right, last question, it's a two-parter, Karl Rove. Can she be beaten by a Republican? And when will the super PACs begin to hammer her as the Democrats hammered Romney in 2012? How early will they open up on her with the big guns in media and social media, etc.?

KR: Let me take the second part of that first. They will begin to open up, or they should begin to open up when she becomes a candidate and not before, because most of the American people, the people that are going to have to be reached, are people who are paying not much attention to politics, and will not pay a lot of attention to politics until next year. But once she becomes a candidate, they will begin to pay more attention to her, and to things that are being said about her. Having made that point, though, I'd say this. She's not a federal office holder. So they're going to all have to go out and raise 527 money in order to attack her. That's going to be hard in 2015, because a lot of the people who are willing to write checks to Super PACs are going to be more interested in writing checks to the Super PAC of their favorite candidate for president for the Republican presidential nomination. The first question, though, that you asked is the important one—can we beat her. And the answer is yes. However, here's the big question mark for Republicans. Will they be able to be articulate and optimistic and hopeful conservative vision for the future of the country that causes people to say you know what, I know what you're running for. We're really good at knocking around Obama. And there's going to be a role for doing that. We're going to be really good about knocking around Hillary. And there's a role for that. But at the end of the day, simply being the best person to knock around Obama, or to knock around Hillary, is going to be insufficient to either win the nomination, or more importantly, to win the general election. They're going to, you know, look, Ronald Reagan spent some time in 1980 kicking around Jimmy Carter. But he spent an inordinate amount of time sharing a vision of what he thought America's promise and possibility was. And he talked about it, and sometimes in very specific fashion. You and I both remember it, Kemp-Roth. He was out there talking about supply side economics in 1980, as well as kicking around Jimmy Carter for presiding over an economic debacle. That's an important lesson for us. We win when we have an optimistic and positive conservative agenda that causes people to say I know what you're going to do. We can attack them, but that serves as an entry point to discuss our values and views, and to draw people to us, not simply push them away from the opposition.

With David Axelrod:

HH: *But speaking about the Secretary of State for just a moment, what did Secretary of State Clinton accomplish when she was secretary of state?*

DA: Well, I think that you, a lot of what the President was working on was also her work. So as I said, you know, we went around the world and worked very hard to cobble together a coalition against Iran. She was very much a part of that effort. I know that she comes under attack now on the issue of the reset. But the reality is that in the first two years of the president's administration, when Dimitri Medvedev was the president of Russia, there was a different opportunity, and we took advantage of that opportunity in terms of arms treaties and a whole range of other issues that were good for this country. It is unfortunate that President Putin has decided to take the kind...his country backward. But both President Obama and Secretary Clinton deserve credit for the advances that were made in that period.

HH: Now you've been advising Hillary for years, though—all the way back to 1992. It was a revelation to me in [Axelrod's memoir] Believer *that you advised against her infamous milk and cookies appearance, right?*

DA: Well, you know, what happened was I was informally advising the Clinton campaign at the time, and Bill Clinton came into Chicago, and I was involved in putting the debate negotiations together in the primaries. He was debating Jerry Brown. And Jerry Brown went hard after Bill Clinton about what would later become known as the Whitewater issue, and drew Hillary into the discussion. And there was a very vituperative exchange, I'll say, between Clinton and Brown in which Clinton said you know, you can say whatever you want about me, but you aren't even worthy of being on the same stage with my wife. And after the debate, there was a meeting, because the next day, both Clintons were due to campaign in Chicago, and my suggestion was that he go out alone, because if she were there, it would elevate that debate exchange. And I was overruled on that, and I was sort of a minor player. I was an interloper, so I didn't have the ability to make a very strong argument or winning argument. And she went out and she did make that comment. That was unfortunate, and something that dogged her for some time after that.

HH: It's going to do her, too, in this next campaign. But since you've given her advice before, you know her so well, you know her record at State, and you're the message maestro, you're the guy who crafts the 30-second pitch, how is she going to craft her 30-seconds on what she did at State? What's she going to say?

DA: First of all, Hugh, I think she'll have plenty to say what she did at State. She just wrote a whole book on it. But this election is going to be, as every election is, where you're going to take the country? Where do you want to take the country? What is the future going to look like? And I think the greatest imperative for her, and frankly, every candidate, and I know Marco Rubio probably was talking about his views about the American middle class on our program—this is the fundamental issue of our time. Are we going to create an economy in which work pays and which people who work hard can get ahead? That value is honored, and or are we going to be a country where people work harder and harder just to try and keep up?

HH: Well, I've got to argue with your premise, David Axelrod, and I want to use the authority of David Axelrod to do so. On Page 194, this is the most important page in Believer, you reproduce your late 2006 memo to the president, then-Senator Obama, about running for president. And you write, "The most influential politician in 2008 won't be on the ballot. His name is George W. Bush. With few exceptions, the history of presidential politics shows that public opinion and attitudes about who should occupy the Oval Office next are largely shaped by the perception of the retiring incumbent. And rarely do voters look for a replica. Instead, they generally choose a course correction, selecting a candidate who will address the deficiencies of the outgoing president." So it's not as you put it, it's about being not Obama. So what are the…

DA: But Hugh, I think, let's separate this out, because a lot of this has to do with the style and approach of a president. You know, one of the reasons Barack Obama got elected was because there was a sense that George Bush was too Manichean in his thinking, too bombastic, saw the world in terms of black and white, didn't see the gray, and people wanted a president who could. And they also wanted a president who was very much outside of the system, who would challenge Washington in a way that they felt Washington needed to be challenged. I think that the prism is a little bit different in 2016 because of what I said. I think that they will, people will choose someone who has different qualities than Barack Obama. And I think the candidate they choose will be someone they see, someone who they feel can master the system in Washington, operate in the system in Washington, not necessarily, you know, operate apart from the system in Washington. They're going to choose someone who is a little less nuanced in their thinking than the President, more direct in their approach or perceived as more direct in their approach. I actually think that's a climate that is much better for Hillary Clinton than it was in 2008, because her qualities are not Barack Obama's qualities. They're friends, they agree on issues, on many issues, but they have different approaches and different backgrounds and experiences. And I think that her profile is much better for 2016 than it was for 2008.

HH: Well, you're taking one for the team there. But I'm telling you, Believer has got a, it's like a game plan for going after Hillary. You talk about "Hillary unchained," how Hillary was "affronted," Hillary and Bill using the race card, playing the old, Southern, white Democrat after the South Carolina primary when Clinton said "no big deal..." He didn't say it, you write [of Bill Clinton's attitude about Hillary losing South Carolina to President Obama], "No big deal, the black guy had won the black primary" [and] "Hillary was baggage you didn't need as veep." This is like a gift to the Republicans, David Axelrod.

DA: Well, if they think it is, and I hope they buy it and read it in large numbers, I really don't think of it that way. The one thing that I've said, Hugh, publicly is that you know, Hillary Clinton was an ineffective candidate in 2007, because she was kind of cocooned in this presumption of inevitability, and very cautious. And once we won the Iowa Caucuses, she was a different candidate and a different campaigner. She threw the caution away. She was much more visceral in her campaigning. She connected very well with people. Her sense of advocacy came through very clearly. And she herself was more revealing of herself. My strong feeling is that if she is that candidate, she can do well. If she's the first candidate, if she retreats back into the cocoon of inevitability and is cautious, then she'll have a much harder time.

HH: Can Elizabeth Warren beat her?

DA: I don't think Elizabeth, I know Elizabeth Warren well, and my strong feeling is she's not going to run. I think she's trying to influence the direction of the party, and you have more influence as a potential candidate than you do if you take yourself out. So she's allowing, she's sticking to this language of I'm not running for president, and titillating people with it, because it gives her more leverage. I don't think she would beat her. I have high regard for Elizabeth. I don't think she would beat her. Look, look at the polling, Hugh. Hillary is probably as well-positioned within her own party as any open seat candidate has been in our lifetime. And you know, she's going to have to go out and work for it. If she assumes anything and doesn't go out and work for it, and earn it, and make her case and present her, a rationale for a candidacy that resonates with people, then anybody is vulnerable under those circumstances. But you know, I know the team she's assembling. I have a high regard for them. I have some sense of the kind of thinking she's doing. I think she's going to come out of the gate very strong.

HH: But then you're saying, you have to be saying, I don't mean to corner David Axelrod, I can't corner David Axelrod. You're saying that Elizabeth Warren is the candidate that Barack Obama was, because Barack Obama was in the same position vis-à-vis Hillary in 2007, and he beat Hillary, and you're saying Elizabeth Warren couldn't beat Hillary?

DA: No, what I'm saying is that 2007 was, is not 2015 or '16. There was a dominant issue within the Democratic Party in 2007 and 2008, and that was the war in Iraq. Obama had opposed it, Hillary had voted for it. That gave him an enormous edge in the race. This is a different time. And so there isn't that kind of galvanizing issue, particularly if Hillary comes out of the box, as I expect she will, talking very clearly about how to buttress the middle class, how to create greater opportunity, how to restore the value that says if you work hard in this country, you can get ahead.

HH: I'm going to try a third time, though, but you're the message guy. How does she capture what was, in my view, a completely achievement-free four years at the Department of State? How do you give me 30 seconds that avoids the reset button, the collapse in Egypt, the Libyan fiasco, the Syrian civil war, the drift with our relationship with Israel, the utter chaos that's become America in the world? How does Hillary escape that anchor?

DA: Well, she'll make her case, Hugh, but as I said, I think there are lot if, there are number of other important advances that she had on her watch, which ended four years ago, that went to helping put together the international coalition in the midst of the financial crisis, putting together international coalitions around arms control, making sure that we had supply routes open so our troops could be resupplied in Afghanistan. There were a wide, you know, she dealt with a broad number of issues on which we had success. And you know, she'll make that case. I do not believe, and you know, and I invite, you know, if folks on the other side want to try, they should. This race is not going to be about that. This race is going to be about the economy, about whether you can be a middle class person in this country and get ahead, whether you can be a striving person who is not well off, poor, and can work hard and make something of your life. That's what this is about. We've got a profound challenge, and every developed economy has that challenge today because of the changing nature of the economy, technology and globalization. We either rise to that challenge or we're going to have great, great disparities of opportunity in this country. And that fundamental value that is the American value, that if you work hard, you can get rewarded for that work and get ahead, is going to be in jeopardy.

HH: You know why I smell weakness there, David Axelrod, is because you have such a command of detail. You wrote at one point that when you picked the voiceover for Spanish ads in the Chicago mayoral race, you found a Colombian-accented spokesperson so as not to upset the Puerto Rican voters on the north side, or the Mexican voters on the south side. That's on Page 90. And when I read that, I realized you know the detail. This is granular. And if you can't get Hillary to 30 second ads on State Department, she's lost. And you can't do it, because no one…

DA: I think she's going to be able to, I think she's going to be able to make a great accounting of her record in the State Department. What I'm telling you, Hugh, is that if that's the fight that the Republican Party wants to fight, and I'm just telling you this as a clinical matter. I'm not saying this…

HH: I get it, I get it.

DA: …for rhetorical purposes. I think that they're going to be, they're, it's going to be a dry hole for them. And I think they know it, because when you see these Republican candidates, this isn't what they're talking about. What they're talking about, you know, Jeb Bush is talking about the right to rise, Marco Rubio is talking about the middle class, Mitt Romney in his brief flirtation was talking about poverty. The Republican Party is talking about economics and middle class economics. And if they're not, they're not going to win this election.

HH: I think they're going to be talking about Reagan's peace through strength, because the President's gutted the military. And we'll come back to that in a second But let me go to the campaign itself.

DA: So you must be for lifting the sequester levels.

HH: I am. Amen. On the Department of Defense only. I've been arguing that for a long time. David Axelrod, a couple of quick questions. Why didn't you guys ever release the President's transcripts from Harvard Law School and Columbia and Occidental?

DA: You know [long pause] honestly, I've got to, I'm not fundamentally focused on that. It's not something that I wrote about. And I'm not sure how relevant it is. What was it that you were looking for in there?

HH: Oh, I just wanted to know how he did. Like. I went to law school at Michigan, and I want to know how he did in Contracts, Crimes. I want to know how he got on the law review. At one point, you know, you're so specific in your book that I notice little things. On one page, for example, you refer to the president as the first black editor of the Harvard Law Review. *Of course, he wasn't that, on page 118. But then on page 142, you correct it. You call him the first African-American president of the* Harvard Law Review. *So you got it wrong when you called him the first black editor. You got it right when you called him the first black president of the law review. So you're very careful. So you had to have made a decision not to let those grades out, and I'm just curious why? It wouldn't have mattered if he was a C or a D student.*

DA: You know, well, I'll tell you something. First of all, the book is about my experiences. And so, you know, I wasn't around when he was at Harvard. But I'll tell you what, I did go and interview some of the people who were his professors at Harvard, and to a person, they said he was perhaps the best student that they had ever encountered there. So you know, I mean, if that's what you're going for....

HH: No, I'm just curious as to why not?

DA: I mean, because I don't think they would, you know, like I don't remember what all the discussions were around these things. But I didn't feel any necessity to go back to law school, college, high school, grade school, because it was apparent that this guy was a bright, accomplished guy, and anybody you talk to or who had dealt with him over the course of his career would tell you that, including the people who I filmed for commercials who were professors of his at Harvard.

HH: Yeah, if you don't remember that, that's the only thing you don't remember, David Axelrod, because you remember, I mean, I found the conversation that you had with Blair Hull, when he was thinking about running for Senate, and he says there's no paper on that with regards to the allegations of domestic abuse. You've got one hell of a memory. There's not much that you've forgotten...

With former Speaker of the House Newt Gingrich:

HH: *I was very surprised to hear Mrs. Gingrich say Hillary's formidable, and maybe the party needs to move to the center. Do you agree with her?*

NG: Well, I think the point she's making is you can't just take for granted that women are automatically going to vote against Hillary Clinton. And I agree with that. I think Secretary/Senator/First Lady Clinton is formidable. If you look at her numbers in the Democratic primaries, they're stunning. And I think we've got to be aware of that as we put together our ticket, and we've got to realize for a lot of women, particularly younger women, there is an attractiveness to the first woman president. I think anybody who thinks that's not real is just out of touch with reality. So we've got to be careful not so much about right versus left, but we've got to find a ticket and a platform that says to younger professional women, who by the way, voted Republican in 2014 in much bigger numbers than anybody expected, a key part of our victory in 2014 is that we were doing very well with people between 18 and 35, much better than we have done in a decade. And I think we want to continue to appeal to those folks as the party of the future.

HH: *What is Hillary's greatest weakness, Mr. Speaker?*

NG: Boring! She's just, you know, she's a celebrity like Kim Kardashian. But I mean, tell me what she's done, and tell me what she stands for. I mean, she currently stands for the idea that it's time for her to be president because she's been standing around waiting for the time for her to be president. So she'd like to be president, because after all, I mean, she and Bill think it would be good to be president, and why don't we make her president. Well, that's not a ticket. I mean, I have no idea is she going to be different than Obama, or if she's going to be Obama's third term. If she's going to be different than Obama, can she take the heat of disagreeing with the incumbent Democratic president? And if she's going to be his third term, do you really think the country's going to vote for four more years of this mess? I mean, I just think her candidacy has some big internal contradictions.

HH: *She sits down for like a quarterly interview with Thomas Friedman or Charlie Rose, or one of the reliables for the safe interviews. Can she keep that up? Will the American media allow her to waltz to the nomination without actually having to answer* *questions about Libya, about Egypt, about Russia and the reset button? Does she get a pass?*

NG: Oh, I think to some extent, she gets a pass, because the elite media's giddy at the idea that there's finally going to be a woman president. Don't underestimate in these newsrooms among the elite media how many of them are not just liberal, but they think boy, wouldn't this be just a wonderful moment in history? You know, we have our first African-American president, now we can have our first woman president. This will be just fabulous. And it's almost like asking the question, so what kind of president would she be? And that seems to be for a lot of these folks irrelevant, because they're voting symbolically in their brains. And that's why you see the elite media pull so many punches with Secretary Clinton. I mean, your point, which is I think very funny, we did research on this. I mean, the reset button story is hysterical.

HH: Yes.

NG: You know, they're in Geneva, they want to do something fancy. They actually get a button from, apparently, a Jacuzzi. It's a red button. They then paint in Russian what they think is the word *reset*, which turns out to be the word *overcharge*, because their translator got it wrong. The Russian foreign minister is standing here looking at a Jacuzzi button with the word *overcharge* on it, turns and says I don't think so. I mean, that was the beginning that led to Crimea. That was a reset? No, that was a joke. That was Keystone Cops. It was the Three Stooges. And nobody holds her accountable and says gee, how can you run a State Department so incompetent that your translator doesn't know the word in Russian for *reset?*

CHAPTER 29

Interview with Mark Steyn, December 11, 2014

HH: Mark Steyn, making news earlier this week, Hillary Clinton, who gave an address at Georgetown University, which includes this memorable paragraph.

HRC: This is what we call smart power, using every possible tool and partner to advance peace and security, leaving no one on the sidelines, showing respect even for one's enemies, trying to understand and insofar as psychologically possible, empathize with their perspective and point of view, helping to define the problems, determine the solutions. That is what we believe in the 21st Century will change, change the prospects for peace.

HH: Now Mark Steyn, I think you may be the most notably unempathetic of all columnists when it comes to our enemies. What did you make of the former Secretary of State's declaration of the need for a universal empathy?

MS: Yeah, I think the first part of that—I'm with her up to a point when she says we should respect our enemies. We should respect our enemies, and we should take seriously their desire to kill us. And we should act accordingly. But the empathy business, I think, is what has led Hillary and this administration so badly astray. And I don't really want to empathize with the head-hackers of ISIS, for example. Far too many young Western Muslims living in Dearborn, Michigan, and Toronto and London and Lyon and Rotterdam empathize and sympathize with them already. I'm far more interested in defeating them. And I think defeating your enemy requires a clear understanding of what's different, what differentiates you from them. And that's where she and the whole smart power thing have completely failed. I'm a believer in smart power in part because we don't do warmongering very well anymore. So you have to use the other levers of power. You have to use economic, cultural power and all the rest. This is what we have signally failed to do in Iraq, in Afghanistan, during the Arab Spring, in Syria, in Libya, in Russia and Ukraine. Where is the evidence for the smart power? For Hillary, smart power means racking up frequent flyer miles and standing there next to the Russia foreign minister with a reset button that some idiot, over-paid idiot at the State Department mistranslated, and turned out to mean something else entirely. That's pretty stupid smart power. But smart power properly deployed is what means you don't have to go to war all the time. And that's what this administration has been so signally inept at.

HH: Bret Stephens, who will join me later in the program today, deputy editorial page editor at the Wall Street Journal, wrote about this Hillary Clinton passage that it shows that Mrs. Clinton is as tin-eared as she is ambitious. It cannot be used except as a GOP political attack ad if and when she runs for president. I'm beginning to really question, Mark Steyn, whether she's viable. Everything she touches turns to stone in terms of appeal to the public.

MS: I think that's right. I think she's one of these people you're always having to explain. She's also, she's not just tin-eared. She's also, to go back to what we were talking about earlier, thin-skinned, so that even friendly interviewers like Terry Gross at NPR, rub her up the wrong way. If you can't handle Terry Gross at NPR, the idea that you're going to be able to withstand a primary campaign and then a general election, I think is slightly dubious. But I think it's actually a, this is a serious flaw. This is someone who has not thought about what's gone wrong in the last four years. You know, Chris Stevens, who died in Benghazi, in part because of the negligence of Mrs. Clinton's State Department, empathized with the Libyan people to an extraordinary degree, and he's dead, and his body was dragged through the streets of Benghazi. In the streets of Cairo, in Tahrir Square, we called it the Facebook revolution, and thought that somehow they all wanted, all the big, bearded men wanted to be like nice, little Obama pajama boys, and all the covered women wanted to be like Sandra Fluke. And it turned out they wanted something entirely different. She's got a tin ear when it comes to empathy. She doesn't, she's not actually capable of getting inside the head of

Iranian mullahs who seriously believe in Islamic imperialism, and exporting their nuclear technology around the world. She's seriously incapable of getting inside the head of Czar Putin in the Kremlin who wants to reconstitute a Russian empire and a Russian protection umbrella over Eastern Europe. And you'd be surprised how far west his definition of Eastern Europe goes. She's totally incapable of empathizing of any meaningful empathy with what is psychologically driving those guys.

HH: Could her presidency turn out to be even worse than Obama's abroad?

MS: Well, I think there's a difference in that I don't think she's as ideological as he is. And in that sense, I don't think she's driven by the same antipathy toward American power. But the fact of the matter is she is largely, she is largely incompetent. And the idea that she has a problem in that she was basically some guy's wife for most of her life, and then she parlayed that into a Senate seat. And then she got her first executive position in which American power drained in almost every corner of the world. And what is she going to say about that? Is she going to say oh, that was all Obama, that was nothing to do with me, I was flying around, I was eating the peanuts and pretzels in the executive jet, so I didn't actually, I wasn't involved with any of that? That's all she's got to run on. For the rest of the time, she's just got this phony-baloney foundation that exists to principally to fly her and Bill and Chelsea to give six and seven figure speeches to bored Saudi princes. And that's a resume for becoming president?

HH: Well, she's got the family business to protect. It's really about Bill's third term and making the way for Chelsea in the world, isn't it?

MS: Yeah, and I really, I've got no time, you know, one of the advantages of a monarchy is that at least it means your political class is non-hereditary. You know, in Ottawa, Stephen Harper's wife, who is a delightful lady and very smart, has got no plans to become prime minister. In London, Cherie Blair is not interested in becoming prime minister. And in Canberra, John Howard's wife does not feel entitled to be prime minister as Hillary feels.

CHAPTER 30

Interview with Bret Stephens, Deputy *Wall Street Journal* Editorial Page Editor, December 11, 2014

HH: I am now joined by Bret Stephens. Bret is of course the deputy editorial page editor of **The Wall Street Journal**. *He is also the "Global View" columnist at the* **Journal** *and the author of a brand new book,* **America In Retreat**, *which we spoke about extensively last week. Bret, welcome back to the* **Hugh Hewitt Show**. *It's great to have you.*

BS: Good to be on the show, Hugh.

HH: I called you because of your column on Hillary, and I want to talk about Hillary, and I want people to hear first and foremost what it is we're talking about. This is Hillary Clinton earlier this week at Georgetown University making a comment heard 'round the blogosphere, cut number five:

> HRC: This is what we call smart power, using every possible tool and partner to advance peace and security, leaving no one on the sidelines, showing respect even for one's enemies, trying to understand and insofar as psychologically possible, empathize with their perspective and point of view, helping to define the problems, determine the solutions. That is what we believe in the 21st Century will change, change the prospects for peace.

HH: Now Bret Stephens, your column is titled "Hillary Clinton's Empathy Deficit." What did you make of those remarks?

BS: Well, the first thing is you know, just listening to her voice, I'm thinking is that the voice I want ringing in my ears for four or maybe eight years? I'm not so sure. But leaving aside just the sound of her voice, what was very striking to me about the comment, I guess two main things, Hugh. Number one, the choice of the word *empathy* was just so politically misjudged. I mean, any one of her speechwriters must have known, or should have known that to say, to talk about empathizing with our enemies was going to be a political soundbyte for her opponents from now all the way up until November, 2016, assuming that she runs for president. The second thing is well, yes, in a sense, it's correct. You want to try to understand your enemy from his own point of view in order to know him better. That's a dictum of war going back all the way to Sun Tzu, the great Chinese military theorist of the 5th Century BC. But when you actually think of Hillary's record when it comes to getting in the headspace of someone like Vladimir Putin, or the ayatollahs of Iran, she did a pretty bad job of it.

HH: You said in your column that she is as tin-eared as she is ambitious. And I have to agree with that. I wrote a book this year called The Happiest Life, *in which I devoted an entire chapter to the glories of empathy, which is actually a harder to develop emotional response than sympathy, because you actually have to have walked in the shoes of the person you're empathizing with. Only someone who's lost a child can empathize with someone who's lost a child. You can sympathize for them if you haven't, but you can only empathize if in fact you've had a shared emotional experience. It makes, what Mrs. Clinton said makes no sense, Bret.*

BS: Yeah, I mean, look, but let's assume, you can, there's a kind of a meta-level of empathy where you can at least assume that your adversary is not simply stupid and ill-informed, and is operating from a deeply-held sense of certain political convictions. And let's just think about that. Let's take a case like, say, the Iranian ayatollahs. We keep negotiating with them with this idea that what they want at the deepest level is to be reintegrated into the global economy, they want better educational opportunities for their kids, better roads for their drivers, and so forth and so on. And that's just a complete failure to accept that the Iranian regime has sincerely-held goals and beliefs that are just at complete variance with our own. And so it's a failure to sort of understand that your adversary is coming from a place of profound philosophical conviction. Now it happens to be convictions I think are odious convictions, but it's coming from a place of profound philosophical conviction. And he's not about to be bought off in the lingo of what

Westerners or all human beings are supposed to want. The Iranian regime wants nuclear weapons because it wants prestige, it wants power, and it wants to defy the great Satan, which is the United States. Give them the benefit of the doubt. Show them that, the other word she used in that interview, Hugh, was respect. Respect them enough not to think they're stupid.

HH: *I want to go back and use a different context to illumine her remarks, because we just passed Pearl Harbor day. Can you imagine FDR talking about respecting the Nazis or empathizing with the Japanese, Bret Stephens?*

BS: Well, as a political matter, it would have been completely stupid for them to do. That being said, certainly with the Japanese, it was very important, I think, for the Americans to really to try to think carefully about Japan's mentality. And by the way, this went especially when you think about the end stages of the war where we seemed to think that, or some people seemed to think in retrospect that we could have defeated Japan without the shock of the atomic bombings of Hiroshima and Nagasaki. And that required really thinking seriously about the Japanese warrior mentality and what would be required in order to break it. But again, this is a matter of politics, too. I can't imagine FDR or Harry Truman speaking about it, because Americans aren't rallied in the language of empathy and respect. And if that's what her notion of smart power is, it equals dumb politics.

HH: *So tell me what you think she was attempting to accomplish, because I have been probing for a year and a half people about Hillary, because I'm writing a book about her. And I keep asking the same question—does she have a glass jaw? Are her political flaws so manifest in this speech overcomeable?*

BS: You know, Hugh, a year ago if you had asked me who's going to be the next president, I would have said it's going to be Hillary. And now, I really, I just, I am being reminded on a regular basis with the publication of her book, with comments about her being "dead broke" when they left the White House, one comment after another, I'm reminded that she is not as smart, at least not as politically smart, as is advertised. And sometimes, you know, I am a dear student of William of Occam. And "Occam's Razor" tells us, in effect, that the simpler explanation is the likelier explanation when you're faced with two alternatives. I think the simpler explanation here is a woman who's slightly out of her depth trying to find a higher purpose for a political candidacy that is driven solely by personal ambition. So what higher purpose is that? Well, there's smart power, the justification for her time in office. And yet the application of smart power turned out to be a four year foreign policy disaster.

HH: After the break, I want to review an earlier speech that she made at Georgetown from five years ago. But the short question, which I probably posed before to you, Bret Stephens, is what exactly did she accomplish at State?

BS: Nothing. That's the short answer.

HH: That's, I think, the answer.

BS: That's the short answer.

HH: I think that is…how do you run for president except on the assumption that the American people won't care, because it's really Bill Clinton running for his third term?

BS: Because this is the Jonathan Gruber view of America—we're stupid.

HH: Yeah, that is, she really does come down to that, because when you look at this paragraph, I don't know what she was attempting to accomplish. And 30 seconds to the break, Bret, what could she have been attempting to accomplish at Georgetown this week?

BS: Well, whatever she was attempting to accomplish, she accomplished the reverse. If it was to polish her brand as a smart diplomat, it didn't work.

HH: I'll be right back with Bret Stephens. He is the deputy editorial page editor of the **Wall Street Journal.**

HH: Bret, when I read the excerpt of Secretary Clinton's speech at Georgetown this week, I was reminded of a speech she gave at Georgetown five years ago. And I've gone back and grabbed four audio clips. This is at the beginning, only shortly after President Obama had received the Nobel Prize. I thought I'd get you to comment on some of her comments from five years ago, Cut number one:

HRC: Today, I want to speak to you about the Obama Administration's human rights agenda for the 21st century. It is a subject on the minds of many people who are eager to hear our approach, and understandably so, because it is a critical issue that warrants our energy and our attention. My comments today will provide an overview of our thinking on human rights and democracy and how they fit into our broader foreign policy, as well as the principles and policies that guide our approach.

HH: I play that excerpt, Bret Stephens, because there is quite a lot of effort in Hillaryworld to distance herself now from President Obama. Is that going to be possible, because she's speaking in the collective we here in Georgetown.

BS: Well, right, and I think whoever runs against her is going to constantly try to remind Americans of the, of just how closely they worked, or at least pretended or claimed to work. You know, I'm just shocked by the human rights case for the Obama administration. You know, we were talking a little bit about Iran just in the first segment, and remember when Iranians rose up in revolt against the stolen election, Mahmoud Ahmadinejad's so-called reelection in 2009. And you remember the images of Neda, Neda Agha-Soltan, the young, brave woman who was killed by Iranian thugs, regime thugs in the streets. And this is a regime that sat on its hands and did nothing. No, excuse me, this isn't an administration that sat on its hands and did nothing. This is an administration that has sat on its hands for two and a half, three years and watched 200,000 people get slaughtered, including a thousand people in one day in Damascus from Sarin gas get slaughtered, and has done nothing. The Sarin gas, it's true, took place after she left the administration. But when it comes to human rights, it's hard, I'm hard-pressed to think of an administration that has a worse record than this one in standing up for basic human rights around the world.

HH: Given what you've just said, listen to this clip from her 2009 Georgetown speech, cut number two:

HRC: This Administration, like others before us, will promote, support, and defend democracy. We will relinquish neither the word nor the idea to those who have used it too narrowly, or to justify unwise policies. We stand for democracy not because we want other countries to be like us, but because we want all people to enjoy the consistent protection of the rights that are naturally theirs, whether they were born in Tallahassee or Tehran. Democracy has proven the best political system for making human rights a human reality over the long term.

HH: "Whether they were born in Tallahassee or Tehran," Bret Stephens, the irony given what you've just said is pretty profound.

BS: Right, and by the way, just take two cases. What is the country that gets the most ire from this administration? It's the one genuine liberal democracy in the Middle East, and that's Israel. It's the one country that actually gets senior administration officials to mouth obscenities to reporters when it comes to talking about their democratically-elected leadership. And we were talking about empathy earlier in the show, Hugh, and it's, Israelis must be scratching their heads and asking where's the empathy towards them? But at the same time, take another country in the Middle East, which is Turkey, which is moving very quickly away from a democracy or at least a liberal democracy, into something much more closely resembling a dictatorship. When was the last time you heard a senior official in this administration, or certainly Mrs. Clinton get up and start to speak clearly about what is happening to liberalism and democracy inside of Turkey under the long rule of now-President Erdogan?

HH: It of course has not happened. And when I come back, a couple more clips from Hillary Clinton's December 14th, 2009 speech at Georgetown. I go out by giving you a repeat of what she said just this week at Georgetown. Here's Hillary just a few days ago:

HRC: This is what we call smart power, using every possible tool and partner to advance peace and security, leaving no one on the sidelines, showing respect even for one's enemies, trying to understand and insofar as psychologically possible, empathize with their perspective and point of view, helping to define the problems, determine the solutions. That is what we believe in the 21st Century will change, change the prospects for peace.

HH: I'll be right back with Bret Stephens of the **Wall Street Journal.**

HH: I doubt, Bret, you could have written your book five years ago

*and imagined as bad a five years as we have experienced.
I don't think it was…*

BS   Yeah, even with my distrust of the administration, it would have sounded like science fiction, and here we are.

HH: And here we are. But at the time that it began, it wasn't that way. Here's Hillary from December 14th, 2009, cut number three:

HRC: Sometimes, we will have the most impact by publicly denouncing a government action, like the coup in Honduras or violence in Guinea. Other times, we will be more likely to help the oppressed by engaging in tough negotiations behind closed doors, like pressing China and Russia as part of our broader agenda. In every instance, our aim will be to make a difference, not to prove a point.

HH: Now Bret Stephens, I bring this up because it reminds us of the first ill-fated step of the Obama-Clinton years…

BS   Yeah, Honduras.

HH: Honduras.

BS   I mean, dreadful. What…the government of, the people of Honduras stood up against the possibility of a new Hugo Chavez and save themselves from a dictatorship, and the United States was simply in the wrong in not accepting that Honduras, for all of its problems, actually has a rule of law, that its then-Chavezista president was attempting to violate. I mean, it's just a stunning, it's just a stunning comment. And again, I get back to this conceit, Hugh, of smart power, you know, this self-belief that they are so smart. And yet on so many levels, not only are they not smart, they're not even well-informed.

HH: Oh, she says she would press China and Russia behind closed doors to make a difference, not to prove a point. She gave them the reset button. They tried to get it back, it was revealed, in HRC, by Jon Allen and Amie Parnes. And in fact, it's a total debacle what's happened with Russia since then. And that's smart power on display, where the really smart guy, unfortunately he's evil, has eaten their lunch.

BS: Well, and you know that that smart button literally had the word *reset* mistranslated in Russian. They used the wrong word. So from the get-go, the State Department didn't even have the linguistic prowess to get the language right. And it was just a kind of a symbol of everything that came after it. This idea that you could charm a KGB agent like Vladimir Putin into being a cooperative member of an international community where as in fact he's hell bent on restoring the glories of the Soviet Union.

HH: One more quote from, in the wayback machine, 2009, Secretary of State Hillary Clinton is laying out the agenda ahead at the end of the first year of the Obama administration. And here's what she says about what we'll hear a lot about in the next two years as she runs for president—women. Cut number four:

HRC: On my visits to China, I have made a point of meeting with women activists. The UN Conference on Women in Beijing in 1995 inspired a generation of women civil society leaders who have become rights defenders for today's China. In 1998, I met with a small group of lawyers in a crowded apartment on the fifth floor of a walk-up building. They described for me their efforts to win rights for women to own property, have a say in marriage and divorce, and be treated as equal citizens. When I visited China again earlier this year, I met with some of the same women, but this group had grown and expanded its scope. Now there were women working not just for legal rights, but for environmental, health, and economic rights as well.

HH: Bret Stephens, I imagine we'll hear a lot of this stuff, and we'll hear a lot about the one Chinese dissident that she did indeed get sprung from China in the course of her four years as Secretary of State. But I don't think we'll be hearing much about what's going on in Hong Kong, and I doubt really, I really doubt that these women that she met with in that dramatic moment in the 5th floor walk-up in the crowded room that was no doubt full of infiltrators and listened to every word by listening devices are actually making much of a difference at all in China.

BS: It reminds me a little bit about her description in one of, during the 2008 campaign, of walking into a hail of gunfire when she landed in the

Balkans, I think in Sarajevo back in the mid-1990s. That should be checked. I would, my instinct as a journalist tells me I want to go back and check on that. Notice, by the way, what she omitted: the greatest human rights violations, or women's rights violations in China, the one-child policy, the forced abortions that go into enforcing it.

HH: And the inability to religious, to worship religious...

BS: Oh, the list is long, but I'm sticking to the women's, you know, specifically the women's agenda, and unbelievably cruel treatment of women who cannot afford to bribe their way out of the one-child policy.

HH: And you mentioned Turkey in the last segment. Women are being pushed back into the veil in Turkey at an alarming rate. They've never gotten rid of it in some places. And her great foreign policy push for Libya has left that country in utter chaos, Bret Stephens.

BS: No, look, I mean, this is one of the hypocrisies that drives especially those of us who are concerned about Israel's well-being and its security, the constant harping on alleged Israeli human rights violations, and the complete failure to take note of what is happening to women, to minorities, to gay people in Muslim societies, to Christians, to people with different religious beliefs all over the Muslim Middle East where this administration walks on eggshells.

HH: Yeah, ISIS threw a gay man from...

BS I mean, it's a disturbing double standard.

HH: Yeah, ISIS threw a gay man from a bridge yesterday and then stoned his broken body. That's who we're dealing with here, and I'm just curious, we have a minute left, Bret. Does the mainstream media indulge her in these fantasies of competence? Or do they attack the narrative as she's attempting to construct it? Not you and me, but the mainstream media.

BS: You know what? I don't know if you saw that *Times* story based on her time in as First Lady. It was a remarkably harsh story. I was struck that on the front page of the *Times*, there was this really pretty dim view of her political savvy or lack thereof during her time as First Lady. I think there are a lot of people on the left who just as in 2008, so, too, going into 2016, are really sick of the Clinton brand of politics, which is about personal ambition above everything else, and all of the policies, all of the ideas, opportunistically constructed to suit that vehicle of their ego and their interest. And I think a lot of, don't be surprised, Hugh, don't be surprised if one of the other candidates who throws his or her hat in the ring, maybe the governor of Maryland or even Joe Biden, might do surprisingly well.

CHAPTER 31

An Interview with *The New York Times'* Peter Baker, December 9, 2014

HH: Okay, second part of the conversation goes back to a story that you and Amy Chozick wrote on Sunday [in the **New York Times***].*

PB: Yeah.

HH: "Hillary Clinton's History As First Lady Powerful, Not Always Deft." Remarkable story, very interesting, and I want to begin with a lot of the source material, which is this oral history project. One of the critiques of that oral history project, it was paid for by Clinton-world. Did that bother you at all in using the sources?

PB: Well, *National Review* made a point of that, and let's just clarify. They didn't pay for the oral history project. They did give some contributions to the Miller Center. That appears to be the case. That was not fully funded by them or something like that. And the Miller Center is an institution that's affiliated with the University of Virginia, you know, a public institution, and they've done oral histories for every presidency going back to Jimmy Carter. So I think you know, it's a relevant fact that we should know, I supposed, that the Clinton Foundation gave them money. Fair enough. It's also relevant to know that the director of the Miller Center from 1998-2005, the one who did this oral history project, was Phil Zelikow, who was a well-known historian who worked for both Bush presidents in the White House and the State Department. So you know, I read the interviews. I don't see anything in there that suggested to me that they were done in any different way than the ones I've read from the Reagan and the Bush 41 administrations. And they produced a lot of interesting material. And we looked through them. We were looking for quotes or stories or anecdotes that told us something from people who were inside the room. By definition, those are going to be Clinton people. But what was interesting about it is it wasn't all, you know, like flattering and you know, puffery. I mean, there were a lot of sort of sharp edges to the portrayal of Hillary Clinton as the First Lady.

HH: Oh, absolutely there were. And in fact, I want to talk about that. You referred to the health care debacle of Mrs. Clinton's time as first lady, and those are the first two years of the Clinton administration. Is she going to be able to avoid in her presidential campaign, Peter Baker, being called Obamacare's grandmother, because it really is her, not her baby, but her grandchild that we're living with now.

PB: Yeah, yeah. What's really interesting is how much she has managed to evolve her political persona from that time as first lady, right? In the 90s, her identity and public perception was a very liberal figure, the liberal voice inside the White House, promoter of health care, government involvement in the economy, you know, a skeptic of welfare reform and so on and so forth. And in the years since then, really, you know, transformed herself into sort of this centrist figure, somebody who's criticized on the left. Gosh, there's the liberals who would like to get Elizabeth Warren out there, and she's seen as a more hawkish figure even than President Obama when it comes to national security. So she's done a remarkable job of sort of changing that perception over time. But any campaign, especially one that will be as hard fought as this one is going to revisit history. That's why we thought it was worth going back, looking at that time that people have kind of forgotten about, and reminding us where she came from, how she got from there to here. And I think health care's going to be a big issue, particularly if the administration can't get it working right by then. It had some success lately, they would say, but there's still two years to go. We'll see what the perception of it is two years.

HH: What's your understanding of Hillarycare compared to Obamacare? Wasn't Hillarycare—it's my understanding—I won't put it in terms of a question. It was my understanding that it was even bigger and more intrusive than Obamacare.

PB: Yeah, yeah, no, much more government-oriented. In fact, Obama's is arguably closer to what the Republican alternative was at the time when Senator Dole and Senator Chafee were arguing for a little bit more of a market-oriented approach. That's closer to what Obama ended up with. It's still obviously perceived by a lot of people as too much government in their health care choices. But it does, you know, provide subsidies for people to buy private insurance, not government insurance. And Hillary Clinton's version of it was much more government, much more bureaucracy. It was famously lampooned on the floor of the Congress with a big chart showing all the boxes and everything. And I think that was one of the things that really brought it down, because the perception that it was going to be the big states coming into your health care choices.

HH: *Now Peter Baker, you also noted in the December 5th piece in the* **New** York Times *that throughout the White House years and since she created her own team, her insiders, her Hillaryland, and that it's insular. Does she take advice from anyone not in Hillaryland seriously?*

PB: Yeah, that's a good question. You know, she's suffered over the years sometimes from having advisors who led her in a direction she might not have wanted to have gone. Obviously, her 2008 campaign advisors overestimated their capacity to take down this young newcomer named Barack Obama, and they didn't compete in a lot of the caucus states. They presented her as this, they were trying to address the issue of being a woman and whether she's tough enough, when everybody pretty much thinks that Hillary Clinton's tough enough, and they didn't address the issues that they really had. She gets caught in, as any politician does, in the network of people you've got around you. The question is in 2016, is she going to have some of those same people, or is she branching out and bringing in a fresh crop? And we'll see. I don't know whether we really know the answer to that, yet...

HH: *You know, you wrote in your piece that she was unsparing in her calculations about her husband's political prospects, and you just mentioned the need to freshen herself. One of the big critiques is that she's past her DC sell-by date. That she's old and tired. Has she heard that? Is she aware of that?*

PB: Oh, I think she's aware of it. She's certainly heard it, yeah. I do think that's an issue. You know, I went back and looked. With the exception of Ronald Reagan, we haven't elected a president since James Buchanan who was ten years older than the outgoing president, right? We tend to move on from generations forward, not backwards. And so she's going to have to address that. She's going to have to make the case for why she's not a retread. Having said that, as my wife reminds me, she has the advantage in some ways of seeming fresh because if she were to win, she'd be the first woman, and that is a barrier-breaking kind of thing. And that, to some extent, is different than if she were a 69 year old man running for president at this point. She can argue that she is moving the country forward in a way that a younger person might. She's got to explain what at 69 she's offering. And I think that even young women who are excited about the idea of a woman being president are still asking the generational question is she somebody who understand where we're coming from at this point. And she's going to find it's going to be a challenge for her.

HH: You mentioned that national security and foreign affairs don't much matter in presidential elections. But what exactly is she going to say she accomplished while Secretary of State?

PB: Well, it's a good question, right? She's a very cautious Secretary of State. She didn't have, you know, a swing for the fences kind of diplomatic breakthrough, you know, a Middle East peace or things like that. I think she'll argue that she took the right side, in her view, on Afghanistan, on Iraq, on being tough with Putin.

HH: Putin?

PB: That's what…

HH: Putin, Peter Baker? I mean, she gave him the reset button.

PB: She gave him the reset button, but it was a policy that was really the President's, and she, within the circles, and you hear Bob Gates talk about this, she always thought it was kind of, you know, not necessarily likely to succeed, and was, had a tougher point of view on him.

HH: She did push Libya. Doesn't she own that? You know, "You bought it, you break it"?

PB: Yep. She did. She did push Libya. That's an area where she'll be criticized. Obviously, Benghazi will still be an issue at least for some people. And I think that you're right. She doesn't have like sort of a bumper sticker kind of accomplishment she can point to. "I was the Secretary of State who did X." I think probably, maybe, the one she would say is "I'm the Secretary of State who helped restore America's position in the world after the Bush years," which will appeal to a lot of Democrats. But I think Republicans will probably argue, well, the Obama years have had their own, you know, problems in terms of international credibility.

HH: Now Peter Baker, you noted in **Days of Fire** *Bush was a pretty robust retail campaigner. He was good at it.*

PB: Yeah.

HH: *Hillary had a terrible book tour, said some terribly flat speeches or controversies about her speaking fees. Does she have a glass jaw that you know, Obama found, and that the next, whether it will be the Republican or primary challenger will also find when it comes to retail politics?*

PB: Yeah, I mean, part of the downside for her of being so dominant on her side of the spectrum right now, in other words, she's probably better positioned to get her nomination any non-incumbent president has been in decades. But the downside is you don't get to go through the paces, right? You know, one advantage of having a rough and tumble primary campaign is you come out of it pretty, you know, pretty warmed up for the general election. You've been hit, you know how to take a hit, you know how to respond to a hit, you've gotten some of the harsher criticisms sort of out of the way, and people absorb them. She's not going to have that, at least it doesn't look like it at the moment. And she does have, you know, she's had some issues, as you point out, with the book tour. It's probably better for her that she got them out of the way with the book tour than when she starts campaigning for real. But it's probably a reminder that campaigning is an art, and something that you can, you know, you need, you get rusty on.

HH: *Last two questions, the role of Bill in the White House, some people say we're not running for Obama's third term. It's really Bill Clinton's third term. What do you think?*

PB: Well, it's a good reminder, right? You know, it, the idea of Bill Clinton as first husband is entertaining and mystifying. What would he be like, a former president in that role? And he's such a character to begin with, and prone to his own issues from time to time. And you can imagine her trying to find ways of keeping him under control politically. But you know, third term, I think they would rather argue the third term of Clinton rather than third term of Obama, because you know, rightly or wrongly, we look back today with Clinton, on Clinton's time as being better than we do right now for Obama's time, you know, much like, you know, people today are very positive on Reagan, even Democrats. I think Clinton has kind of turned the corner, historically, a little bit, and that people forget how much they were polarized at the time.

HH: *Okay, last question, who's going to be her vice president, Peter Baker?*

PB: That's a great question. Well, we're already, it tells you a lot about her position in the party.

HH: Sure, it does.

PB: We're already talking about that, right?

HH: It does.

PB: You know, a couple of names, obviously the new HUD secretary, Castro, is a possibility. Senator Tim Kaine, I wonder, in Virginia, might be an interesting choice, right? He's Catholic in a purple state. He's been critical of Obama on some things. You know, it's an open, jump ball.

HH: What do you think of Deval Patrick?

PB: Maybe. Maybe. I mean, he comes from Massachusetts, which is a state presumably you're supposed to get anyway. But you know, he's an attractive figure, and then they would argue that that would look new generation as opposed to…

HH: Well, he's my class. He's class of '78 at Harvard, so he's…

PB: Young guy, then.

HH: Fifty-eight-years-old. Yeah, young guy. But I mean, the African-American vote has been so central to President Obama's electoral majorities.

PB: Yeah.

HH: Do they have to, in essence, either put one of the Castro brothers or Deval on there in order to energize that community?

PB: Well, they would energize that community. And I think they would probably energize, to some extent, the youth vote that she otherwise has to have a way of selling, right? Now her argument would be, you know, look at this, this is not your grandfather's ticket or your father's ticket. It's a new generation ticket. And we'll see. You know, I mean, I think that the danger, of course, is you don't want to look anything like the last administration when you're trying to sell a new administration, but you know, Deval Patrick is a very talented campaigner, and would probably bring something to the ticket.

CHAPTER 32

An interview with your biographer,
The Hill's Amie Parnes, who co-authored
HRC with Jon Allen, December 4, 2014

HH: An interesting article appeared in **The Hill** *by my guest, Amie Parnes. She is the co-author, along with Jon Allen, of* HRC, *that wonderful biography of Hillary Rodham Clinton. And today, she wrote in* **The Hill** *about the people that Hillary fears most. Amie, welcome to the program, it's great to talk to you.*

AP: Thanks for having me, Hugh, I really appreciate it.

HH: Now it's very interesting to write that piece today. I wonder if you've heard anything from Hillaryworld about it.

AP: It's been silent ever since this piece came out. But I did talk to them quite a bit before the story came out. So I know, I knew exactly where they were all coming from.

HH: So summarize for our audience who the four people Hillary should be most afraid of come 2016 are.

AP: So what we have are Jeb Bush, Rand Paul, Chris Christie and Scott Walker, who many are labeling a dark horse. But, you know, they're taking him rather seriously, actually.

HH: In Hillaryworld, they're taking Scott Walker very seriously?

AP: They are. You know, I first started hearing rumblings there was a Ready For Hillary meeting in New York two week ago where lots of donors came, hundreds of donors, and staunch Hillary supporters, and a lot of them talked to the press. And we were sort of picking their brains on who they were most concerned about, and who had a good shot at becoming the nomi-

nee. And you started hearing rumblings of Scott Walker. And I started looking into it, and sure enough, you know, that Democrats are very interested in
what he has to say. And you know, this is someone who has run successful, a
successful campaign in a Democratic-leaning state, and someone that they
are very concerned about.

**HH: *Now Amie Parnes is my guest, author of* HRC *with Jon Allen,
author of a piece in* The Hill *today. Do they worry about my guest
from last hour, Senator Ted Cruz?***

AP: I'm not hearing that name so much. You know, I actually talked to
them about Ted Cruz. You know, there are these four guys that I mentioned,
and they're really focused on them. I think the DNC is keeping, you know,
they're making books, as they call them, on all these different candidates, but
their focus is basically on these...people.

**HH: *Amie Parnes, what does she perceive as her own
vulnerabilities?***

AP: I think they're quite a few when you talk to people. I think inevitability
is one of them. It's a huge factor, and we heard that again and again at this
Ready For Hillary meeting a couple of weeks ago. They think that inevitabil-
ity could hurt her in many ways, and they saw how it hurt her in 2008. And
I think, you know, I think people are just, they have Clinton fatigue. And
I think a lot of aides are very concerned about that. So they're looking to
repackage her in a way that makes her sort of seem fresh and of the moment.
And I think they're going to have to, you know, work hard on that. It's hard
for her to seem, you know, of the people, and not seem, and not have that
Clinton name with her. So they're going to have to work on kind of humaniz-
ing her, if you will, and making her into a candidate that people want to have
a beer with, as they say.

HH: *Oh my gosh. Isn't that impossible?*

AP: I don't know. It remains to be seen, but yeah, I think a lot of people
would agree with you that you know, it is tough for her, because she does
seem so, you know, behind the scenes, she can be very kind of funny and
candid, but she's unwilling to let that side show. And I think that hurts her....

**HH: *And does she have a record that she's proud of? I mean, what
are they going to say about her years at State other than trying to get
people to look the other way and play Burma Bingo?***

AP: I know, I think they're going to have to try to really play that up, because there is no real bumper sticker issue, you know, where, that she can campaign on. You know, I think that they're going to play out, as we talk about in our book a lot, you know, there were certain moments where the President really counted on her—the bin Laden raid, for instance. She was instrumental in sort of making that all happen. And Leon Panetta came to her very early on and wanted her buy-in to make that happen, because he knew that she sort of had these hawkish views. And I think they're going to play that up a little bit, especially in a general election. I think that would play well for her....

HH: Here's my last question. What will Bill's role in the White House be if she wins her first election?

AP: I have a feeling she would use him as, you know, he would be the guy, he would be the conduit between Capitol Hill and the White House. She would send him, he has so many contacts on Capitol Hill, on both sides of the aisle, and I think she would use him effectively in that way.

HH: Would he be co-president?

AP: No, I think she would work very hard to sort of make sure who the president is, and I don't think that would happen. But I think he would be almost like a senior advisor to her.

HH: They must be vetting VP's already. We have one minute. Who's on that list?

AP: Oh, that's a good question. We're still trying to figure that out. You know, Jonathan and I are working on a second book right now, and so that's at the top of our list.

HH: And if you had to just speculate, give me three.

AP: Three? That's a tough one. I would say maybe a Castro, maybe, you know, it's hard to say. It would have to be someone. I don't think it's going to be an Elizabeth Warren, for sure.

HH: Could Deval Patrick be on that list?

AP: Maybe, maybe. I think someone, I don't know, I'm not quite sure. I think he might be on the list. It's hard to say at that point.

CHAPTER 33

Interview with Dr. Charles Krauthammer, November 27, 2014

HH: *[Hillary] immediately signed on and endorsed the President's, in my opinion, lawless immigration executive order speech earlier this week. What did you make of her decision to endorse that action, and of her positioning for the 2016 election?*

CK: Well, I think, Hugh, the key word there is *positioning*. I think she made a choice. I think she believes, I would guess, as most people do, and particularly if you're a liberal Democrat, that the policy was a good one. I don't agree, but I can see how many people do, but that the process was abominable. But thinking of her electoral prospects for next year and the year after, particularly among Democrats, and for the general election, that it would be more advantageous to her to grab onto the policy and to get the support from many liberals, and from, of course, many Hispanics, rather than to dwell on the process, because I don't think she would calculate that the process is necessarily going to be determinative, and it may not, since she isn't the one who made the decree, it might not hurt her. So she's on the right side of the issue, wrong side of the process, and I think that if that's her calculation on balance, I think she made the right, in other words, the more accurate calculation of what would help her.

HH: *With Benghazi back there and her immigration position, do you think former Senator Webb is in a position to give her any real problems?*

CK: You know, I think that Democrats are in such a swoon over Hillary, it's sort of all, it's not at the level, the emotional level of the 2008 swoon for Obama, but they are committed. I mean, they've already, they are betrothed. You know, this marriage has already been set. I don't think anybody's going to give her serious trouble. I think Webb might actually just be an interesting counterweight to her, but I don't see it as a serious challenge to her getting the nomination.

HH: Then what do you guess she's going to run on? Or are we in fact really just electing Bill for the fun of it for a third term? Or does she actually have a platform that we can expect to see?

CK: Well, you know, I think she's running on nostalgia for the 90s. I don't think there's a platform at work here at all. And it's not as if she's the only one. You know, George W. Bush sort of ran under the aura of people who thought you know, maybe we should have reelected his dad. People, Kennedys all run on the Kennedy name. With her, it's not so much on her husband, but on the feeling the 90s was a time of peace and prosperity. It was that decade, that holiday from history, between the fall of the Berlin Wall and the fall of the Soviet Union, and of course, 9/11. It's a time that people remember as a good time, and it was, in fact. So that's what, you know, that's the subtext of her entire campaign.

HH: All right, two last questions, then. Has she been around too long? I don't mean in age, but she's been around DC for a quarter century.

CK: Yeah.

HH: She's been in reruns a long time. Is it too long for the American people?

CK: Well, except for the fact that she's Clinton, and that she's the wife of the president who people remember as being a really good decade. So I think that works somewhat against her. But it's not as if she's a hack politician like a Harry Reid who's been around forever, and people say do we really want him in high office? You know, it's a person associated with a certain time. I'm reading the biography of Napoleon by Andrew Roberts, and I'm thinking of, you know, his nephew, Napoleon III, who came around 50 years later. I don't know what Louis Napoleon's platform was, and I'm sure he was running on the Napoleon name, and a bit of gauzy nostalgia for his time.

CHAPTER 34

Conversation with President George W. Bush, November 25, 2014

HH: [T]his is very interesting, the relationship between the Bushes and the Clintons. And at every level, it's very interesting. And your father and former President Clinton, and you and former President Clinton get along well, and they call them the black sheep of the Bush family. Is that going to mean hands behind your back if Hillary's up against Jeb in two years?

GWB: Well, if that happens, and I don't know if it is, I of course will be all in for Jeb, and I'll still maintain my friendship with Bill, as will Dad.

CHAPTER 35

An Interview with Josh Kraushaar, the Politics Editor of *The National Journal,* November 22, 2014

HH: Here is the most significant tweet of the night following President Obama's speech. Less than 10 minutes after it concluded, Hillary Clinton tweeted out thanks to POTUS for taking action on immigration in the face of inaction. Now let's turn to permanent bipartisan reform immigration action. Were you surprised, Josh Kraushaar, that she moved that quickly to endorse the President's sweeping and unprecedented action?

JK: Not entirely surprised. I was actually more surprised that it took this long for her to take a position, but you know, the President's speech sort of forced her hand, to some extent. And to me, her positioning vis-à-vis the President in the next year is going to be one of the most fascinating political stories, because she sees the polling as closely as we all do, and she sees the disparity between most Americans, you know, if you ask them broadly do they support comprehensive immigration reform, you do see it. It depends on how you ask the question, but you see majorities of the public expressing sympathy towards that position. But then you see the two polls that came out in the last week when it comes to the executive order, and you have large pluralities, 48% opposing, and 38% approving in the NBC/ *Wall Street Journal* poll that came out this week. She is trying to thread that needle. She wants to make it seem like she's for that legislative process to take place, but she's not against the actions that President Obama undertook. She needs that Obama base. She needs the Hispanic vote when she runs for president in 2016, and she needs to have the base enthused. But she also needs to broaden the coalition beyond just the base. So this is one of many, you know, tactical decisions she'll be making to sort of try to stay with Obama, but also keep a little bit of space. She's tied in more with Obama, though, than keeping the space on this one...

HH: *What is going to be her claim to success at the Department of State? What's her record at State that she can tout as an achievement?*

JK: Well, I mean, she and her advisors have talked about how she's visited a whole lot of countries, and actually being the first woman, or I guess the second female secretary of state...

HH: *Third.*

JK: ...and trying to promote issues that are of importance to women. I mean, that's something that she's talked about, that she's traveled quite a bit to make that case. But you know, look, Benghazi's going to become an issue. The Republicans are already bringing it up in the run up to 2016, and you know, she doesn't, in terms of, I think a lot of what happens in the second term for President Obama, whether there's an Iranian deal reached, and that was something that sort of began under her watch as Secretary of State, diplomacy with Iran. So I think she is going to have a lot to answer for. Foreign policy is, I think, going to be a significant issue in 2016, and isn't always in a presidential election. But I think if she runs on her record as Secretary of State, and runs on foreign policy, she's really going to have to answer to a lot of the President's foreign policy decisions.

HH: *And is there, by third Secretary of State, I meant Madeleine Albright, obviously, Condoleezza Rice.*

JK: Oh, right, right.

HH: *Yeah, but when you, if you're the writer's room, if you're a fly on the wall in the writer's room for Hillaryworld, what do they put on the white board as having been an actual honest to goodness achievement? Forget Benghazi, about which she has to answer the questions, but Libya's a mess, Egypt she got wrong, the reset button with Russia was a disaster, Ukraine's been carved up. How in the world does she run on competence?*

JK: I mean, it's a challenge when it comes to foreign policy. I mean, it's hard for any, someone in anyone's administration to create that space when a president is facing vulnerabilities on that specific front. So the president, when you look at the specific issues and job approval, and President Obama and all the various areas, foreign policy is one of his lowest points at this moment. It was higher when she was Secretary of State, but I think she's going to have to answer, and perhaps bear some responsibility for some of the decisions that the President has made. So it's going to be a challenge. There's no doubt about it. You know, I think they're going to talk about the fact that she traveled, that diplomacy was emphasized, that she tried to work with a lot of other world leaders. She's going to point to a lot of her travel. But I think she's going to have a challenge to really defend the President's foreign policy at a time when a large majority of Americans are very skeptical about it.

HH: With Webb in, O'Malley moving around, Joe Biden still there, Jerry Brown may be running as Yoda for president, does she have a glass jaw, Josh?

JK: You know, the thing that she has going for her is that she does have a brand. I mean, generic Democrat running as a third term of the president might have a bigger challenge than someone like Hillary Clinton, who is well-identified, for better or for worse, with the American public. But you know, and I think that she's been able, we've seen through polling throughout the last few years, her numbers have gone down somewhat, but she still has higher approval ratings than President Obama. She still has higher favorability numbers than, say, Joe Biden. So I mean, she, and she definitely has an experienced political team who's been through the trenches, who went through a very tough 2008 presidential campaign. So I mean, I don't think she has a glass jaw. I think she's, you know, she's prepared for 2016, and she's very well-attuned to all of the vulnerabilities that she faces. But she also sees her campaign as a real opportunity to be the first female president, and to forge a new coalition for the Democrats.

HH: But with her tweet, you know, she's sort of mini-me on immigration. And I'm just, I'm curious, because I'm not referring to the fact that she'll be 69. I'm wondering if her brand is so old. She's been around DC for a quarter century. Young people don't get excited by Hillary Clinton. It's like getting excited about your grandma running. And she's the grandmother of Obamacare. How in the world does she refresh the brand? We've got about a minute.

JK: Well, the big question, I mean, I think that's the big question. A lot of Republicans, I mean, there's a lot of debate within Republican circles over whether they want to nominate someone like a, say, Marco Rubio, who's a younger, less, you know, a lot less experienced compared to Hillary Clinton, but someone who's a fresh face who can almost, you know, argue the Bill

Clinton 1992 campaign theme about talking about the future, and really being a contrast. But other folks think that Jeb Bush or someone with more experience is a necessary type of challenger Republicans should nominate against Hillary Clinton, because that will, you know, people are worried about the state of the world – foreign policy, you know, it seems like the Middle East is falling apart, you know, we have the instance of Ebola just a month ago. So there's another alternative Republican point of view that thinks that Hillary Clinton probably, her experience can be an asset in this type of volatile environment, and Republicans might actually need to match her experience with someone like a Jeb Bush...

HH: *I didn't want to let you go, Josh, because I wanted to get you live in the middle of sort of Grand Central Station of politics, and this goes to branding. Is Hillary stale?*

JK: I don't think that she's stale. I think that part of branding is coming up with strategic ways to, I mean, there are a lot of brands that have been around for a long time. And smart marketers have been able to refresh those brands and make them more relevant going forward. I think that's the big challenge, though, for her campaign team. Do they have, I mean, you brought it up first, Hugh, like what is their message? What is going to be the argument for Hillary Clinton's 2016 campaign? I think it could be fresh. I think it could be, she could be coming up with something that talks about her experience, but also talking about how she differs from previous presidents, and how she, say, a third way, a different approach from President Obama and President Bush. But we haven't heard that from, she hasn't announced her campaign, we haven't really heard that from any of her advisors at this point. So I mean, I think it remains an open question.

HH: *Do you think we're really going to end up being asked to put Bill Clinton back into the Oval Office a de facto third term for Bill, not really a first term for Hillary?*

JK: I think it'll be fascinating to see how active a role Bill Clinton plays on the campaign trail. I mean, that was an issue in the 2008 primaries. And he was as smart and savvy of a politician as he is. He would get the Clinton folks, the Hillary Clinton folks, in trouble quite a bit for making off-message comments. And I think that will be the biggest question for her campaign going around. I thought it was also notable that you know, a lot of people have made the connection between Hillary's campaign and Bill's late in the '90s. But you know, if you look at the Senate races where both of them campaigned in, I think there was a lot of hope that the Clintons could sort of make some inroads in blue collar parts of the country, states that they won, or states that Bill Clinton, rather, won in '92, '96—Arkansas, Kentucky, in those two big Senate races in 2014. And they didn't make inroads. And the working-class voters that supported Democrats back in the '90s ended up voting Republican in this past election. So I think that's a big warning sign for both Bill and Hillary, in terms of their ability to kind of recreate that magic from the early 1990s. It's going to be a lot harder this time around....

HH: *You know, there was a very famous exchange in British politics in the 19th-century where Disraeli charged his great rival, Gladstone, with being an exhausted volcano. Do you think that's what Hillary might be, exhausted?*

JK: I mean, she's had time off from serving in the White House, so I don't think she's exhausted. I think she's actually been preparing and thinking about how she's going to run a campaign, and she hasn't told us much. And her staff hasn't been very open, either, even when she's going to announce, if she does announce a 2016 campaign. But I do, I don't think she's exhausted. I actually think that she's been very strategic, and has been resting and relaxed and ready to launch this....

HH: *Last question, then. She's inextricably bound up with his foreign policy failures, probably with the Iranian deal. And I just want to know if you think she can unglue herself from this immigration executive order if it becomes operational, as I think it will, as bad a rollout as the Obamacare website. I think it's going to be phenomenally difficult to administer this. It's going to be a practical nightmare as well as a Constitutional fiasco. But can she get away from it now? Or did she flypaper herself to the President's lawlessness, in my view? I know that's not your view, but my view, lawlessness, is that stuck to her in such a way that it cannot be unstuck?*

JK: And I would never say, I mean, there's a lot of time to go before she even announces her presidential campaign. The point, I think one of the other reasons why the President did what he did is he thinks he can bait Republicans to saying out of the mainstream type comments, things that make them do things, threat of impeachment or the threat of a government shutdown.

HH: No one's going to do that, though, right?

JK: It'll make it easier for someone like Hillary to run against. So I think there's a lot left to be determined. I feel like it's too early to really make a judgment on how the immigration play turns out. But I think if Republicans don't self-destruct, if they don't do things that hurt their own brand, I think the burden is on Hillary. The burden is on the Democrats to really show how they're in the, how they get the majority back with supporting this executive order, with supporting the process of this executive order.

CHAPTER 36

An Interview with NBC's Chuck Todd, November 21, 2014, November 9, 2014, and March 26, 2015

Interview, November 21, 2014

HH: *Are you going to cover Webb, because I think James Webb presents a very interesting problem for Hillary Clinton.*

CT: To a point, I do think he could. He could. He presents, put it this way, if you were to go into a factory and say who's the perfect potential challenger for her, I think the only thing, the only problem is I think demographically, having, he doesn't necessarily, a southern white guy isn't necessarily the perfect primary challenger to her. But he's to the left of her in economics, will come across as stronger on national security, even as he's more to the left of her, less hawkish, certainly will be incredibly critical of her, particularly on Libya. He's been, he was from the beginning critical of the entire Libyan operation, and being somebody who wore the uniform doesn't hurt. The question is, can he raise money? I thought it was fascinating, if you saw the Jim Webb news, within 12 hours, Tim Kaine puts out a PAC email talking about being ready for Hillary. It tells you that, you know, I think the Hillary people, that wasn't an accident. I think they are nervous about him if he ever got traction.

HH: *And I have been watching, I put in an interview request which has not been responded to earlier today of Senator Webb's office, because I am curious about...*

CT: I would bet you he comes on.

HH: *I know, and he told me to contact the office. And I am curious as to what he's going to do on immigration, because it seems to me the opening against Hillary.*

CT: Right, he was not in favor, you know. I'm old enough to remember when there were a whole bunch of Democrats who weren't supportive of some of these immigration reforms, particularly having worried about the idea of basically wages going down. And that suddenly, you know, and there were a lot of labor unions members worried about that.

HH: *And jobs being taken. So I'm curious, were you surprised that former Secretary of State Clinton, it took her less than 10 minutes to issue a full-throated endorsement of the President's action*

CT: Oh, if it's not a reminder that this was, look, I know we're all shocked that everybody plays politics with issues, but this was pretty, I mean, that the politics of this has been pretty obvious from the get-go, which is the Democratic Party, and look, and if you look at it from Obama's point of view, he broke promise after promise with Hispanics. And he felt like he had to come with something, or they risked alienating Hispanics for a long time, which is why I think you saw Hillary Clinton so quickly do that. But I have to say there's another part of this story that we haven't talked about enough, and I think we're going to play the demographics game, and that is white working class voters are, you know, dealt a thumping to Democrats in 2014, and immigration is one of the reasons. So you know, yes, for every gain they make, and maybe long term, the demographic trend will be better off for the Democrats, but they also have a white working class problem. I think a Minnesota, I think Iowa, I think Wisconsin, I think you're going to start seeing that for every Arizona that the Democrats think they're going to bring into play, I think some of the northern Midwestern states are going to come into potentially being in play for the Republicans.

Interview November 9, 2014

HH: *I want your take on what [Tuesday's vote] means for Hillary.*

CT: You know, I've been thinking about this a while, and I think, I'll tell you, she's got pressure on her to now get in earlier maybe than she wanted to. I think there is a sense, there's the sense of some Democrats are looking for somebody to sort of start rallying the party. But I have to say, I think a long presidential campaign's not going to be healthy for her. Like I don't think that's a good, it's just not good for anybody to be in the spotlight for as long as she's going to be in it. And I think a bigger problem for the Democrats this election is the fact that Harry Reid and Nancy Pelosi, everybody decided to run again. You know, the fresh faces, the young faces in Washington are Republican faces. And the old faces or sort of the veteran faces are Democratic faces. And so I think that's something that the party in general, and you wonder if you're Hillary Clinton, you know, she's the youngest of that group of Harry Reid, Nancy Pelosi, Steny Hoyer, Jim Clyburn, those folks, but you know, I think you want to present yourself as the next generation, you know, sort of the party of the 21st Century. And maybe demographically they feel like they're there, but I think their leaders, I think the faces of the party, I think that's something they have to think about.

Interview, March 22, 2015

HH: Would you be surprised by a 69 year old at the time former Senator and Secretary of State declining to run, because boy, the news today was bad on her. And Gawker's got a story out with Pro Publica about the Sid Blumenthal story. The Washington Times has Trey Gowdy, who you had last week, blowing up because she wiped her server clean and she's not turning it over. Hillary's at the center, and this new poll shows only 26% of Americans now have a favorable view of her, 37% unfavorable, another third are undecided. And it's dropping like a rock, Chuck Todd.

CT: Well, and this is the pattern of Hillary Clinton, something I brought up last week. The pattern of her political career is when she is front and center, the polarizing view of Hillary Clinton comes into focus. And when she is off the front pages and is sort of a player but on the sidelines, like when she was a Senator or when she was Secretary of State, her numbers go up. And as a presidential candidate, and when she's at the center, you know, I think all of a sudden, there is, and she might blame that press, that the press has old habits die hard, they only cover her like she's a Clinton from the 90s, and so it doesn't matter. But all of a sudden, I think this is such a big challenge in the email story, is not the email story itself, it's the idea that it creates the 'oh, there they go again, this is the 90s all over again.' And if Clinton fatigue, which is already a disease in the press corps, actually becomes a problem with the voting public, and these polls, maybe this is the first time that it's becoming a problem, that is doom for her.

HH: It is a rumbling drum in the background. Now the Blumenthal story is different. I thought until today, actually earlier this week when I began to get wind of this, that Blumenthal would send her emails and she would write him back, and it was the kind of thing where you had a former aide, a hanger-on, and you stay in touch with everyone. No. He's running a private intelligence operation on the Libyan-Tunisian border through former CIA operatives. Chuck Todd, if W. had done that, or actually, Condi Rice or Colin Powell would be the appropriate analogy...

CT: Yeah.

HH: ...people would be tearing their hair out.

CT: And yet I have to say nothing involving Sid Blumenthal surprises me. Zero. And I agree. I think this, I saw this Gawker stuff. You know, you've got, it's Gawker and all this stuff, but I've learned over the years, nothing involving Sid Blumenthal is surprising. And you know, for some reason, they've had, he's blindly loyal to them, and I think the Clintons have always had a blind spot with him, because he skirts the rules.

HH: Yeah, this is going to...

CT: He's, you know, he likes to leak stuff. He likes being described, I think, as a practice of the dark arts in politics.

HH: Well, Murray Chotiner...

CT: And this goes right into his pattern of practicing dark arts. And in this case, instead of politics, it's world diplomacy.

HH: Yeah.

CT: I agree it's, if proven, and I think more of us are looking into this, I think it just, it only, all it does is no one thing will take her down. It's the accumulation of bits like this that then feed the narrative of oh, do you want ten more years of what you didn't like about the Clintons.

HH: You know, Richard Nixon had Murray Chotiner. Reagan had Lyn Nofziger. Lee Atwater was George Herbert Walker Bush's guy.

CT: Yeah.

HH: But Sid Blumenthal is known as Sid Vicious for a reason, and none of those people, to my knowledge, ran a foreign private intelligence operation, because it raises, Chuck Todd, and this would go...

CT: Well, I don't know about Nixon. Don't forget ol' G. Gordon. But when he was around...

HH: *Well, he was [acting] domestically, domestically. But here's what [the Sid Blumenthal story] raises. If [Hillary Clinton has] got a private server and a private citizen collecting private intel [and sending it to her], it is highly likely it's compromised going into the Secretary of State's server. I mean, it's just going to raise all sorts of fun. If there was on the right someone with the chops of some of the famous investigative reporters for* The New Yorker, *this would be keeping them up all night.*

CT: I think, and look, I think all things Sid are going to become a big part of our, I think this is going to get a lot of attention. And I don't think it's a right, left, right, center. And you know, this is going to be, I think, the more explosive part of the first time she testifies on Benghazi. I mean, I think the Blumenthal stuff is going to be the stickiest wicket for her.

CHAPTER 37

An Interview with the *New York Times'* Mark Leibovitch, November 19, 2014

HH: Mark, let's talk about Hillary. You have these letters, these Peavoy letters. Did you copy all of them?

ML: I did.

HH: That's just…

ML: I mean, I think all of them. There was all, the one that filled the box were about 30 of them. And yeah, no, I have them in a file cabinet about 10 feet from my desk right now.

HH: Now one, you might get a break-in very quickly, but you wrote in your profile of Hillary from July 29th of 2007, that once she became aware of them, she respectfully wrote Mr. Peavoy, Professor Peavoy, and requested copies, which he dutifully sent to her.

ML: Yes, it's true. So she knows they exist. I mean, she obviously knows after I published some of them. But no, I think he then told me that like he kind of dropped off the White House Christmas card list.

HH: You also update, though, your portrait of Hillary by noting in the introduction a 2014 speech that she gave that there is, "a relentless scrutiny that now stalks not only people in politics, but people in all kinds of public arenas, and it gives you the sense of being kind of dehumanized." You're struck by the words stalking and dehumanization.

ML: Yeah, those are pretty strong words. I mean, *dehumanize*, especially, is the kind of word you would associate with people who have been exploited, who have been, you know, imprisoned or abused, or something like that. So yeah, you don't very often hear someone worth a hundred million dollars

using terms like that, but I see what she means. I mean, it is not a digni-
fied exercise to go through the scrutiny that someone at that level has to go
through. But at the same time, you know, this is what they're signing up for.

**HH: *It's also another reason to read* Citizens Of the Green Room.
*I had missed this entirely, this speech that she gave, which was
apparently fairly self-reflective, saying as well, "You can't really ever
feel like you're having a normal day. It can be done, but you never
forget that you're in that public arena." As I thought about that, you
really don't want to be a 69 year old woman who's going to get
photographed in their bathing suit, do you, Mark?***

ML: You know, I wouldn't know, just because I've never been a 69 year old
woman, but I'm guessing that that wouldn't be her first choice of photograph
attire. But I can't say for sure.

**HH: *But it also applies to everything else that she does. You remark
that all public people are almost always on.***

ML: Right.

HH: *She can't be anything but on, on, on.*

ML: Well, that's the thing. I mean, I think in a case like the Clintons, you
just, I mean, you have to wonder do they even know what normal looks like,
or what does normal look like. I mean, forget the things that people fixate
on, like she hasn't had a driver's license in X number of years and all that. I
mean, that's, part of being an ex-president and an ex-first lady, and being
Secretary of State. I mean, it's just the bubble of public life. I mean, that's
one thing you can sort of intuit that it not something any of us will ever identify with. But no, just knowing, and being accustomed for, what, I mean, she
was first, they first went to, he was first elected governor in '78, right?

**HH: *Yeah, but being first lady of a state, it's really '91 that she be-
comes part of the public possession.***

ML: Yeah, right. And you know, 23, but not only just part of the public
possession, but being arguably the most famous woman in the world. Now
she was always saying I'm the most famous woman in the world, and nobody
really knows. And I think that's fairly common for a lot of politicians to think
that they're fundamentally misunderstood and shallowly drawn. And I think
that it's true to a point, but at the same time, it's a familiar lament. I mean, I
actually have a profile of Governor Christie that's coming out this weekend,

and he says something similar about how he has been portrayed. But no, I think look, it is not an easy thing, I imagine, to be defined publicly in just sort of the shorthand of modern journalism and the internet and TV and so forth.

HH: Yeah, no know is ever known, but just a very few are studied. My question is they all choose it, right? It's their choice. She could vanish tomorrow.

ML: Sure.

HH: She could go Salinger if she wanted to.

ML: Yeah, I don't know if she could go Salinger, but she could certainly just, you know, make a definitive statement that she is done with public life and ask everyone to leave her alone, and I'm guessing that quite a few people would. So yeah, she can opt out.

HH: Would you have been up to the profile of Jackie O.? Do you think you could have cracked the code?

ML: Oh, sure, I would have loved to have tried. I mean, you know, it doesn't always, you don't always... First of all, that would be a case where I doubt she would have let me in. I mean, it would probably been done despite her. But sure, I mean, there's always someone else who can tell you something. And I think people give up too easily.

HH: Good note to young journalists. I agree with you a thousand percent.

ML: Yeah.

HH: If you have editors who will let you hunt long enough, right?

ML: Yeah, I think so. I mean, look, I am extremely lucky. I mean, I do have, in many cases, a lot of time and a lot of space to explore this stuff. But I think the principles are the same for everyone, whether you have a couple of days or a couple of hours to work on something, or a couple of weeks or a couple of months or whatever.

HH: Having studied so many adults who've lived in the spotlight, do you think this is why so many young stars go crazy, spin out, do stupid things, because they're just, they have no maturity on which to handle this?

ML: I think that's a great, great question. I think yes, I think it's absolutely true. I can't imagine a worse scenario in which to try to grow up and to try to learn about the world. I mean, I suppose it's possible. I mean, always, I'm always amazed by the relative normalcy that a lot of presidents' kids seem to sort of emerge from, whether it's the Bush daughters or the Obama daughters or Chelsea Clinton or whoever. I mean, obviously, it's not a picture book childhood that anyone would consider typical by any stretch. So yeah, no, it's tough, and I think that's why you see so many problems, especially out in Hollywood.

HH: Would you use the word ruthless *in connection with Hillary?*

ML: Yeah, I think in some ways. I think they want to win. I think they're willing to, you know, fight pretty hard to win. I don't, I mean, *ruthless* is, maybe it's a pretty strong word, but I think these are as competitive and combative a public, couple of public figures as you can imagine.

HH: See, I don't, I just think it's a descriptor, sort of like Margaret Thatcher, I think, was ruthless, and I think Golda Meir was ruthless. But I think women are afraid of that adjective more than men.

ML: Yeah, I mean, Bill Clinton was ruthless. I think George W. Bush was ruthless. I mean, I think, you know, in order to be elected president, or even to be close, you have to, you've got to be a killer. I mean, Mitt Romney, I mean, these are very, very competitive people, and I think that that's part of, you know, what gets people elevated to that level.

HH: Now I'm talking with Mark Leibovich. His brand new book, Citizens Of The Green Room, *must reading for anyone who cares about 2016, if only because Jeb Bush, Rick Santorum and Chris Christie are all in here, and they're all going to be part of that...*

ML: And Hillary, don't forget Hillary.

HH: And Hillary, of course, and Hillary.

ML: Yeah.

CHAPTER 38

Excerpt From An Extensive Interview with Chuck Todd, November 13, 2014

HH: Chuck Todd, host of NBC's **Meet the Press** *is with me. Chuck has just put out his brand new book,* **The Stranger: Barack Obama In the White House.** *It's linked over at* **HughHewitt.com.** *It's an incredible read. Chuck, welcome back to the* **Hugh Hewitt Show.**

CT: Thank you, sir.

HH: How many times did you sit down with Joe Biden to talk about **The Stranger?**

CT: (laughing) I did not have any official book interview with him.

HH: (laughing)

CT: So the answer is no.

HH: I tried my little **Meet the Press** *trick there, Chuck.*

CT: Yeah, nice try. Neither the president nor the vice president ever did a book interview with me....

HH: Hillary was badly banged up by the elections of 2014. She went to Kentucky and held a fundraiser for Alison Lundergan Grimes. She held a fundraiser for Mark Pryor, and Bill actually went to Arkansas three times for Mark Pryor, and Tom Cotton wins by 17, and Mitch McConnell wins by 15. Does [Hillary] have a glass jaw?

CT: I don't know. You know, look, I think that surrogates are always over-rated in general, right? At the end of the day, are you going to tell me that all the work Rick Santorum did for Joni Ernst is the reason why Joni Ernst is the new seantor from Iowa? You know what I mean? So I do think that we take the surrogate stuff, you know, we overrate it. But I think that she didn't use, what I would say that Hillary Clinton didn't do in 2014 that she should have used 2014 to do, I didn't feel like she campaigned. I didn't feel like she, you know, instead she was doing fundraisers. Instead, she was trying, you know, I didn't see her doing retail politics. I didn't see her sort of taking batting practice, essentially, when it comes to retail politicking, that you know, that has been a weakness of hers. It was a weakness of hers in '07 and '08. And so why not use 2014 to start honing a message, and more importantly, to also start doing some campaigning, doing some retail campaigning. So instead, she just simply was somebody to show up at a rally in order to get TV cameras to show up.

HH: *Does she have a message? Does she have a platform?*

CT: Well, you know, that's a great question. I don't think she does, yet. Like what is, you know, she's got to answer the why, right? She's got to answer the whole Roger Mudd question. Why do you want to be president? And maybe it is to break the glass ceiling. That is a reason. And that's going to be a reason for a lot of people. That's going to matter to a lot of voters, which is you know, let's, it's time to have a woman president, and that is a reason. She needs another why.

HH: *You know, a lot of people say she's too old, and I don't mean chronologically. I mean that everything has a sell-by date in DC when it gets stale.*

CT: You know who is a great, who sort of coined this in politics? Jonathan Rauch.

HH: *Oh, sure, and one of the great proponents of same sex marriage.*

CT: He has said that there is a sell-by date for politicians, and he figured it out once. He said basically, it's somewhere between, the sweet spot is something like eight to fourteen years on the national stage. And once you've been on the national stage more than fourteen years, then if you look back, you just have a higher hurdle in order to be seen as the future candidate, the change candidate.

HH: *And was Rauch one of the big proponents of Obamacare as well, Chuck Todd?*

CT: I don't remember on that.

HH: *I can't remember, either. I think he might be. He's a Yalie, and I've been following his career for a long time. But I think he was also, which brings me to this question. Is Hillary the grandmother of Obamacare? Is she going to get tagged in 2016 for the ongoing collapse of this fiasco?*

CT: Well, and it's funny, it's like that's, I think that's something she's got to get her arms around, because the irony is, of course, is candidate Obama campaigned against the [individual] mandate. Candidate Obama campaigned against taxing the big health [plans], you know, basically campaigned against two parts of Hillary Clinton's health care plan in 2008, and a part of John McCain's health care plan in 2008. And then he adopted both of them. I think she has to own it. I think she can't run away from it. I think the lesson for Democrats in general in '14 is if you try to run away from it, the voters are going to say well, you know, then what are you for? You know, I think that she's going to have to own it, and I think in an interesting way that you're going to call it grandmother, that's going to, some people are going to take that the wrong way. But I do think that she's going to have to own it and figure out how to be the person that says okay, this is how I would fix it. This is how…you know, Democrats have to stop saying they want to fix health care. They actually have to say what they want to fix.

HH: *As she is to her granddaughter, so she is to Obamacare. I mean, she started it. And no Hillary, no Chelsea, no granddaughter. No Hillary, no Obama, no Obamacare. Let me ask you about State. What is she going to say about State, Chuck Todd? It was a fiasco?*

CT: Well, I had one former Democratic senator say to me, "You mean the Secretary of Myanmar," that basically, that that's her best…

HH: *Yeah, we call that Burma Bingo.*

CT: Right.

HH: *Whenever I ask this question, we wait for someone to bring up Burma, and then we yell Bingo.*

CT: And that's the, and you know, that's the best, that's the best part of her record to tout. And I think that that's, you know, at the end of the day, I think that the best thing going for her is that it's Obama's administration, it wasn't hers. And I think one thing that I think I made clear in the book is that you know, he directed foreign policy, she represented it.

HH: You know what's interesting, in The Stranger, *Jon Allen's been a guest for a lot of time as well when he wrote HRC. He had part of the Benghazi story. You've got another part of the Benghazi story. But you both put Hillary in the room with Cheryl Mills in the State Department Sensitive Compartmented Information Facility, or SCIF. She was right in the middle of it, and then she goes home at some point, and she never calls back Greg Hicks. She called him once, but after they confirmed Stevens was dead, and the embassy burned, she never called back her number two in the country. Does she have explaining to do?*

CT: I don't know if she thinks she does anymore. I think she feels like she did it during the book tour. I think it really, I think when it comes to Benghazi, I think that the bigger problem she has to answer for is the Libyan intervention, right, which was the decision to intervene without leaving a footprint, and was there a rush to intervene? Was it necessary? Should it have been done? And I think that that's, you know, that to me is the larger question. That, to me, is the larger debate. And I've always thought, frankly, Republicans have spent too much time worried about Benghazi as an incident and not enough time asking larger questions about the decision to go in and not have a, if you're going to go in, then you need to have some sort of footprint after the fact to stabilize the situation, because guess what we got?

HH: You know, Chuck, though, that always strikes me as like my saying I think Democrats have always spent too much time on the 17 minutes of tape that are missing, and you know, it was those 17 missing minutes of tape that cooked Richard Nixon's tail, right?

CT: Well, I'm not saying, but look, and I think it certainly shines a spotlight on a larger policy issue.

HH: Exactly, or a set of competencies.

CT: Okay, which was intervening in Libya without a plan to win once you've toppled Qaddafi.

HH: Now I also want the audience to know, one of the reasons I think they need to read The Stranger *is I think whoever it was that gave you the Thomas Donilon account of what happened that night, this is the first time I've seen anywhere an account of what the president was doing that night. And it's not much of an account, but it's more than we've got anywhere on page 418. Donilon says he kept the president informed throughout the evening, and that Martin Dempsey had ordered military units, and he had ordered Martin Dempsey, the chairman of the joint chiefs, to get military units into the area as fast as possible. It doesn't really make sense to me, Chuck, because he's not the combatant commander. I mean, you can call up your JCS chairman, but you should be calling the guy at CENTCOM, whoever it was at the time, I think it was Mattis, I'm not sure, and saying what have we got, what do we have, and that's not happening here. And nevertheless, someone gave you an account that no one else has had, yet, of what was going on in the White House that night.*

CT: Well, I mean, you know, I'd like to think it was putting some more pieces together. I mean, look, I think that there was, there has been, I think there is more attempts at assuming conspiracy, and I think it was not a conspiracy. I think there were just mistakes made in the heat of the moment.

HH: Oh, I agree with that. I think it shows that she broke. They sent her home at 1:00, according to Jon Allen, and I think that the 3:00 AM phone call ad from 2008, which you talk about in **The Stranger,** *is going to come back around to the Secretary of State when she runs for president, if she runs. Do you think she's going?*

CT: I can't imagine she doesn't. I, you know, look, I think she is really, though, in a weird box, because she's getting advice that says if you're going to run, run early, because you need to put up an infrastructure, because frankly, you know, the Republicans are ready to go. They want to, there is going to be a concerted effort to not let her have a free ride. If she's not going to have a competitive primary, and if Republicans are going to be busy beating each other up in a primary, somebody's going to focus their fire on her. And that's certainly, I think the RNC has made it clear that that's what they view their job in 2015.

HH: Has the White House's political operation, which you detail so well, polling, polling, polling, has that disbanded now? Or is being shifted over to Team Hillary?

CT: There's not, I mean, I was just going to say if they have a political operation, it's not a very thorough one anymore. I mean, basically, once Plouffe left, so went the political operation, for what it's worth.

CHAPTER 39

Interview with *The New Yorker*'s
Ryan Lizza, November 11, 2014

HH: I begin today with Ryan Lizza. Ryan is the chief
Washington correspondent for **The New Yorker,** *the cover of which is*
this rampaging elephant. I love the cover. But Ryan's article is actu-
ally about Hillary Clinton and her inevitability problem. Ryan Lizza,
welcome to the **Hugh Hewitt Show.**

RL: Hey, thanks for having me. I thought you'd like that cover.

HH: I love that cover. In fact, I think I'm going to frame
that cover. But I loved your article as well, because if Hillary Clinton
has an inevitability problem, the Republicans have
got a shot at winning the White House.

RL: I think so. Now you know, I'm sure the people in the Hillary camp
would say well, we'd rather have the inevitability problem than not have it,
right? But yeah, I'd say look, it's really hard. Republicans have a shot to win
this in 2016. It's hard to win a third term in politics. We all know that, and
you know, you look at all these forecasting models that look at the fundamentals, and they always, you know, they give a few points off for the party that's
been, if you've been in power for two terms. Historically, it's hard to pull a
three-peat off, right?

HH: Now your piece, Ryan Lizza, begins by talking about
Hillary being next to Jeanne Shaheen, one of the few Democratic
victories on November the 4th. But Hillary's record of delivering the
goods was not very good in 2014. She was in Kentucky and [Bill was
in] Arkansas on the last weekend campaigning for Alison Lundergan
Grimes, and Mark Pryor, respectively. The former lost by 15 points,
the latter by 18 points. And that's Hillary's second home state. [Bill

Clinton in fact campaigned for Pryor in Arkansas three times in the last month of the campaign.]

RL: Well look, let's be forthright about this. No Democratic surrogate was good at helping any other Democrat anywhere in the country, right? I mean, you can't really point to anyone who was out on the stump and made a difference for Democrats. So you know, Martin O'Malley, one of the people I focus on, he's campaigned all over the country, and he didn't win any races, either. But you know, the one that I happened to go to, the one event that I happened to go to in New Hampshire is where you know, the two statewide Democrats did win, right? So Maggie Hassan, the governor, she got reelected, and Jeanne Shaheen, the Senator, beat Scott Brown, one of the few bright spots in the whole country. So I think you know, if you're Clinton, you probably take a little bit of solace from that, because obviously, New Hampshire's always been good to the Clintons. And the two female candidates won there that she stumped for. But you're right. There was no magic in the Clinton's surrogacy this campaign.

HH: More than no magic. Going to Arkansas, and Mark Pryor's a storied name down there.

RL: Yup.

HH: He's a legacy candidate, Tom Cotton, a freshman Republican Congressman, and yes, a war hero and a Harvard Law, Harvard undergraduate. But Hillary manages to, what she'd go? Did she drive Pryor down? 18 points is the worst loss.

RL: You know, you probably disagree with me on this, but Hugh, I basically see the Senate races, I think the gubernatorial elections are much, much, different story on the gubernatorial side. But the Senate races, I basically see as a hardening of the red and blue divide, with the obviously important exceptions of Iowa and Colorado, and you know, arguably North Carolina. Basically at the federal level, we are turning into two countries, right? And the Senate is looking a lot more like the presidential divide. And it'll bounce back depending on who's up every two years. It'll bounce back and forth, excuse me.

HH: Does Hillary have a glass jaw?

RL: You know, I don't think she does. I mean, she's been in politics for a quarter century. And you know, everything's been thrown at her. She's still surviving. She's the overwhelming frontrunner for the Democrats. I don't know. I mean, what's the evidence that she has a glass jaw?

HH: That she cannot help these candidates when she is supposedly the prohibitive frontrunner, and she goes into Arkansas. This is, to me, the most telling race about Hillary's lack of appeal.

RL: Yeah.

HH: She lived there for 15 years.

RL: Yeah, and I think you know, it's an open question of whether she's actually on the ballot in a general election, could she and her husband actually win Arkansas. And you know, I think that's an open question. I haven't looked at any polling about her down there. But you know, but Hugh, you've been around long enough to know that no surrogate can pull a weak candidate in a bad period for his party over the finish line, right?

HH: Well, I agree with that, but an 18 point loss isn't pulling them over the fishing line.

RL: Maybe he would have lost by 25 without her.

HH: It's impossible. It's actually impossible to lose worse than Mark Pryor did. I think Hillary was an anvil, that they threw Mark Pryor an anvil in the form of Hillary, and that...

RL: You know, I'm not convinced. I think surrogates are overrated. People don't vote on whether someone comes down and says, you know, and campaigns for someone.

HH: Okay, let me put it this way then. Is Hillary Clinton too old? And I mean not just chronologically, but in terms of DC sell-by date? She's been there.

RL: I think that is the number one most important question, and that is her biggest vulnerability. You know, as Howard Dean told me in this piece, and Howard Dean, this is a person who is already saying if she runs, he will support her. He made the point that we rarely go back a generation in presidential politics, which I thought was very interesting. And he pointed...

HH: Thought he was quick to say but I'm not talking about you, Hillary.

RL: He was very quick to clarify that you know, he still thinks she can pull it off, because he thinks that the Republicans will nominate someone too far to the right. But I think it's a good point. You know, that being around in politics, a public official at 25 years in an age where everyone is very excited about something that's new and shiny is something that she's going to have to overcome.

HH: *She doesn't strike me as particularly supple.*

RL: Yeah.

HH: *We're going to get to the competitors here.*

RL: Yeah.

HH: *When it comes to new media, she doesn't get it, in fact.*

RL: No, I don't think so. And you know, I don't know this for sure, but the sort of conventional wisdom is that none of that matters in the Democratic primary, that there's no Barack Obama on the horizon, and sure, she will have some kind of testing by someone, but basically could run the same campaign she ran last time, and she'll win it.

HH: *Ryan Lizza, let me begin by asking you what is she going to run on? She had a horrific four years at State.*

RL: I don't think we know. I don't think we know. I think on foreign policy, I think you'll probably have some, look, she doesn't know what she's going to run on, because she doesn't know who she's running against, both in the primary and in the general election. And let's be honest. Candidates don't like to figure out their exact campaign agenda until they know what the contrast is going to be with the other side. And so she has some idea that the challenge in the primaries is going to come from the left as it always does if you're the establishment candidate, and she has some idea what the general election Republican might look like. But there's no incentive for her to lay out anything until she sort of has a clear sense of the battlefield.

HH: *So her campaign until then will be as boring as her memoir from State?*

RL: (laughing) You know, I don't know if I agree with you about the memoir. I thought there were some moments in there that I found interesting. But I think so. I think it's going to be very, very vapid, and not a lot of detail until she absolutely has to fill it in. And she's not going to listen to us in the press who pressure her into filling in those details before she's ready.

HH: *She's been around forever, and still new stuff pops up. The* **Washington Free Beacon** *found her Alinsky letters.*

RL: Yeah.

HH: *And they found her files down at the University of Arkansas. And I thought there wouldn't be...*

RL: Yeah, I wasn't really impressed with the Alinsky letters are far as, like, you know, proving that she was at the heart of some crazy, left-wing conspiracy, to be honest. But it was a very interesting reportorial find.

HH: *Yeah, but it's just that something can show up this late in the game. I mean, maybe we'll find...*

RL: Well, fair enough, and it's a bad, it's a statement about the press, frankly, that it's been sitting around and nobody found it before now.

HH: *The Whitewater files may show up again. Who knows what we'll find with her? But is she, is in fact the fact that we won't find anything make her boring?*

RL: I think it's part of it. I think you know, the communications consultants, the political consultants always say it's, the views of someone who's been around a long time are set in stone, right? So there's not a whole lot of new information that I can tell you, Hugh, about Hillary Clinton that's going to get you to change your mind about her, and there's not a whole lot of new information that you can tell about her to get some unpersuaded voted to change his or her mind. And that's sort of her burden, but it's also, it might be what, you know, an advantage, depending on who she's running against.

HH: *Well, some people buy day-old bread to save money, Ryan Lizza.*

RL: But if she's running against someone who's got, from a reporter's perspective, an interesting history and a lot to uncover and learn about, that can be an advantage going against someone who's been around so long that nobody cares about anything in her history.

HH: *Absolutely true. What about Benghazi? Will it matter at all?*

RL: I thought we were going to get through 15 minutes without Benghazi?

HH: Never, and that's one of her problems, right?

RL: You know, my view of Benghazi is, and I don't know what this says about the press, but it's one of those issues that is almost completely now seen through a partisan filter. And the right will view it one way forever, and the left will view it one way for another, and there are almost no facts that can come up, the new facts that'll change people's minds about it. I don't think it's going to be a big deal, Hugh, to be honest. I think in a Democratic primary, nobody will care about it, and in a general election, people will care more about what is she going to do about troop levels in the world, how's she going to handle Iran, how's she going to handle North Korea.

HH: I'm going to talk about the three people profiled along with Hillary in Ryan Lizza's brand new **New Yorker** *story. And one of them will bring up Benghazi.*

In that piece are profiled the three candidates who are thinking about running in the Democratic primaries for president in 2016, 2015 and 2016, one of whom will almost certainly bring up Benghazi, Ryan Lizza. Which one do you think I'm talking about?

RL: Webb will bring it up.

HH: Webb will bring it up. James Webb, and the reason, do you know that he wrote **Rules of Engagement,** *the screenplay, for that movie?*

RL: That's right. No, you know, I did know that, and I'd actually forgotten that until you just brought it up. I wrote a much more extensive profile about him for *GQ* in 2007, and I read all of his books back then.

HH: Well, Webb served with my brother-in-law in Vietnam. And I've known him, I don't know him well, but I've met him.

RL: Is that right?

HH: And I've had him on the show a number of times. He'll be a tough candidate. And he will bring up Benghazi, not because of scandal, but because I think Hillary cracked that night and she went home and wasn't in command and control of the situation.

RL: Look, I think the case for Webb, you know, here's the big, missing component for all these guys, is what demographic group in the Democratic primaries can they pull away from Hillary Clinton, can they steal. We all know what group Barack Obama stole in 2008. He did what no, you know, he did what no sort of, for years, the challenge to the establishment candidate always won over the college-educated whites in the Democratic primaries. But there was never enough to win the whole thing, right—Gary Hart, Jerry Brown...

HH: *All the way back to Eugene McCarthy.*

RL: All the way back to McCarthy, right?

HH: Yup.

RL: And that group has grown on the Democratic side, but nobody until Obama could pull in another group. And obviously, Obama pulled in African-Americans. And so that's the demographic box that frankly any of these, you know, white, male candidates have in running against her. So you know, and I think that's the problem that O'Malley has. Webb arguably, maybe he can cut into her appeal among white working-class voters, because remember in 2008, people forget this, Obama was sort of the candidate of the, you know, what the strategists sometimes called the wine track, right? And Hillary was the candidate of the beer track. She did better with white working-class Democrats. If Webb can steal that in addition to the more college-educated liberals, that would be an interesting coalition.

HH: There's also, Ryan, a growing concern, and this surfaced in the 2014 cycle, about international chaos. Whether it's Ebola—the impersonal killer—or ISIS—the very driven killer—having someone who can speak directly to national security.

RL: Yeah.

HH: And I thought your comments from Webb about the three kinds of national security candidates out there are very revealing. He intends to be in category three, behind door number three, and there might be national security Democrats and some Republicans, if the isolationist wing of the party spring up who would love a James Webb.

RL: Yeah, and I don't know if you got it from the quotes, but in my conversation with him, he is really close to Rand Paul on foreign policy right now. He's dead set against any kind of humanitarian intervention. He would not have bombed Benghazi, or excuse me, not bomb Benghazi, but he would not have bombed Libya's, Qaddafi's forces that were outside of Benghazi. He, you know, he didn't believe in any of the humanitarian interventions of the Clinton 90s. And you know, he believed in Congress having a stronger role when we go to war. He's definitely not an isolationist, but he's much more of a non-interventionist than a lot of Democratic elites saw.

HH: *But he'll be for a very big stick.*

RL: Exactly.

HH: *And Hillary Clinton, do you think she has any credibility on defense issues in terms of, you know, a 350 ship navy, or a steroided-up Marine Corps or anything that would normally go with a national security Democrat that Webb would have?*

RL: I don't know. I mean, the armed forces, when you look at the opinion polls, they're mixed, ideologically are much more mixed than people usually assume. and I think they're, you know, I think Hillary would have quite a bit of support, if you're just talking about...

HH: *Democratic primary voters.*

RL: Well, not, even in a general election.

HH: *Oh.*

RL: Remember in 2008 how well Obama did with military voters.

HH: *Again, that's disputed, but it's also the national...*

RL: Well, it was certainly not 90/10, right?

HH: *No, it wasn't 90/10. But the national security voters are a very small slice of the electorate. But in a Democratic primary, it could have an enormous resonance if Webb is running both for the NRA vote and for the DOD vote.*

RL: I think, what happens if Hillary Clinton runs against Rand Paul? What happens to national security voters in that race?

HH: *I think they split decidedly. That's what Howard Dean told you. He's counting on that, actually, for the Democrats.*

RL: Yes.

HH: Let me turn to the other two you profiled, and we'll talk about the two that you didn't. Bernie Sanders...

RL: I only put, look, my rule was I was only profiling people who are openly talking about running.

HH: And there are two who are kind of openly talking about that you gave them a pass.

RL: Not open enough.

HH: Martin O'Malley and Bernie Sanders. First, Bernie Sanders. Now this is a joke. This is like Ben & Jerry's ice cream meets the presidential campaign.

RL: Oh, I can't believe you're not a Bernie Sanders fan.

HH: Oh, no, I love the guy. But it's just a joke. It's like Peter King running for president, right?

RL: Well, of course, but you know what? I think it's, I'm honestly a little, I think this is a little bit of a media bias going on with covering the Democratic side. Anyone who goes on TV and says they might run for president on the Republican side gets all this coverage, you know, Ben Carson, King. And on the Democratic side, these guys are like screaming from the sidelines they want to run for president, and nobody's covering it.

HH: That's because Bernie Sanders is a self-described socialist.

RL: Yeah, but so what? Ron Paul was never going to win. Ron Paul ran as a third party candidate on the Libertarian ticket, which was pretty radical, and still was covered...

HH: You don't really know the answer? Come on, you know that answer. The reason that Ron Paul was covered and Bernie Sanders isn't is that Ron Paul coverage hurt the Republicans, and the MSM wants to do that.

RL: Well Hugh, well, I'm surprised that, I'm actually surprised that conservatives are not making more of a media bias case on this, saying hey, Why isn't the MSM covering Bernie, Webb and O'Malley, who are willing to go after Hillary? Everyone's just saying it's over, it's a coronation. Hillary won.

HH: *Well, because generally, we're realists. And the MSM have agendas. We're fair and balanced...*

RL: Well look, I state very clearly in the piece that you know, Sanders will be like Ron Paul of the Democrats. He's not going to win, but he will raise issues that will speak to certain Democratic voters, and that the frontrunner, Hillary Clinton, will have to address, especially if he's in the debates, as he surely will be.

HH: *Now the most interesting bit of the piece is, I think, about Martin O'Malley, about whom very few people know much. I only know that his anointed successor got crashed in Maryland.*

RL: Yeah, big problem for him.

HH: *Martin O'Malley apparently is running a very successful campaign for vice president already.*

RL: You know, that is a good point. Is he jumping, do you jump in the race against Hillary to try and become her running mate? And you know, the Democratic strategists have argued this both ways to me. Some say that is the worst way to become her running mate, because the Clintons, as soon as you start attacking her and running against her, and give her any bit of a hard time in a primary, you have been put on the naughty list, and you're not going to be her running mate. Other people say well, if you run a clean race and you acquit yourself well, then maybe you can heighten your profile, and since the Democratic bench is so weak right now, maybe that is the route to the...

HH: *Are you saying that she's not a* **Team of Rivals** *type?*

RL: That's the reputation. And you know, that's the conventional wisdom. But you could run a race where you're not necessarily attacking her, you're just being positive, putting out your own issues, and maybe not whack the Clinton hornet nest....

HH: *Two people not there who should have at least cameos are the ancient of days, Jerry Brown, and the new Elizabeth Warren lefty insurgent type. What about those two, Ryan?*

RL: I think Warren is still a question mark. And I sort of dealt with her simply by saying she's insisting she's not running, so she's not talking about running. And I actually wanted to talk to the candidates who are thinking about running. But the piece is really about in general insurgents, and what you have to do, and the sort of rules for insurgents. And so if you read the piece, you know, it's sort of a strategy guide to an insurgent run against Hillary, and it would apply to Elizabeth Warren, right? You've got two big ways to run against Hillary. One is new/old, right? You've got to be the new, tag her as the old. And the other is an ideological challenge, you know, challenging her from the left. And Elizabeth Warren would be able to do both of those...

HH: Okay, so let's just limit it to, if Elizabeth Warren gets in on the left, and James Webb runs as a national security, traditional Scoop Jackson Democrat on the right...

RL: Yup.

HH: Hillary's in a vise.

RL: I think so. I think she's going to have to decide where does she come out on these questions that liberal Democrats care about more than ever, inequality, right, too big to fail? What is she going to say about the banks? What is she going to say about Clinton era deregulation? What is she going to say about Clinton era policies that don't look so good to liberals in hindsight, like the Defense of Marriage Act?

HH: Ryan, what is she going to say qualifies her to be president? Is it because Bill is her husband?

RL: Experience.

HH: Experience at what: leaving the State Department on the night of Benghazi? Experience...

RL: She's going to have to deal with Benghazi for people like you. There's no doubt about it. But she's also going to say hey, I've been around. I've seen two White Houses now, I've been, traveled the world as Secretary of State, and there will be a lot of people who say you know what? We can't afford someone new. Even people who think Obama was a failure will say yeah, maybe the reason was he was too new. Maybe we should try someone who's...

HH: Ryan, that's an argument for making the White House chef the president. They've been there longer than anyone. It matters what you do. And I'm serious here. What has she done?

RL: She's been first lady. She was a partner in what is regarded historically as a very successful presidency, in the Clinton administration. And as Secretary of State, you may disagree with this, Hugh, but she does have something she can brag about. Some of the policy in Asia, I think, doesn't look so...

HH: Give me a country. Give me a country.

RL: Well, look, and this is one I mention in the piece, and you can, although Obama's going to be there this month, but the opening to Burma has been more of a success than a failure.

HH: You just played Hillary...Duane said Yahtzee. I was going to say Hillary Bingo. Burma always comes up. They have a genocide underway in Burma, Ryan Lizza.

RL: Look, there was a genocide...turning Burma into an ally rather than a country completely isolated in China's orbit is better for America. Am I right or wrong about that?

HH: It's our genocide partner. You're wrong. It's a friendly genocider. You know, that is...

RL: Whether it's genocidal has nothing to do with whether we are more allied with it than China is, right, Hugh?

HH: Well, no. It does, because her own husband said Rwanda was the biggest mistake of his career.

RL: Let me ask you this. How can you, what's a better way to have influence over a country that's genocidal? If it's completely isolated and there's sanctions against it and you have no influence, and it's in China's orbit, which doesn't care about genocide? Or if it actually listens, you actually have a relationship...

HH: It's a great question for her on the debate stage, because I think she'll stand there and go, "Dabba dabba dabba, what about the girls?"

RL: Yeah, if Rand Paul's the nominee, what's he going to say about that?

HH: Oh, well, if Rand Paul's the nominee, whoever they nominate is going to have a more robust foreign policy interventionist, right?

RL: Yeah, and look, let me make the other case. I'm not saying that Burma, you know, Hillary Clinton running on a Burma policy is what gets her elected, but having eight years in the Clinton administration, which is what will be regarded historically, even in 2016, and perhaps more so after the, depending on where Obama ends up, I think it will be more of a plus than a negative in a general election.

HH: Ryan, so we're really voting for Bill Clinton, aren't we?

RL: Do you agree with me there?

HH: No, I don't. I think we're really voting for Bill Clinton.

RL: Hugh, wait, so of the three, the last three administrations, you don't think the Clinton administration is looking pretty good right now?

HH: Absolutely not. Oh, absolutely not, back to the 90s.
But very quickly from you, we're really voting for Bill Clinton, right?

RL: I think she's going to have to deal with that. I think she's going to have, she can't do what Gore did, right? She can't pretend to run away from Bill Clinton. And she's got to run on Clinton's record for the most part.

HH: She's got to attach herself at the side of Bill if she wants to win.
Ryan Lizza of **The New Yorker.**

CHAPTER 40

Interview With Guy P. Benson
and Senator Marco Rubio, June 9, 2014

*HH: Joined now by United States Senator Marco Rubio.
Senator Rubio, great to have you in studio, thank you.*

MR: Thank you.

*HH: Now I want to talk to you about Hillary Clinton's memoir,
but the very first and most important question, the Browns drafted
Johnny Football. What do you think?*

MR: I think it was a nice move by them. They'll sell a lot of tickets. He
might go play baseball.

HH: No, he's not going to go...

MR: Did you see he was drafted in the 180th round or something?

HH: He's not too short?

MR: I think he'll be all right. He's a unique player.

HH: All right, just...

MR: Yeah, did you read the leaked report the Patriots have the last scouting
report?

HH: I did indeed.

MR: Yeah. And you're not concerned with that?

HH: I'm not worried. Bill Belichick was just messing with our mind.

MR: You're right.

HH: Now I want to talk to you about Hillary Clinton's memoir. What do you think? Is this the first time you've seen Hillary's memoir?

MR: Well, the cover, yeah. I haven't read it.

HH: What do you make of her using on the back flap a picture of the return of the dead from Benghazi?

MR: Yeah, well, I mean obviously, I think many people are going to question the use of a photo like that. And by the same, I mean, especially when it's surrounded by just about everything else there is in the picture, other than the bin Laden raid, all are upbeat things. But I think more importantly, is what she'll say about it or has said, and I haven't read that account. But I think that's a huge unanswered question, as far as her time in the State Department. Look, here's what's, I think, not been covered nearly enough, certainly by the mainstream media, and that is one of two things is true. We either should not have been in Benghazi, there should not have been a facility there given a consistent threat stream that had been arriving at the State Department, or they decided to still be there. Remember, the Brits had pulled out by then, the Red Cross, if they decided they were still going to be there, then they should have had a sufficient security plan in place not just to protect the people on the ground, but to be able to extract them. And that clearly was not the case. So I think it's questionable whether they should have been there. You sit there now and look at that stream of reports that were coming in, and it was clear how dangerous it was, but at a minimum, should have had sufficient security, which certainly was not the case, and no extraction plan.

HH: I'm going to have you put on the headphones so you can listen to a conversation that Secretary of State Clinton had with Diane Sawyer earlier today about the security situation in Benghazi. Diane Sawyer posed it this way.

DS: Is there anything you personally should have been doing to make it safer in Benghazi?

HRC: Well, what I did was give very direct instructions that the people who had the expertise and experience in security…

DS: But personally, you…

HRC: Well, that is personal, though, Diane. I mean, I am not equipped to sit and look at blueprints to determine where the blast walls need to be or where the reinforcements need to be. That's why we hire people who have that expertise.

DS: I wonder if people are looking for a sentence that begins from you "I should have…"

HH: *Do you think they are, Senator? Diane Sawyer's question, are they looking for Hillary to admit responsibility and accept it?*

MR: Yeah, I mean particularly because no one at the State Department's been held responsible for what occurred on that day. Clearly, at some point, and I actually, when we had a hearing that she appeared before us, tried to dig into the bottom of that in terms of understanding why it is that they didn't take this more seriously, but here's what was pretty clear, is that no one did, that it didn't happen, and no one's been held accountable for it. So at some point, someone made the decision that what they had in place in Benghazi in that consulate facility was sufficient. That buck needs to stop somewhere, and it never has.

Guy Benson: Senator, good to see you.

MR: Good to see you.

GB: If you were in the House, hypothetically, and on this Select Committee…

MR: Yeah.

GB: And if Secretary Clinton were to show up, what is the number one question you think that she hasn't sufficiently answered that you would put to her?

MR: And I think that question would be explain to us the process by which the decision was made to keep that consulate open, given all of this information that's out there, and I think it'll be very important to see whether this Select Committee will be able to hold hearings in a classified setting, where the details about some of that reporting stream will be, they'll be able to delve into. And then the second question I would have is tell us at which point you were involved in that decision-making process, or how much you had individually gotten involved in it, and I'll tell you why that's relevant.

During our committee hearing in the Senate during the Foreign Relations Committee where she appeared before us, I asked her about some of the meetings she had had with Libyan officials where this idea that we had outsourced a lot of the security for that facility had been outsourced to Libyan militias. I mean, people have forgotten this, but a lot of the perimeter security in that facility was being handled by Libyan militias. And they were the first people to leave as soon as any of the fighting started. So again, I think the buck, we need to understand who made that decision, and how high up the chain did that reach.

HH: *She mentions in this book that she talked with Gregory Hicks along with eight other members of the State Department, confirmed some of his decisions, and said, stay in touch. She never called him back. We know that there's got to be a recording of that, because there was a transcontinental phone recording. To your knowledge, has anyone subpoenaed that conversation?*

MR: No.

HH: *Should it be?*

MR: And again, I'm not sure that there is a transcript of that conversation, certainly probably a read out of some sort. But I wouldn't assume that there is. But again, that was, you're talking about now once it was underway?

HH: *Yes.*

MR: Yeah, and so that specific question, I'm not sure, has ever been posed in terms of any sort of subpoena. Certainly, the Senate's not issued any subpoenas for anything from this White House or the State Department.

HH: *You think the Select Committee should go and ask if that recording occurs?*

MR: Sure, I think we need to understand, and I'll tell you why this is important. This is not just about embarrassing Hillary Clinton like some people say or what have you. It's about, the bottom line is that we have multiple facilities around the world, including in Tripoli right now, that are in a dangerous place. And is the same process being used to make decisions there?

HH: *Senator Rubio, in this book, and you spent a lot of time on foreign policy in the last few years, Hillary writes in page 470, "It is impossible to watch the suffering in Syria, including as a private citizen, and not ask what more could have been done." How does that strike you?*

MR: Well, again, I mean, I've read excerpts where she said she actually argued that in meetings within the White House about what the steps should be taken in that regard. So I'd say two things about the Syrian conflict. Clearly, the humanitarian aspects of it are important, and we need to care about that. But more important from the political perspective, or from an administrative perspective, is the national security interests of the United States. Is it not in the interest of the United States for Syria to become a vast ungoverned space where foreign fighters stream in and use it as a base of operations like they used to use Afghanistan? That's what it's becoming. That's why I argued in the early stages of that conflict that we should try to identify the more modern elements, and ensure that they were well-equipped and armed so that there wouldn't be a vacuum created. That didn't happen. And I know she argues in the book that she advocated for that. That may or may not be, but the White House didn't pursue that track, and now what you've seen is that the majority of the rebels that are fighting in Syria are not Syrians. They're coming from all over the world including Europe, and they're radical jihadists.

HH: *If it turns out that she runs for president, and it turns out that you run for president, will you be afraid of debating her foreign policy record with her?*

MR: You know, anyone, whoever runs for president against Hillary Clinton, I think, is going to have ample space to criticize foreign policy. What is the signature foreign policy achievement of this administration? If you look at the world today from where it was a few years ago, doubts about America's leadership have never been higher, certainly in the last decade. You know, with George W. Bush, people can disagree about different decisions that he may or may not have made with regards to foreign policy. But there was never any question that the US was going to lead the free nations of the world. Around the world today, perhaps, the most common theme is one of serious doubt about the US' willingness to lead or ability to lead, whether it's in Asia or Europe, or in any part of the planet, so what is the signature achievement of her four and a half years at the State Department?

HH: Do you think there is one?

MR: I do not. In fact, I think if you look at the administration's foreign policy especially during her watch, it completely lacked any sort of strategic vision of what America's role is in the world in the 21st century.

HH: Before I turn this over to Guy, on page 205, she writes that, "Many in Europe were put off by the 'you're either with us or against us' style of President George W. Bush's administration, exemplified by Secretary of Defense Donald Rumsfeld's dismissive description of France and Germany as old Europe at the height of the Iraq debate in early 2003. By 2009, positive views of America across Europe had eroded significantly. We had our work cut out for us." True or false?

MR: Well, again, there might have been elements in Europe that didn't like the direction George W. Bush headed, but at least they knew where he stood, and they respected it. I think the even worse problem that we face now is the significant doubts among our allies around the world that the US is still capable of living up to their defense obligations. You look at Asia as an example, and this is a promising development, in my mind, but the fact that Japan is now spending more money and trying to define their Constitution in a way that allows them to participate in collective self-defense, is, one of the reasons why that's occurring is because of significant doubts about whether the US is still willing or capable of playing the role that it has historically in the Asia Pacific region.

Guy Benson: Senator, the Clinton camp has sort of pushed back, and sort of trying to have it both ways on the Bergdahl situation, where Secretary Clinton has been supportive of the deal. But then there is reporting in **The Daily Beast** *that said she was skeptical about the deal and wanted more out of it. A: Your take on that trade?*

MR: Yeah.

GB: And more specifically, B: Where do you come down on the argument about the president was bound by law to inform Congress, versus he had as commander-in-chief executive power, he didn't have to do that?

MR: So he does have executive power to act in a national security interest. So for example, if there was clear evidence that the sergeant was in imminent threat for his life, that some dramatic instances had changed and he wanted to move forward on a deal for whatever reason, he certainly had the constitutional power to do that. They've offered no evidence of that. And in fact, their story, just the health concerns they had about the sergeant, have now changed a couple of times over the last week since this deal has been announced. Beyond that, my take of it is that for American service men and women around the world, they're in greater danger today than they were before this deal was made. There's been a very clear message and incentive sent now that if you get your hands on an American service man or woman, it proves greatly valuable. I'm not making that up. The Taliban has said that, including last week in an article in *Time* magazine. And then beyond that, I would argue that we've released five extremely dangerous individuals, some of whom have been accused of atrocities, war crimes, and I say accused, but quite frankly, they did it, they admit to this, have been released, and by the administration's own assessment. You can anticipate almost all of them, if not every single one of them, will return to the fight against America fairly soon.

HH: *Senator Rubio, there is exactly one reference to Valerie Jarrett in this memoir. Do you understand Ms. Jarrett's role to have been more significant than that in the last five and a half years? And if so, what do you think her role is?*

MR: Well, I don't know what it is. They've certainly, I'm not an insider in that White House, so I would probably be the last one to know what her role is. I know she's a prominent player in the White House, but at the end of the day, I would imagine her role cannot extend beyond making, giving advice. The ultimate responsibility is on the President, and on the members of his cabinet, like Hillary Clinton, who guide policy and who make decisions on management and so forth with regards to the decisions that were made with security at this facility in Benghazi. And for the President, he's the one who has failed to lay out a strategic view of what America's role in the world is. To the extent that there is one, it seems to have been that America's problems around the world were created by a robust foreign policy through the Bush administration, and that his job was to extract us from these things around the world. I think that's proven to be a disaster.

Interview with United States Senator Marco Rubio, March 24, 2015:

HH: *I begin today's show with United States Senator Marco Rubio.*

Senator Rubio, welcome back to the **Hugh Hewitt Show,** *it's great to have you.*

MR: It's great to be on, thank you.

HH: You know, my tradition, I always start with a couple of sports questions with you.

MR: Yeah.

HH: The Heat are at 33-37…

MR: Yeah.

HH: The Dolphins are drafting 14 after an 8-8 year. The Marlins only won 77 games last year. The Gators lost five games. I mean, are the sports gods auspicious for a presidential run for you this year?

MR: (laughing) It's been a good year, I mean, a bad year, but I think that's always the beginning of a good one. So the Marlins have actually put together a Major League roster. I mean, so they're excited about that. The Heat is struggling, of course, because they've had a lot of injuries. But they've made some, you know, Dragic, the Dragon, who they've just added, is a real point guard and gives them, they hadn't had a point guard on that team in ten years. So the combination of that and Bosh coming back next year hopefully from the blood clot, I think they're one good scorer away from being a very legitimate contender. And the Gators just had a tough run, but they'll be back.

HH: All right, then a second question, the MVP debate is hot. Westbrook-LeBron, you do remember LeBron, right?

MR: I remember LeBron. We beat him last week, actually.

HH: (laughing)

MR: We beat him for the second time this year. I do remember.

HH: Westbrook-LeBron-Curry-Harden, who's the MVP, Senator Rubio?

MR: You know, I think Westbrook's had a great year. LeBron can be the MVP any year, but you know, Kyrie Irving has really been more of, has kind of really stepped up and taken leadership on that team in ways that no one had anticipated. Now you could argue that that's LeBron opening up the floor for him, but you know, it's interesting. I just think Westbrook means more to his team right now.

HH: All right, now to the serious stuff. I see that you and Senator Cotton have co-authored an amendment. I have been talking about Defense spending for the last two weeks on this show. Tell us about the amendment and about the prospects for a serious return to serious funding limits for the Pentagon.

MR: Well, let me begin by saying that the fundamental obligation of the federal government, beyond almost anything else, is the national security of our country. That doesn't mean you just throw away money on programs that don't work. But I do believe that when you put together a federal budget, your number one object should be how can we protect the country from foreign adversaries, threat of terrorism, etc.? And once you've funded that, then I think you begin to fund the other things. But it should not, it is not an equal part of the budget when it comes to the federal government, and we're not doing that now. We are well below, you know, $487 billion dollars over ten years are the cuts that have happened under this administration. It'll add up to over a trillion over the next decade as you move forward. These, this is just an incredible decline in spending at a time when the risks are continuing to grow. This country has tried to take peace dividends in the past, after Vietnam, after the Cold War. But at least, that was not a good idea. We had to come back and reverse all that, and it costs more money. But at least at that time, there seemed to be some sort of prospect for peace. This is not in any way a peaceful time. This is a time of increased threats, whether it's the Asia Pacific region with China's growth and militarily, in the Middle East with the threat of both an Iranian nuclear weapon and also the threat of ISIS/al Nusra/al Qaeda and all these other related jihadist groups in the region. And of course, NATO needs to be reinvigorated as well. So these cuts couldn't come as a worse time. So we just want to take it back to the numbers proposed in the Gates budget that was offered up in 2012. And it reflects what the bipartisan, Congressionally-mandated National Defense Panel stated was the minimum required to reverse course and set the military on a more stable footing.

HH: Do you have the votes for that, do you think, on the Senate side? The House will be different. There'll be a conference. But first, you've got to get serious funding out of the Senate to at least get to the conference to get to serious Defense funding?

MR: Well, we hope we do. Obviously, it's going to be a heavy lift, because we'll need some Democrats to come on board, and we'll need all of our Republicans. And we do have some fiscal hawks in our conference that don't want to see anything that isn't paid for. My argument is I want to balance the budget, too. But we can only balance our budget through entitlement reform. You can't do it by cutting Defense spending. There's just not enough money there when you're talking about an $18 trillion debt, and it's a very dangerous thing to do in terms of putting us at risk. So it's unlikely we'll get to 60 votes. Maybe we can convince some people, and of course, Democrats, some even the pro-Defense ones, are insisting on a commensurate increase in domestic spending to support any increase in Defense spending. So that proves to be problematic. But we at the very least have to lay down, we need to know who's who around here when it comes to making Defense spending a priority.

HH: All right, now you mentioned NATO as well, and I asked Dr. Ben Carson this last week, I want to ask you as well. Putin does not appear to be checked by anything. There is a threat to the Baltic states. Do you believe NATO would back up their commitments to their Baltic members if Putin made an aggression there, and ought they to?

MR: Well, a couple points on that front. The first is that I think we've got some European partners that quite frankly are not excited about the prospect of having to have someone invoke the common defense agreement, the collective defense part of NATO, and they're worried about that to begin with. You've seen some of that already, although Ukraine is not a NATO member. You've seen some reluctance there to do things like arming the Ukrainians, beyond just the capability argument. I mean, almost all of our NATO allies have significantly reduced Defense spending over the last few years. Virtually none of them except Poland, and I might be mistaking one other country, is meeting at the threshold number that's been set for NATO membership. So part of it is just a capacity argument. And the notion that America, there's never been a NATO without America. You really can't have it. We're still the cornerstone of it, and we have our own capacity issues that we're facing. So I would hope that NATO would live up to its defense agreements. It certainly, I think, says it would. But the question is one of capacity, and cost benefit analysis for a lot of these countries. And I think that it's a challenge, because Putin has made a very clear decision, and that is he wants to rewrite the European order in the aftermath, and he wants to rewrite post-Soviet Europe.

And I think Moldova is the next target, and you're already starting to see moves in that direction in terms of supporting separatist groups in Transnistria and other places.

HH: *Now today, the President announced that he is going to delay the departure of at least half of the 9,800 troops that remain in Afghanistan. Did he make the right decision today? And ought he to extend that decision through 2016 as it seems the Afghan president is asking for?*

MR: Yeah, I think he made the right decision, but I think the better decision would have been to follow some of the military advice that he'd gotten in terms of troop strength. And I hope he's learned from the mistake of Iraq, where the rapid exit of American troops left behind a vacuum that was ultimately filled by these radical elements that now find themselves there, these, through ISIS and others, and has created basically an Iranian invasion of Iraq in terms of being on the front lines of controlling these Shiia militia, which they do, and have an increasing and exorbitant influence over Baghdad and over the Iraqi government. And you could make the argument that had the U.S. remained, it would have been a check on Maliki's abuse that certainly occurred when his abuses of the Sunnis in the country, which created the conditions for a lot of what we're facing. So back to Afghanistan, absolutely, I think it's important. And by the way, something that's not being covered enough, there is a growing ISIS presence in Afghanistan. They are actively fighting with, not warfare, but they're actively competing with al Qaeda and Taliban elements for influence in a post-U.S. Afghanistan. And you worry about where some of the mid-level Taliban officers are in terms of their true allegiance at this stage.

HH: *Well now, speaking about the ISIS threat, I spent an hour yesterday with Benjamin Hall, who wrote* **Inside ISIS: The Brutal Rise Of A Terrorist Army.** *He spends a lot of time talking about the fact that Qasem Soleimani, the head of the Iranian Quds Forces, actually got operational control over the Shiia militia. Petraeus mentioned this, General Petraeus mentioned this last week in the* **Washington Post.** *It appears as though we've lost Baghdad, Marco Rubio, and that in fact, it's already under the operational control of Khamenei. So if that is in fact the case, why in the world are we negotiating with them in Switzerland?*

MR: Yeah, and that's the argument that I've made. I mean, first of all, I believe a lot of what's happening in terms of U.S. strategy against ISIS and Iraq is being driven by our desire not to turn off the Iranians, because they certainly don't want us there at all. And I know John Kerry testified to the opposite. He's wrong, and he knows he's wrong. They don't want us there at all. They're suspicious of what we're doing there now. And they foster all sorts of conspiracy theories and lunacies about who we're really helping, and accuse us of double playing and so forth. So I think that's a big problem. And the second problem is the one you've outlined, and that is that the Iranian influence over the government in Baghdad has grown exponentially in the absence of a stronger American presence on the ground. I still think there are elements of the Iraqi government that are distrustful of Iran, and would want to work with us. But we don't have the footing to do it. And I think long term, our personnel there are in potential danger from the Shia militia, who aren't fans of the United States, and could easily turn on us at any moment.

HH: Should we walk away from these negotiations in Geneva right now because of the conduct of Iran in other places than that negotiating room?

MR: Well first of all, we need to remember what's not being covered by these negotiations, which are just as important as their nuclear ambition, and that's the intercontinental ballistic missiles that they're developing. And it's very reasonable that before the end of this decade, Iran could possess a long range rocket that could reach the United States, the Continental U.S. They're rapidly, that's not even being covered by these negotiations. They're not even the subject of sanctions. And I think that alone is a reason to be imposing sanctions on Iran, not to mention their state sponsorship of terrorism. That being said, any agreement that allows Iran to retain enrichment capability, leaves in place the infrastructure they will need in five, ten, eight, whenever they decide to ramp up enrichment and produce a weapon, if the only thing standing between them and a nuclear weapon becomes, and the ability to deliver it through a long range rocket becomes the ability to enrich at a higher level, that's the easiest switch to flip. And you saw the North Koreans follow a model such as this. So I just think the deal is premised on an agreement on something that is totally unacceptable, and quite frankly, abandons almost a decade of sanctions built on the idea originally that they would not be allowed to enrich. And by the way, the Saudis, the Turks, the Egyptians, even the Jordanians have made very clear that whatever Iran is allowed to do under this agreement, they will expect the same. So if Iran is

allowed to enrich up to 5%, 20% for research, the Saudis are going to insist on the same capability. **HH:** *Then let me ask you the three ifs. If that deal is in fact signed by President Obama that allows them to retain enrichment, and if you run for president, and if you win, would you revoke that deal?*
MR: Yes.

HH: *Would you go on record and just let them know that's not going to…*

MR: Absolutely, and I already have. And the point, because it's not, first of all, it's not an enforceable deal as we made clear in the Cotton letter. It won't survive this president in terms of you know, a future president will have to decide whether to live by it or not. It's not enforceable. It doesn't have the force of law. Now if he brings it to the Congress and can get it passed, that's a different story. He's indicated that he prefers to take it to the United Nations instead of the U.S. Congress. The second point I would make is that I think it'll be difficult to reassemble the international sanctions if this falls apart, but nonetheless, we should be willing to lead unilaterally. And I think others will ultimately see it. And the third is I anticipate the Iranians will take advantage of any loopholes they can find in the deal, and I think they'll flat out try to violate portions of it. You know, Iran has other challenges ahead. They're going to have a succession fight fairly soon when the Supreme Leader passes from the scene. And it's very possible that the new leader of Iran, after the current leader vanishes, could be someone even more radical, as hard as that is to imagine. And that's something to keep an eye on as well.

HH: *Now Senator Rubio, next hour, I've got Dan Balz coming up. Last night, he was honored with the Toner award for excellence in political journalism. And when he accepted, he looked out and he saw former Secretary of State Hillary Clinton sitting there, and here is what he said.*

Dan Balz: Please, thank you very much. Secretary Clinton, thank you for continuing to sit here through this. I didn't expect that you were going to be here. I'm happy to yield my time back to you if you want to take some questions.

HH: *And Senator Rubio, she shook her head and she took no questions. Now she tweets occasionally. Is it admissible, is it acceptable* *for the former Secretary of State and probably Democratic nominee to say nothing about these Iranian negotiations as they unfold right now?*

MR: Well, I don't think it is, but ultimately, as of today, she's still a private citizen that has no formal obligation. The minute she enters the race for president, she'll have to answer plenty of questions. And she's the chief architect of the failed foreign policy. I mean, in essence, during her time as Secretary of State, the U.S. has no measurable real achievements in terms of making the world a safer place. And in fact, many of the causes, the root causes of what is global instability from a U.S. perspective were put in place during her leadership at the State Department. The reset in Russia was a failure. The inability to follow through and complete the mission in Libya left behind a vacuum that's now turned into one of the premiere operational spaces in the world for global jihadists to operate from. The list goes on and on.

HH: I asked your colleague and friend, Jeb Bush, a couple weeks ago if he would be hampered if he became president by the legacy of Bush War I and Bush War II in Iraq. And that actually is for all Republicans. Republicans carry that burden of having to prosecute war in the face of what is alleged war worriedness. What would Marco Rubio say about having to persuade people to go abroad again in defense of interests that may not be so obvious to people?

MR: Well, part of the leadership is explaining what the interest is. And certainly, the American people are not a war-loving people. We really don't want to be in war, and we would prefer these things not to exist. I would prefer ISIS never to have existed. I would prefer for Assad never have to govern Syria. I would prefer for Iran to by governed by normal people and not a radical jihadist cleric. But that's the world we have, and we have to confront it. Now here's the question. If we don't lead the world in confronting it, who will lead the world in confronting it, because the truth is, no one can. The United Nations can't do it, the Russian obviously are in many ways supportive of some of the things that are happening. China has no interest in it. There is no substitute for American leadership on the global stage. And you can ignore our foreign adversaries, but they won't ignore us. And eventually, you're going to have to deal with them. So more often than not, the choice before us is do we deal with them now, earlier, when they are easier, not easy, but easier to confront, or do we wait for this problem to grow bigger, costlier, more expensive, and more difficult to confront? And that's one of the lessons of foreign policy. When you do something is almost as important as how you do it, in many instances. And again, we're not looking for wars to be engaged in. We'd prefer not to. And in some instances, we don't have to be involved in war in the traditional sense. As an example in Iraq today, I mean, we should have really taken a lead early on in putting together a Sunni coalition in the region to confront ISIS on the ground with U.S. air support. Instead, we've outsourced it to Shiia militias under the control of Iran, and I think we're going to pay a terrible price for that in the years to come.

HH: Do you still see the opportunity to find people left in Syria under the banner of the Free Syrian Army or any that would stand both against Assad and al Nusra and ISIS?

MR: I still think there are individuals that are capable of that. I think it's harder than ever. They've been decimated by attacks from both the regime and competing other groups on the ground. My argument always was that we wanted to get in front early and in power some group that would not be a radical group, and make them the strongest and best-armed group, because if we didn't, that vacuum that it left would be filled by a more radical group. That's exactly what happened. ISIS is a result of that vacuum, stepped in, flooded the region with foreign fighters, and as a result, we've seen what's happened. I think it's more difficult than it's ever been. It's still worth trying, but it's no longer the linchpin of our strategy in the region, because those groups have either folded up under the groups that actually have guns, or are dead, or have left the battlefield.

HH: Last question, Senator Rubio, your speech about Israel last week, I replayed most of it, it was warmly received by most people. Today, the President got a question about his relationship with Benjamin Netanyahu. This is what he said:

President Obama: I have a very businesslike relationship with the Prime Minister. I've met with him more than any other world leader. I talk to him all the time. He is representing his country's interests the way he thinks he needs to, and I'm doing the same. So the issue is not a matter of relations between leaders. The issue is a very clear, substantive challenge. We believe that two states is the best path forward for Israel's security, for Palestinian aspirations and for regional stability.

HH: *Senator Rubio, do you believe him on the "businesslike relationship"?*

MR: No.

HH: *And what about this two-state solution at this time in this place?*

MR: No. First of all, he's wrong on both counts. Number one, he can't say he has a businesslike relationship or that it isn't personal when his entire political machine, virtually, some of the top people in his political operation were in Israel, on the ground, trying to defeat Netanyahu, which is unprecedented. You know, he didn't send anyone in any other country to try to influence the outcome of those elections. And from Jeremy Bird down to others that were deeply and intricately involved in his campaigns in the past, he sent them down there to start the equivalent of a superPAC to try to oust Netanyahu. So I mean, what he's saying is absurd in terms of it not being personal. That sounds pretty personal to me. As far as the two-state solution, I would say what many Israelis say, which is yeah, that's the ideal outcome. It's also the least likely. And here's why, because you don't have the conditions today for that to happen. You have a Palestinian Authority that has no interest at this point. Certainly Hamas has none, but the Palestinian Authority has no interest at this moment on being a serious partner for peace. They continue to reward and elevate people they call martyrs, who we call terrorists, who have killed Israelis and even Americans. They've walked away from very generous offers over the last, at least twice over the last 15 years that have been made by the Israelis. The conditions just do not exist at this point. They teach their children to hate Jews, that it's a glorious thing to kill Jews. These are the sorts of things that make it impossible at this moment to have an agreement. And in fact, if you're standing from the Israeli perspective, what you see is the possibility that that second state that some are calling for would be nothing more than a launching pad for further attacks against Israel in the future.

HH: *Senator Marco Rubio, always great to talk with you.*

CHAPTER 41

An Interview with then-*Bloomberg*'s Washington Bureau Chief now with TheVox.com. and co-author of *HRC*, Jon Allen, April 18, 2014, discussing comments about Hillary Clinton from *The New York Times*' Mark Leibovich, *The Washington Post*'s Dana Milbank, *The New York Times*' Maggie Haberman (then of *Politico*), MSNBC's Joy-Ann Reid and *The Daily Beast*'s Jonathan Alter

HH: I'm talking about Hillary Rodham Clinton. Specifically, I'm talking about a brand new New York Times bestseller about her titled HRC: State Secrets And the Rebirth of Hillary Clinton by Jonathan Allen and Amie Parnes. And I want to begin by saying it's an absolute must-read for the center-right, especially for conservatives who are interested in 2016. It is the best portrait of Hillary available that is not comprehensive, because it begins in 2008 through the present day. But it is detailed, it is insightful, and I am pleased to welcome the co-author, Jonathan Allen, who is the Bloomberg White House correspondent. Jon, welcome, it's great to have you.

JA: Thank you.

HH: I want to begin at the end of the book, because you tracked down Jason Chaffetz, who's the rising star of the House Oversight Governmental Affairs Committee, and I think he got it exactly right. Prior to the attack, he said Libya could have been Hillary's swan song. It could have been her major achievement. But the whole deck of cards fell out from underneath her. Is that the widely shared view on the right?

JA: I don't know that it's the widely shared view on the right. I think one of the reasons that we spent so much time talking to Congressman Chaffetz is he seemed to have a handle on the big overall question which is what was driving all of this, and what was motivating Secretary Clinton. And you know, I don't know, people can make a judgment about what they think was motivating her based on all the evidence, but you know,

Congressman Chaffetz took a shot at that, and had a theory about. And I think it's actually a more important question than whether or not there was extra security in Tripoli. You know, we talk about rejections of requests for security, but very seldom does anybody point out that those requests were for Tripoli, not for Benghazi, and that it may not have made a difference on the ground that night. But the bigger impact in question, of course, is why did we go in, in the first place? Were we ignoring dangers on the ground? Were we trying to do too much there? And I think Congressman Chaffetz is really focused on those larger questions, and they apply, I think very importantly, to Secretary Clinton's perspective on the world and the United States' role in the world.

HH: We have a lot of ground to cover about Hillary, and I'm start-ing with Benghazi only because I want to assure my conservative audience that you are thorough, fair and detailed, and that you do not spare the criticism or the insight into it so that they'll not believe that it's a Beltway book for Beltway insiders, but in fact, it does dig in to the good, the bad and the ugly of HRC's four years at State. So I want to start with Benghazi, but we'll move on from there fairly quickly. Chapter 15, Pages 283-309, is all about Benghazi. Earlier, you quote Hillary as saying we came, we saw, he died, referring to Qaddafi on Page 252. But the attack begins on Page 283, and I'll summarize so that we can save your voice for your response. Stephen Mull goes into Hillary's office to inform her of the attack at 4:05 p.m. DC. You go on to write when she heard Benghazi had come under attack, Hill-ary gathered several of her staff in her office on the 7th floor to get a full briefing on what was happening in Libya and give orders—Mills, Sullivan, Burns, Boswell and an aide from their Near Eastern Af-fairs Bureau, were among the group assembled. By the way, Jon, was Philippe Reines there?

JA: You know, I'm not entirely sure. We listed the people we knew were there, and in fact, it's interesting. We said one of the aides from the Near East Bureau, because were two women who worked in that bureau, and we talked to people who were aware of that meeting, and there were disagreements about which of the two women were in the room.

HH: Interesting, interesting. Very careful. Was Huma Abedin there?

JA: I don't know for sure.

HH: Do you suspect that she was?

JA: You know what? I couldn't say.

HH: *All right.*

JA: We really put all the people that we knew who were there into the book.

HH: *You go on to give the narrative. Around the same time, one of Pat Kennedy's subordinates told Hillary Clinton that Smith had been killed. That's one of the people at the embassy who was with Ambassador Stevens, and that Stevens was missing. Hillary called Tom Donilon, the NSC advisor. We have an issue here, we need you to be on it. She called David Petraeus, and then you say by 5:30 DC, an hour and a half into the attack, deputies meetings began, a rolling teleconference run from the Situation Room—Brennan, Biden staffer Blinken, Ben Rhodes, Tommy Vietor. "Mills represented Hillary from the 7th floor of the State Department, but at one point, Hillary walked into the Operations Center to participate in the meeting." Now here's where it gets interesting to me, Jon. You write on Page 295, "People got fairly frantic, particularly when they couldn't find Chris." And between 4 pm and 8 pm, we really don't know what Hillary is doing, do we?*

JA: Between 4 p.m. and 8 p.m.? I mean, I don't have a minute by minute timeline of what she's doing. What I do have is pieces of that timeline. I know there were conversations with foreign officials. I know that she was on these teleconferences with American officials. I know she called Petraeus. I know she called Donilon. But it's true, like, it's not like there's a transcript of every minute that is available. I do know the State Department put together a timeline for people who had to testify on this, and nobody was willing to make it available to me or my co-author. So there is a timeline that exists. I don't know how much more detailed it is than what we got into the book. But I presume that there's probably more detail into her account.

HH: *This is the most detailed timeline of the most important night of her Secretary of State tenure. And you did the best job of reporting it. That's why I like* HRC, *including the fact she called Gregory Hicks at 8 pm in DC, and she never called back. Does that strike you as odd, Jon Allen, that she never called Hicks back that night?*

JA: I think there was a lot going on. It doesn't necessarily strike me as odd, but again, without knowing what she was doing minute by minute, you're having to figure out what are the priorities. And if somebody else is in contact with him, is able to handle that end of the discussion and she's needed for something else, then it might make sense. If she's kicking back and drinking lemonade by the poolside and not calling him back, I think it does sound odd. And without that full timeline, it's hard to know. I do know that of the public, of the major public officials involved in that incident, we know more about her timeline than anybody else's.

HH: *We certainly know more about hers than the President's. But I have always asked the question out loud to people both involved with the investigation and not, your number two is in the middle of Tripoli. They've got the axes out. It's like a scene from Argo. They're smashing up the computers in Tripoli. Benghazi's under attack, Stevens is missing, you talk to Hicks at 8 pm, he gets the okay to retreat to their CIA annex. A few hours later, SEALs are dead, another attack is underway, and you never call back your number two on the ground. It just seems like a massive leadership default.*

JA: It's a good question, Hugh. I mean, you're right. You're right that as Chris Stevens is missing, the head person in charge there, and de facto, because Chris Stevens is in Benghazi, but if he wasn't missing, you know, Greg Hicks is the one that's in charge. And I think it's reasonable to ask that question and it's not one that I have an answer to. If she runs for president, I think it's one she'll get.

HH: *Again and again… We'll move on from Benghazi fairly quickly. But this does not spare Hillary. She goes home at 1a.m. She checks in with Cheryl Mills, her chief-of-staff, at 2:30 a.m., and it is not a flattering portrait. You bluntly state the attack at the annex begins, officials were shocked by the second-round attack, you quote. Administration officials didn't anticipate the second strike. People got fairly frantic. You know, at one point, I wrote in my notes, I wonder if they sent Hillary home. Do you think she stressed out, and they just said go home?*

JA: I don't. I think at that point, they, and remember, this is now, by the time she goes home at 1:00 in the morning, we're talking about, forgive me, after putting together that timeline, it's escaping me right now. But I think it's about 7:00 in the morning, 7:30 in the morning in Benghazi. They know that Chris Stevens is dead by that point. I mean, they're waiting for the official confirmation, but at that point, they know that he's dead. They know about the second attack at that point. And so my guess is that they were pretty confident, there were no other American outposts to attack. The group that had been at the CIA annex was on its way to the airport or had arrived at the airport by the time she left. So I don't think it's a matter of them shooing her out of the building so much as her role in being able to affect anything at that point was probably somewhat minimal. I will say this, though. I think it's shocking, as you do, that nobody in the American government anticipated that there might be an attack on the CIA annex a mile or so from the diplomatic compound. It never occurred to them that this could be more than a one-off. I mean, I think it's a startling admission that they were caught flat-footed. And obviously, we know that, obviously.

HH: And you do not spare that. And I want my listeners to realize that's why **HRC** *is like crack cocaine for political junkies, but this is also very, very good reporting.*

[Tape transcript of congressional hearing]

Senator Ron Johnson, (R-WI): We've ascertained that that was not the fact, and the American people could have known that within days, and they didn't know that.

HRC: And with all due respect, the fact is we had four dead Americans.

RJ: I understand.

HRC: Was it because of a protest? Or was it because of guys out for a walk one night or decided to go kill some Americans? What difference at this point does it make?

HH: That, of course, is Hillary Clinton sparring with Senator Ron Johnson, an exchange which is deeply detailed and backgrounded in the brand new book, **HRC: State Secrets And the Rebirth Of Hillary Clinton,** *co-authored by Jonathan Allen,* **Bloomberg's** *White House correspondent, Amie Parnes of* The Hill. *It is a* **New York Times** *bestseller, and with good reason. It is absolutely riveting on the entire tenure of Hillary at State, not just Benghazi. But I do want to finish up that conversation about Benghazi. Your book opens, and no one noticed this, Jon Allen. I did. With Hillary watching videotape* *with senior staff, including the very controversial figure of Pat Kennedy, in early April, 2010, this was 30 months before the Benghazi incident, and the video she's watching is about embassy security in Peshawar, Pakistan, where the compound was almost overrun. And so at the very beginning and the end of the book, you open with her duty as the steward of the professional FSOs, and being aware of the problem, and then not having acted in a way to prevent the murder of four Americans.*

JA: Yeah, I was shocked that people didn't make more of a big deal out of that when the book came out. And maybe it's because it's in the introduction, and people sometimes skip the introductions to books. But yes, she's, in 2010, an attack at the Peshawar compound in Pakistan sort of, like Benghazi, one of these outposts sort of in the middle of nowhere with a lot of terrorist activity around, it comes under attack. The attack was thwarted by some of the defenses of the compound which were better than what we had in Benghazi, and she wants all of her aides to watch this, to see what happened, to know that the diplomats were in these places, are in peril, to know that safety measures can thwart attacks, but to be aware of the general situation, because in Washington, I think it can be easy to forget that a lot of the diplomats, a lot of the people in the Foreign Service are, you know, under threat. They're in places that don't like us, and necessarily sometimes in places that don't like us. And I was a little befuddled that that wasn't one of the big headlines coming out of the book.

HH: Jon Allen, I actually don't think conservatives have read your book, yet. And I'm trying to urge them to do so, because I think it is so fascinating and detail-filled. And they may not have read it, because the **New York Times** *reviewed it favorably. They said it's a largely favorable portrait of Hillary. I just think it's a largely objective portrait of Hillary. And you, like me, have been a partisan in the past, and so maybe conservatives don't think you're bringing the dish. But I mean, the dish is here, starting with the story that did get a lot of play, the enemies list. And I love this line. "Special circle of Clinton hell, reserved for people who had endorsed Obama or stayed on the fence after Bill and Hillary had raised money for them, appointed them to a political post, or written a recommendation to ace their kid's application to an elite school." It includes Rockefeller, Casey, Pat Leahy, I love seeing him on that list, Chris Van Hollen, Baron Hill, Rob Andrews. There's even a sub-basement in hell, and that's for Claire McCaskill.*

JA: Yeah, she's never getting out of there.

HH: *(laughing)*

JA: She's like the walking dead to the Clintons. Put her in the basement and don't ever let her out.

HH: *There is a quote. "Hate is too weak a word to describe the feelings that Hillary's core loyalists still have for McCaskill." But I must say, the arc of the story of Jason Altmire, which begins on page 16 and ends on page 274 that was a creative decision that you and Amie Parnes made. You use him as a sort of a totem of what happens when you cross Team Hillary.*

JA: Yeah, we loved the idea of drawing that out and sort of, because one of the big themes of this book is the way in which Bill Clinton and Hillary Clinton interact, and how their operations support each other and are integrated with each other.

HH: *She drops the F-bomb. And that, by the way, is itself a story. Hillary seems fairly comfortable with the use of that term.*

JA: Yeah, I think she uses it a lot.

HH: *And see, that's going to, you know, when Nixon's tapes came out and all the expletives were deleted. They should have left them in, because they weren't the F-bombs people thought they were... Let's go out with a little [of* The New York Times*'] Nicholas Kristof on what he thought of her accomplishments:*

NK: You know, the…the gains were in many ways fairly modest. You had, you know, the success at Burma, which as you say, sort of pales next to some of the difficulties. On the other hand, we did de-escalate, we did move down from a mess in Iraq. And for now, it's a somewhat better mess than it was. That may also be true of Afghanistan. And the crisis in the Middle East was, I don't know that it was handled brilliantly, but it was a mess for anybody who would have been dealing with it. Likewise China, North Korea, I don't think that those are shining successes.

HH: *Look in the dictionary under faint praise and you'll see Nicholas Kristof on Hillary.*

HH: Jon, I have made a habit over the last few months of asking a variety of people, and I'll play some of these clips for you today, what they thought of Hillary's tenure... the last segment with Nicholas Kristof damning with faint praise. Here's Jonathan Alter of **Bloomberg,** *one of your colleagues there, and a pretty good historian himself:*

JA: It's a really good question. You know, I traveled around the world with her when she was secretary of State for an article that I wrote about her for *Vanity Fair*. And I gave her, you know, decent marks for essentially for being a goodwill ambassador. You know, she was met very enthusiastically every place she went. She did these town meetings that were very effective in building goodwill for the United States in many countries around the world. That's an important part of the Secretary of State's job. It is not, however, fair to call her an historic Secretary of State. Now part of that is not her fault. You know, the stars were not aligned properly for her to make peace. The truth is that you have to go back to Richard Holbrooke, who wasn't even secretary in the Clinton Administration to find an American diplomat who was actually, really brokered peace in a real way, which he did in the Balkans. So I have a feeling that when we look back on it, if John Kerry catches a break and his persistence pays off in one of these areas, that we will see him as being a more historic Secretary of State than Hillary Clinton.

HH: And Jonathan Allen, one more for you to comment on, Mark Leibovich of **The New York Times,** *a shorter one, cut number 8:*

ML: Geez, look, I think, I don't cover the State Department. Look, you have that look on your face like you expect me to duck this question.

HH: No, I expect you not to be able to say anything, because she didn't do anything.

ML: I actually didn't, I don't, here's the deal. I have not written any stories on Hillary Clinton since 2008. About, what's like the graceful way to duck a question?

HH: Not even ducking, just this is, we're playing Jeopardy!

ML: Yeah, I honestly don't know.

HH: Nobody can come up with anything, Mark.

ML: Yeah, let's see, what did she do? Yeah, I mean, she traveled a
lot. That's the thing. They're always like, well, she logged eight zillion
miles. It's like, since when did that become like, you know, like diplomacy by odometer?

*HH: Jonathan Allen, this is where your book is a great assist they
think, because you chronicle what she did. But boy, the conventional
wisdom, Kristof, Alter, Leibovich, it's pretty settled that it was an
undistinguished four years.*

JA: Yeah, she's no Thomas Jefferson or James Monroe when you look
back historically. So you know, I agree with you. We put together what she
did do. I think there are things you do as a diplomat that are important that
are not a marquis peace deal creating a harmonious Middle East. Obviously,
everybody goes in wanting that. I think averting problems is a big part of
the Secretary of State's job. I think advising the President is a big part of the
job. I think being a goodwill ambassador for the United States is part of the
job. All those things are part of the job. But let's not forget making big strides
on big issues are also an important part of the job. And you know, for that,
there is no big deal. There's no Clinton doctrine, not that Secretaries of State
really have doctrines. They're usually the President's. But there's no doctrine,
there's no big deal to create peace, to extend peace. A lot of what she did was
to, I think, you know, particularly in war-torn areas, was to keep partnerships
going, to try to keep the Pakistanis on board so that our intelligence community could work in Pakistan. But again, yeah, it's fair to criticize her or fair to
look at her record and say there's no big agreement there.

*HH: 956,733 miles traveled, 112 countries visited. You're very care-
ful to include the specifics of that. But you know, cruise directors go
farther than that. Is that going to actually become a negative? We've
got about a minute to the break Jon, for her to bring up the odometer
diplomacy? Or is it going to remain a positive?*

JA: I think it's a mistake to bring up the odometer diplomacy. It just invites
the contrast of what she accomplished to how many miles she logged, and
nobody really thinks that's the measure of what a good Secretary of State
is. You know, we make the point in the book that her aides are very quick to

point that out. They were very quick to keep a record of it and put it on the front page of the website. But you know, when you examine her record in deeper detail, it definitely invites comparison of what she actually got done to how many miles she went, and that's not good for her.

HH: Jonathan, voice-challenged though he is, he sounds like those days when I would come in and put lemons on my desk and take steroid packs. And I sent him a note this morning when he was struggling to get ready for the interview. I said you know, Carville played hurt on a Dallas debate that I moderated with Mary Matalin the day after the Denver debate between Obama and Romney, and I complimented him on it. He said if you can't play hurt, don't get in the game in his typical Louisiana drawl. And then I noticed Jon Allen, that Carville's not in this book. And I'm kind of amazed by that. The old team is sort of gone from Hillary's new team.

JA: Yeah, it's really interesting. Carville and Begala win two elections for President Clinton, and they are not part of the inner circle of Hillary Clinton. That said, their voices are still influential. They still can get Bill Clinton on the phone when they want to. If they had some advice for her, I'm sure they could get it to her. But it's not like they brought those guys back. And you know, I think both of them are pretty good political strategists. And the people that she had running her 2008 campaign were not particularly good political strategists as it turned out. So there may have been a mistake there.

HH: Here is Dana Milbank of the **Washington Post** *talking with me about what Hillary got done, and I think he is just absolutely pin perfect on his assessment:*

DM: Well, she, I suppose what she accomplished for her reputation was she increased her standing to the point of invincibility.

HH: But what did she actually do, Dana Milbank?

DM: Well, I don't know. What did Lawrence Eagleburger do? You know, I don't believe we had any major peace treaties under her. We had some brief military actions, but basically cleaning up the ones that were in play. So I don't…

HH: You're a columnist. I'm just asking. Do you think she accomplished anything? Or was she basically a non-entity at State?

DM: I think she was successful in the sense of projecting a strong American image abroad, and of restoring American standing and reputation in the world. But these are nebulous...

HH: Dana, how do you get there? How do you measure that? How do you, I mean, under that talking point, what are the data points?

DM: Well, right. What I was saying before you said that is these are, that's sort of a nebulous notion of American standing. You know, and so whether we are more popular in European and foreign capitals, I'm not sure whether that particularly matters. But you know, I mean, I certainly didn't come on this call to be a defender of Hillary Clinton.

HH: And he wasn't Jon Allen.

JA: No....

HH: Jon, I want to talk just briefly about the people who aren't there. Now did you watch **The Sopranos?**

JA: I did.

HH: You know, Big Pussy was a big character in the first couple of seasons. Then he's gone, right?

JA: I don't want to, I don't want to know where this is going.

HH: Well, I'm just saying, people like Mark Penn, Patti Solis Doyle, Howard Wolfson—they're like Big Pussy in **The Sopranos.** *They're gone. They're put over the side.*

JA: Yeah, they didn't do a very, well, let's put it this way, they were unsuccessful in a campaign. And that usually means you didn't do a good job, or at least you get blamed for not doing a good job. Hillary's, some of her aides came to her after the campaign and tried to outline what had gone wrong. She had a bunch of one-on-one meetings in her Senate office and at home, and they told her what they thought she had done wrong, and what others had done wrong. And some of those big name people were considered to be toxic. Mark Penn was certainly considered that way. Patti Solis Doyle was considered to be less than able, less than up to the job, in over her head, if you will, and also, if you will, a bit arrogant. So some of these folks, you know, they're not going to, they weren't around for her time at State. They're not going to be back around if she runs for president.

HH: *And you know what's fascinating about that...*

JA: And by the way, some of it's by choice. Howard Wolfson, for instance, her communications director, became a deputy mayor of New York under Bloomberg, who I work for, full disclosure, Michael Bloomberg. But you know, so he had a second act in politics, just not with the Clintons....

HH: *Jon Allen, I want to go back to a couple of quotes about what she did and did not do before we turn to her substantive record at State. Let's do E.J. Dionne, of course,* **Washington Post** *columnist, friend of the show, cut number 9:*

EJD: I think there are, first of all, her accomplishments inevitably are going to be linked to what we see as Obama's accomplishments. And if you see, as I do, ending the war in Iraq, knowing the place is a mess now in many ways, but getting our troops out of Iraq, that's part of it. I think that for the period she was Secretary of State, opinion of the United States rose in the world. I think that she did a lot of work on human rights and women's rights around the world. I think that you know, and you and I will just plain disagree on this, I think at the end of her four years, we were in a better position in the world than we were when she took the job. And that is the old Ronald Reagan question.

HH: And here is Lanny Davis on my show answering the same question, cut number 16:

LD: Well, the biggest thing of all is goodwill around the world, which is what secretaries of State do. I don't know what any...

HH: Like in Syria and Egypt and Libya?

LD: I don't know, well, Libya and certainly the intervention in Libya, getting rid of Qaddafi, you would say is a pretty good achievement for the President. But these are presidential achievements with a partnership with the secretary of State. What do secretaries of State do? For example, she was very instrumental in the details of the Iranian sanctions program, which has produced apparently some results. I'm very skeptical about this deal in Iran on the nuclear weaponry, but the credit she deserves on this sanctions program, which literally was her program in the State Department to enforce, but in partnership with Barack Obama.

HH: *Let's go right there, Jon Allen. You spend a lot of time on Iran sanctions in here, and you know it's falling apart. I'm not sure she wants to run on this. But you write that she was caught in an administration that did not believe in the blunt force of sanctions, and that she also kind of botched the Green Revolution, because while Jared Cohen got the Twitter thing going, they didn't really stand with the Green Revolution. How is Iran going to play when HRC gets evaluated for president?*

JA: That's a great question, Hugh. I mean, I think there are a couple of things to look at here as far as the Green Revolution goes. I think it's hard to step out from where the President is. If the President is saying we're not going to interfere in their elections, and you're the secretary of State, if you go out and talk about interfering in elections, if you talk about supporting the Green movement, you're being disloyal to the president of the United States. And that could be a problem. What we saw in the book, and we go into this story in detail, is that one of her guys, Jared Cohen, who was actually a Condi Rice protégé, and is now at Google Innovation. He's the head of Google Ideas. He had basically gotten in touch with Twitter, and tried to get them to help with the Iranian Green movement, revolutionaries being able to keep in touch with each other. And you know, we go through this sort of dramatic thing in the book where there's a big question at the State Department over whether he should be fired for contravening what the President had said in terms of not interfering. He was supporting the Green movement. The President said we're not going to do that. And ultimately, Hillary Clinton comes into the room the next morning after the New York Times has written a little bit about this, and plops the paper down on a table and says this is exactly what we should be doing.

HH: *And that is, by the way, for people who want to know from the foreign policy specialist standpoint, the chapter on the Twitter revolution in foreign policy is worth the price of the book, because very few people understand how this has dramatically altered. You know, I got into this, Jon, working for Richard Nixon in San Clemente in exile writing the book,* **The Real War.** *And so I've been following foreign affairs for 30 plus years. And Twitter has changed everything, and Jared Cohen got that. And Hillary kind of gets that she needs to get it, and you illustrate that. I'm not sure she managed it very well, but on page 188, you summon up the final judgment. "She was always for turning up the heat on Iran. She just took a more nuanced view of*

*it when she got to the Department of State." You quote an unnamed
State Department official, or a national security official saying this.
It looks like a White House source. You know, whatever her nuance
is, Iran's going to be nuclear when she runs for president, and that's
going to have happened on her watch.*

JA: Yeah, I mean, so we don't know obviously where this latest round
of negotiations is going. And frankly when we wrote the book, we didn't
know that there were these back channel communications going on with the
Iranians, which was reported I think either at the beginning of this year or
very late last year. We'd already gone to print with the book at that point, or
were about to go to...somebody did some good reporting on that. But there's
no doubt that the sanctions were aimed at dragging the Iranians to the table.
And I think they were successful at that, but the question is, is it good to have
them at the table. If they're not good faith negotiators, if they're stalling for
time, if they are going to nuclearize while negotiating, then of course that's a
problem.

HH: Yeah, huge.

JA: So they accomplished the goal, but the question is whether the goal
was the right one.

*HH: Yeah, it reminds me of the '94 negotiations with North Korea
led by Bill Clinton and Madeleine Albright. They got the North Koreans to the table, and they got taken to the cleaners when they got
to the table. So they managed to get the poker game going, and then
they lost all of America's chips. I mean, it's going to be ugly when it's
over. Let me play for you one more cut, I'm trying to save the Allen
voice here, Maggie Haberman, your old colleague from* **Politico,** *who
came on the show and talked to me about Hillary's accomplishments.
Nere's that cut, number 12:*

HH: How long you been with **Politico**? Five years?

MH: Four years, three and a half years.

HH: Okay, so almost her entire tenure at State, and I've been on the
air since *2000*. And I can't think of anything, and I'm giving you the
floor if you can come up with anything for her on her case, lay it out

there, just from the top of mind. It should be front shelf, right?

MH: It certainly is not, there is not a giant list that I think people can point to.

HH: There's no list.

MH: And I think are a couple, and I think there is a couple of reasons for that, like I said. With the major issue of dealing with Israel, she was not front and center. And she certainly received some criticism early on in terms of how the US dealt with Russia. I think these are all going to be issues that she is going to have to address, and I suspect she is going to get asked about them repeatedly, and by many, many outlets.

HH: Well, we're done, but go around the bullpen at **Politico** and ask them what did she do, and it's going to be a giant whiteboard, and there's not going to be anything on it, Maggie.

MH: I like the invocation of whiteboard, though.

HH: It is a whiteboard.

HH: Now Jon, I wasn't very fair, because you can write on here Burma and Chen Guangcheng. So she's got...

JA: (laughing)

HH: You detail that, right? You give a lot of space to Burma and Chen Guangcheng. But what else is on the whiteboard?

JA: Well, I mean, there are some smaller things. And in fact, it's interesting in the Middle East...

HH: Smaller than Chen Guangcheng?

JA: No, no, I meant smaller than the big things that you're looking for. No, Chen Guangcheng is a very small thing compared to most countries. But I think if you look, for instance, the last temporary peace deal between the Palestinians and the Israelis was one that she went to the Middle East. She broke off of a trip with Obama, actually to Southeast Asia, and went and negotiated a temporary ceasefire that has held since the end of 2012. So I mean, there's an example, but you're right. If you're looking for the big things, and

I know you're probably going to play me as a cut for somebody else at some point, if you're talking about the big things, they're not there. One other measure, I know you're asking for metrics, I think it was with Dana Milbank earlier, one of the clips you played, one metric is that when she took over, the United States approval rating in the world was 34%. When she left, it was in the 40s. I think it was 41% at the very end. There was an uptick. The United States regained the place of being the best approved of country in the world in terms of leadership role. And I think that matters. I think the public liking the United States in the country gives us leverage with their leadership. It matters. It doesn't matter on the scale, it's not a bumper sticker. It just took me five minutes to come up with an explanation. Certainly not the kind of thing you can campaign on, even competent leadership at the State Department—not a bumper sticker. The best thing that she did was spend four years at the State Department without, with the exception of Benghazi, without major disasters. And so Benghazi is the one thing…

HH: Well, you know, that's interesting. We're going to talk about Egypt and Russia, which I believe are major disasters, and sort of epic failures, like Iran for Jimmy Carter, that are unfolding in real time. And so I do think we've got a couple of epic disasters that are happening, and I've got to say about HRC, you chronicle them, Egypt less so than Russia. Russia actually, Philippe Reines, is never going to read HRC, he's going to be so embarrassed by this book. Have you heard from him since it came out?

JA: I have. I have.

HH: Is he a happy camper?

JA: He's alright with it, because he knew what was going to be in it. I mean, in terms of, we asked him the hard questions. We gave him the opportunity to present his side of things.

HH: Man, it's tough.

JA: So he wasn't surprised by it.

HH: It's tough. I'll tell you about that.

[Coming back from commercial break, I play Allen a tape of MSNBC's Joy-Ann Reid]

Joy-Ann Reid: Thank God she didn't do what Kissinger and others did. We've had some secretaries of state who really messed things up in the world. I don't think she did that.

HH: But what is anyone going to say about her? She was an abject failure?

JAR: Managed, she did what secretaries of state are charged with doing, which is manage the foreign policy priorities of the president she's working for, which in the case of Hillary Clinton's tenure, was the Arab Spring, keeping the United States from...

HH: Did she do a good job in Egypt?

JAR: Really? I think in Egypt, absolutely. We saw a change of regime in Egypt. Egypt is obviously a troubled country when you have a dictatorship for forty-something years. You're not going to have any smooth transition. But I think the United States actually managed that pretty well. We managed to keep our troops out of there. We didn't get involved on the ground in Libya or in Egypt. But that transition in terms of management....

HH: But Joy, is Libya better off today than when Hillary took over?

JAR: What could we do? We're still in...excuse me?

HH: Is Libya better off today than when Hillary took over? And is Egypt better off today? I mean, which Egypt do you like? The one with the Muslim Brotherhood or the one with General al-Sisi?

JAR: Excuse me, if you don't think Libya is better off without Muammar Qaddafi in power, then maybe you want to revisit your views on Iraq.

HH: That was Joy Reid of MSNBC... And let's go to Egypt, Jon. I love the fact that you point out the Clintons' relationship with the

Mubaraks dated back to April, 1993. You quote Hillary as saying "I consider President and Mrs. Mubarak to be friends of my family." That's another Sopranos quote right there. But you do leave out the kind of clown show that went on. They sent Frank Wisner over to Egypt, and then he made an announcement, and they pulled it back, and we ended up toppling Mubarak. And then we ended up being with the Brotherhood. And we got it so bollixed up that al-Sisi is now dealing with Putin. I mean, Egypt is a colossal failure, isn't it?

JA: Yeah, you need more than a scorecard to figure out how many teams the United States was on during all of that. I mean, it was embarrassing. It was a disaster in terms of our foreign policy, one of a series of things over the last few years that I think points out that American, the American ability to influence world events is somewhat less than certainly the President gives it credit for, and I think that most of the American people give it credit for. And so we sit there trying to figure out how to look like we're on the winning side instead of doing something that actually promotes whoever is in our best interest, if we can figure out what that is. And you know, we have a scene in the book, I think this is one of my favorite scenes in the book. Mubarak goes out and speaks to the Egyptian people, and he says something, this is like early February of 2011, and he basically says I'm not going anywhere, and he says some pretty inflammatory things. And in the Situation Room, all of the big leaders—Obama, Clinton, Gates, they've all stopped, and they're watching this on television together in the Situation Room. And Obama's like this guy's gotta go, like what he's just said will inflame the Street. He's going to be going anyway. Let's get ahead of it, and let's put out a statement that pushes him out. And so his speechwriter, Ben Rhodes, writes up a statement that basically says it's time for Mubarak to go. There needs to be a process immediately to like get that going. And Hillary Clinton and Bob Gates, two of the people who were much more hesitant to want to push Mubarak out, start editing the remarks on the table in the Situation Room. They're hand-editing it. It's like, if you saw that in a movie where the Cabinet secretaries are hand-editing a statement before the President gives it, you would think to yourself there is no way that happens like that.

HH: *No way, yeah.*

JA: And American foreign policy was being made on the fly in the Situation Room, and not with like an unpredictable event. I mean, this was something that they could have prepared for. So they go out and they say it's time for Mubarak to go. We push Mubarak out. The revolutionaries come in. Turns out we're not real big fans of the Muslim Brotherhood leadership, and neither are the Egyptian people. And now we've got the military leadership there again. There were three possible factions. We picked two of them, and it was the third that ended up winning.

HH: Yeah, it's shockingly amateuristic. And Hillary's, of course, running State through the whole thing. On page 143, you write in HRC, along with Amie Parnes, "Within the State Department, some senior level foreign policy experts strongly believed at the time, and still do years later," I made a note of that, "that Obama's White House aides were a bunch of piker neophytes whose desire to keep a tight leash on foreign policy wasn't nearly as limited as their real world experience. These are not your Kissingers or Brzezinskis, one miffed former State Department official said." You know, Jonathan, Condi Rice, fluent in Russian, PhD in Russian studies, Colin Powell put his time at the NSC after the Pentagon. The guys who ran Bush's NSC were extremely deep in their experiences. This really has been a clown show for the last five years when it comes to foreign affairs. And how does Hillary manage to deliver the message, which I think this State Department official is trying to say, it wasn't our fault, those bozos at the White House don't know what they're doing?

JA: I think that's a real difficult message to deliver certainly herself. I think there will probably be people who try to put that message out on her behalf. I mean, I would ask you, Hugh, and you know, obviously it's not my job to interview you, but I would ask you, what do you think it would have been like if Hillary Clinton wasn't in the room from the foreign policy perspective of conservatives?

HH: It's a great question, and you're right. It's not a debate. It's an interview. But I do think that a powerful voice for strength in the world would have been, a realist would have been good. I actually think Hillary was as much of a neophyte as the White House staff. She isn't anymore, but I think that that showed up time and time again, and that Gates, Gates' memoir, and I interviewed the former Secretary of Defense, he was very gentle on Hillary for whom I think he likes. And I told, I called an old Clinton staffer yesterday before I interviewed you, and a pretty senior staffer, a very good friend of mine, I'll tell you off air who it is, and I said boy, I put this book down, and she is tough, tough, tough. She is tough as leather. She is the toughest person I think in politics that I've ever come across

other than my first boss, Richard Nixon. But that didn't make her
competent to run State. I mean, that's what I think it comes down to.
She didn't really have a vision of the world. She had a vision of politi-
cal rehab, Jon Allen.

JA: Yeah, I mean, as you point out, she's not somebody with the academic
credentials in foreign policy. She's not somebody who has spent years toiling
at the National Security Council or the State Department or the Pentagon
for that matter. Her knowledge of foreign policy is, you know, acquired and
learned, is studied. And there's nothing wrong with that, but I think you're
right. I mean, to the extent that she has experience, it's coming out the door,
not going in the door.

HH: *Yeah, and in fact, you provide a nice catalogue of the failures*
of the "smart power doctrine." She sent Ross and Cohen off to the
Congo. They tried smart power. They came back empty. She sent them
to Syria to threaten Assad. They came back empty. Egypt, empty,
Libya, a fiasco. I mean, "smart power" sounds good, and I had Joe
Nye in college, by the way, so I've been hearing this for like 40 years.

JA: (laughing)

HH: *But it doesn't work. I mean, when we come back from break,*
my guest, Jon Allen and I will continue. Now we're going to turn to
Russia, which is the worst part of the Clinton legacy. And believe it
or not, HRC: State Secrets And the Rebirth Of Hillary Clinton, is
toughest on Russia, and on Hillary and her team's absolute, com-
plete bollixing up of Russia, which is why HRC is a book you ought
to read. You ought to memorize it. It's like oppo research for us going
into 2016, even though conservatives, they refuse to believe that any-
thing good can come out of Nazareth or Washington, DC. Well, this is
good, and it came out of the Beltway.

HH: *But now I come to, actually, it is painful to read, to me, "the*
reset button." It's the red button's episode. It is so painful to go back
over how Lavrov played her, and how Putin and Medvedev and Lav-
rov have played her and Obama. And you don't spare the ink on this,
Jon Allen. You've got the details here. This was ugly from the begin-
ning.

JA: It's almost comic how they botched that from the beginning. And you
know, we're seeing, the reset button itself is a funny story. It's a little bit of
an alarming story, but it is also one of the things that I think sets the table

for what we're seeing right now with the United States' inability to influence events in Russia, with the United States' inability to really assert itself.

HH: *Philippe Reines is Hillary's senior aide who comes up with the red button, the reset button that has the wrong translation. He tried to get it back. That's the stuff I didn't know about that's in HRC. And the Russians won't give it back. I think it's on Putin's desk. I think he looks at it every day and laughs as he invades Ukraine. Honest to God, I do, Jon.*

JA: (laughing) Yeah, I have no idea what actually became of that reset button, but you could certainly picture that. Maybe there'd be a good comic strip with that as the end, Putin laughing and looking at this reset button that says *overcharged* instead of *reset*. They put it through a couple of Russian speakers who were at the State Department, but not exactly the experts on that stuff. And it was just a last minute gambit that was intended to be warm and gracious, and instead was just a, kind of made the State Department look like a clown car.

HH: *Now so tell me at the end of all this, before we turn to sort of the politics and the staffing in Hillaryland, which is the other fascinating part of this, the geography of Hillaryland is charted here. It's like Captain Cook for the first time for me laying out the various players in Hillaryland. But we've been through Benghazi, Libya, Egypt, Russia, the failures in Congo, the failures at...you know, there's just nothing there except Burma. So I want to give you like one minute to, you know, here, hey, let's talk about Burma, because you know, we've got to give her her due, Burma.*

JA: Yeah, I mean, this is an issue that she brought to the President. The Burmese junta has been extremely repressive for many years, a lot of political prisoners. It's an issue that people on the right and the left care about, the kind of thing that brings together Mitch McConnell and Nancy Pelosi, actually, and for years, we've been sanctioning the regime in Burma. And Hillary Clinton's idea was if you give them an off-ramp, if you say to the Burmese military officials that we will release sanctions or will relax sanctions if you start moving toward democracy, we will bring businesses into Burma that wouldn't otherwise be there, if you start relaxing your stranglehold on your people. And the Burmese actually listened to that. And by the way, Burma is within China's sphere of influence. So even though it's a country we don't think about a whole lot in terms of geopolitics, it holds some significance to, at least symbolically, in tearing a country away from China's circle a little bit.

HH: Yeah, that's interesting, although the downside is I just finished interviewing Robert Kaplan in reading Asia's Cauldron, *and China is pushing the Philippines islands around, they're claiming the Japanese islands, they're surging a blue water navy and an anti-navy navy out, and vis-à-vis China, we've got peeling off Burma a little bit, and she ran a successful Shanghai Expo. I mean, that's it. China played her, too.*

JA: Well, and to me, the real story in the Shanghai Expo isn't that it was a success, although that is a story. We were not going to have a pavilion at the World's Fair. Congress had decided to cut off money for that some years back. The Chinese told her that they would take it as a great insult if we didn't have something there. She raised a lot of money to get that to happen. But the real story to me is how she raised that money, which is she tapped a couple of long time Clinton fundraisers, and they went to the corporate friends of Bill Clinton who were big donors to the Clinton Foundation, and asked them for money. And so when you talk about potential conflicts of interest, when you talk about the ties that bind the Clinton operation to a whole lot of people in the world, you know, that was the way they went about it. It was this whole big deal about how Bill at CGI was going to step away from what she was doing at the State Department. Instead, the very first thing she does out of the box is get her fundraisers to start calling the people that he raises money from to get money for this World's Fair...

HH: Jon, I almost blew right past, and I've got to go back on Russia. You detail Hillary's deep involvement in the New START Treaty, including how she worked Corker and Johnny Isakson, Senators from Tennessee and Georgia respectively, and it makes it sound like Corker could just be bought for the nuke industry in Tennessee. But here's the problem. New START's a disaster. It turns out that the Russians have been lying to us on the development of their intermediate nuclear weapons. Jon Kyl was right. I mean, New START's not something she's going to be able to walk around tattooed on her forehead, is it?

JA: I think she'll try to do that. I think they'll talk about it. We're already seeing her minions, the Super PAC group, Correct The Record, has put out stuff on the New START Treaty. But you know, as is the case with all foreign policy, it's very fluid. And the thing that looks good for you today could very much look bad for you tomorrow. I think the START Treaty is certainly one of those things. It's something that I think, while she probably cared about it, it was really something that Barack Obama wanted desperately. He had campaigned on doing nuclear non-proliferation in a bipartisan way in the Senate, with Dick Lugar, the former senator from Indiana, and I think he wanted to put his money where his mouth was. And so I think it only works if the Russians are allowing us to verify, not just trust.

HH: Yeah, Ukraine and New START together, plus the red button's reset button, that's, it's a bad...here's a few more quotes about Hillary. Governor Scott Walker on my show talking about Hillary:

> SW: I have a hard time pointing to many successes. I mean, you look at, you mention the problems around the world, I mean, she was good at flying around and traveling, but I have a hard time seeing any major victories for this country.

> HH: Here's Bill Kristol talking to John Heilemann on *Morning Joe* about Hillary, cut number 14:

> BK: What achievement of Hillary, I'm serious, what achievement, one sentence, what has Hillary Clinton done? What's her achievement in politics that qualifies her to be president of the United States?

> JH: I'm not going to do a Hillary Clinton ad...I think they will say that she did a big, she repaired, had a big role in repairing America's battered image around the world through all of her travels around the world.

HH: And here's Chuck Todd, no apologist for anyone, on again, Hillary's accomplishments on NBC:

> CT: I think that they wouldn't try to do it as one issue. I think they would say that she was pushing her passions of expanding women's rights, she'd talk about what happened in Burma. She'd talk about the de-escalation that they had in Gaza preventing at the time when they thought that there was going to be an escalation in Gaza between the Israelis and the Palestinians, and getting Egypt to back off. So, but look, there isn't, is there a one, big, crowning achievement where you see her right there and then in a crisis moment as secretary of State,

especially compared to, for instance, John Kerry? I mean, in many ways, the problems she's got about her four years as secretary of State is the comparison to John Kerry, who's been, he throws himself into every controversy. And Secretary Clinton, she'd get involved, but she played a much more quiet role. She never liked to play as public of a role as John Kerry. So I think that that comparison is going to be something she has to deal with on the campaign trail....

HH: *I'm going to get sued by Jonathan Allen's employer, because I'm going to ruin his voice by keeping him one more hour to talk politics and Hillary Clinton. I want to finish the foreign policy conversation with Jon Allen, the co-author of* HRC, New York Times *bestseller, by playing Hillary on stage with Thomas Friedman, cut number 16 from a couple of weeks ago:*

HRC: Look, I really see my role as secretary, and in fact, leadership in general in a democracy, as a relay race. I mean, you run the best race you can run, you hand off the baton. Some of what hasn't been finished may go on to be finished. So when President Obama asked me to be secretary of State, and I agreed, we had the worst economic crisis since the Great Depression. We had two wars. We had continuing threats from all kinds of corners around the world that we had to deal with. So it was a perilous time, frankly. And what he said to me was, look, I have to be dealing with the economic crisis. I want you to go out and represent us around the world. And it was a good division of labor, because we needed to make it clear to the rest of the world that we were going to get our house in order, we were going to stimulate and grow and get back to positive growth and work with our friends and partners. So I think we did that. I'm very proud of the stabilization and the, you know, really solid leadership that the administration provided that I think now leads us to be able to deal with problems like Ukraine, because we're not so worried about a massive collapse in Europe, and China trying to figure out what to do with their bond holdings, and all the problems we were obsessed with. I think we really restored American leadership in the best sense that once again, people began to rely on us, to look at us as setting the values, setting the standards. I just don't want to lose that because we have a dysfunctional political situation in Washington. And then, of course, a lot of particulars, but I am finishing my book, so you'll be able to read all about it.

HH: Now Jonathan Allen, put aside the Alice In Wonderland, allow us to deal with things in Ukraine. When she writes about, when she says she had a good division of labor with the president, that is at odds with HRC's account of her first year, year-and-a-half when the White House just didn't trust her as far as they could throw her. He didn't turn the world over to her. They basically tried to keep placing people in her inner circle.

JA: Yeah, I mean, one of the very first staff decisions that was made was to make Jim Steinberg her deputy secretary of State. And her people accepted that. He'd worked in the Clinton administration, but that was not who she would have chosen. I think she would have chosen Holbrooke, perhaps, for that job, certainly wouldn't have gone with Steinberg. I think you know, the foreign policy, generally speaking, was run by the National Security Council. Now I don't think that's all that unusual. I think in most presidencies, that really is the case, that the NSC gives the Secretary of State as much latitude as it wants to, as much of a leash as it wants to, but is really the master of that. With Hillary Clinton in particular, they kept a pretty tight rein on her early on. I think it's one of the reasons that she really cozied up to Gates and Petraeus and some of the other military leaders, because that allowed her to get their support for things that she cared about. And we sort of go through that in the book, too.

HH: Oh, in great detail. I'm just saying that her line to Tom Friedman, and he didn't follow up, and maybe he hadn't read HRC, yet, it's just not factual.

JA: Right. It does not hold up.

HH: It does not hold up at all.

HH: Today, I want to talk about politics. And Jon Allen, I want to begin with a funny place. I want to begin with a purse. Now you and I, not that there's anything wrong with that, do not carry purses. But women do. And you have a little anecdote in HRC about Hillary and the purse gambit which I think people just, you've got a bad voice,

you've been out promoting the book, but tell people this story, be-
cause it's why she's so good, and why Republicans especially had
better be prepared for a masterly retail politician.

JA: Well, there was a woman who was interviewing for a job in Hillary
Clinton's Senate office, and was very, very nervous about it. She was meeting
Hillary Clinton for the first time, and whatever you think of her, just like anybody else you've seen on television a lot, but don't know, you get a little nervous the first time you meet them. So this woman's in and she's interviewing
for a job, so even more so. So Hillary Clinton walks in, shakes her hand, and
immediately picks up her purse and says this is such a wonderful purse, look
at this beautiful purse, turns to him and says look at this great purse. And
where do I get one like this? Can you fine me one, makes a big deal about
this woman's purse. Well, the effect of that is to make the woman feel at ease.
The effect of it is that the person who is interviewing for the job suddenly
feels like oh, okay. She's a normal person, like I can have a normal conversation about something like purses rather than deep policy intrigue and things
like that. And then the woman, who ultimately takes the job watches Hillary
Clinton do this time and again with people....

HH: Yeah.

JA: ...that this was, and you know, it wasn't a one-off thing where she
loved the woman's purse. She'd pick out a purse, a necklace, a tie—make a
big deal about how much she liked it. And so it's calculated, but also something that makes people feel good. And I think Hillary Clinton's kind of the
master of calculating those things that are intended to make people feel a
certain way, positively inclined to her, generally speaking.

HH: *There is nothing like saving someone who you could crucify to*
make them grateful towards you, and there's nothing like sympa-
thizing with people. And there are a couple of anecdotes in HRC that
I want to call out. One, Jon Favreau is the president's chief speech-
writer, and he gets in his cups. And he gets photographed—dumb kid
move—cupping the breast of Hillary on a cut-out. And she calls him
up and says I haven't seen the picture, yet, but I hear my hair looks
great. Great story, page 61 of HRC. Another story, young Tommy, is
it Vietor?

JA: Vietor.

HH: *Vietor, breaks his arm, or dislocates his shoulder when she*

breaks her arm. She, you know, he's young and he's intimidated. He sees her in the West Wing, and she's got a sling with a State Department seal on it. And he's nervous and makes small talk. Your sling is so much cooler than mine. Two days later arrives a State Department sling for Tommy. These are the sort of things, the forgiveness of Favreau, the sling for Tommy, these are very artful details of a masterful politician. Bill gets all the credit, but she's awfully good.

JA: Yeah, he's got that mass charisma, and even the one-on-one charisma. He doesn't have to do that kind of stuff. He doesn't have to say thank you to people. They watch him, and they're like excited to see him. She's the exact opposite. She has to work people that way. I think she likes to do it as well. I mean, I think she sees it as being polite, good company, good manners. But she needs to show people that little extra bit of attention, that little extra bit of affection for them to really grow on them. And I think some of it's genuine, all of it's strategic, but people, even when they're being worked over that way, tend to appreciate it. I mean, it's just like you get a thank you note from somebody. It may be political, and it may be them trying to get something from you, but at the same time, you appreciate they made the effort to write the thank you note. A lot of people would try to get something from you and not do that.

HH: *Yeah, there's a very great difficulty in* HRC *of keeping score between Hillaryland, the Planet Bill and Clintonworld, and the overlapping territory between them. Doug Band, for example, lives in Billworld. Huma Abedin lives in Hillaryland. How do those worlds get along right now?*

JA: I think better than they have in a while, in part because Doug Band is gone. He was the longtime gatekeeper to Bill Clinton, and I think he caused a lot of irritation within Hillaryland about the way that Bill dealt with the Hillary staff. And I think him being pushed out of the picture, and in part, that occurred simultaneously with Chelsea Clinton coming into the Clinton Foundation. I think that's had an improvement on some of the relations, but they're still pretty scrambled. I mean, it is three different entities. It is Hillaryland. It is the Billworld, and it is the Clinton universe, which is the conjunction of those two things. There are people who have worked for both, and there are people who are loyal to one or the other and not the other, and it is a very hard thing to unscramble, not just for us as viewers, as observers, as voters, but also for the people who are involved in it.

HH: Now at the middle of the web, and I called my friend to compliment this person, is Cheryl Mills. Now Cheryl Mills is Hillary's Haldeman. She is really the center of her political, she's the consigliore. She ran Benghazi night. She keeps her informed. She's brilliant, and I don't know that anyone's really reported on her much other than HRC.

JA: Yeah, the other time that she was in the news, she was defending Bill Clinton in the Senate during the impeachment. And she gave, she was very young at the time, early 30s, and gave an impassioned defense of him. And she was in the news then in the late 90s. And the most people that pay much attention to her, she was brought into the 2008 campaign when it was sort of going overboard to help rein it back in. She was brought into the State Department not just in one top job, but two. She combined the jobs of chief of staff and counselor, which were the two top jobs on the secretary's personal staff. She did both of them. There's nobody who is more important to Hillary Clinton than Cheryl Mills in terms of her political future, and in terms of her ability to manage when she's in government.

HH: Am I right about the Haldeman gatekeeping function?

JA: Yeah, I think there's a part of that, although a lot of the gatekeeping actually falls to Huma Abedin. You know, I think it's both of them, to some extent. But you know, in terms of being completely trusted aide, somebody that gets the unvarnished Hillary Clinton, and is there to try to guide her away from pitfalls, Cheryl Mills is that person.

HH: Yeah, you know, when you talk about Mills and Abedin, I'm thinking Haldeman-Ehrlichman, that there is, I was going to bring up Huma in just a minute, but you know, I worked for Richard Nixon. I knew Richard Nixon. Richard Nixon is no Hillary Clinton when it comes to revenge politics spread over 30 years. I mean, he usually gave up and let it go after a while, because he was always running again. They've got a memory in Hillaryland, which is deeper than any when it comes to keeping score, don't they?

JA: They do. In fact, you know, one of the fun things, I think, in the book that was the first time it was ever revealed is they kept this, after the 2008 campaign, kept this enemies list. We call it in the book a hit list. You can call it what you want. But there were, every Democratic member of Congress was assigned a score from 1 to 7, and the 1's were people that they felt were most loyal to them, followed by 2's who were little less loyal, 3's who were a little less loyal, 4's who were somewhere in the neutral, sort of Dante's hell of neutrality, 5's who were disloyal, 6's who were very disloyal, and 7's were the most disloyal, the people who should be never given anything, the people who should be gone after if ever the opportunity presented itself, particularly on the political battlefield. So yeah, they have long memories, and not only that, they have Microsoft Excel spreadsheets.

HH: But you know what's interesting, and I point this out to people, they are not obsessed with my side. You know, I looked in. I looked for Limbaugh, for Hannity, for Levin, for any of the critics, for George Will, for Krauthammer. They're not here. They don't worry about the other team. They beat the other team when the time comes to beat them. They worry about Democrats. That's where they run their operation.

JA: Absolutely. I mean, you know, are there people on the right that the Clintons don't like? Of course, but that's not where they spend their energy. They expect that their opponents are going to hit them. What they worry about, and what they were so angry about in 2008, is they felt like longtime friends had done it, too.

HH: Yup.

JA: You know, they could name, you know, a million different things that they had done for each of these people. Not everybody had been, you know, had gotten some gift or whatever from the Clintons over time. But they had employed some people. They had given them jobs within the administration. They had written letters to schools to get them in, you know, to get their kids into school. They'd done all these things for people, and then they watched these folks endorse Barack Obama. And they think to themselves, you know, what is wrong here, and we have a point at which Bill Clinton says if you don't have a loyalty in politics, what do you have? And that is their motivating force.

HH: And loyalty, by the way, defined Nixon as well. I never want Cheryl Mills to get into a big, black limousine and pick up the phone and say "We have to talk about Hewitt." I don't ever want that to happen, America. Jon Allen is my guest. HRC is his brand new book, along with Amie Parnes...When you, did you get access to Hillary, Jon? Did she give you time?

JA: So I have to answer this carefully. We got access to every level of the Clinton operation from the very bottom to the very top....

HH: *Page 68, "Informal power gained through Hillary's favor is far more important than the formal power of a particular title." Now this is hardly new. Harry Hopkins defined this, right, for FDR? He's only, he had no title, and no job. He just lived on the second floor of the White House. And so there's this informal power network. Jake Sullivan is the name that I had never seen before. And you know, I kind of know who Huma is. And Cheryl Mills, I've been following since impeachment. But tell people about Jake Sullivan, because that's a new player.*

JA: Yeah, Jake Sullivan kind of came out of nowhere. He's a very young guy. He worked on Hillary's 2008 campaign. He had previously been on the Hill working for Senator Amy Klobuchar, so he did a lot of the foreign policy stuff on, the national security stuff on the Clinton campaign. He was headed back after the campaign to go back to Minnesota, and he wanted to run for a House seat, and he was asked if he wanted to take over a new job that was being created essentially for him, a deputy chief of staff for policy. Once he got in there, he proved himself. Hillary Clinton loved him. She thought he was extremely sharp. I think he shared some of her nerdiness on policy, really wanted to get into the weeds. And he was a turf eater within the State Department. And by that, I mean he started out as the deputy chief of staff. By the end, he had subsumed the policy planning office at the State Department, which is basically the office that does all the future planning for State. He was heavily involved in speechwriting. He was the person that the White House went to. So he became the liaison between the State Department and the White House. And I think he could channel Hillary Clinton's thinking on policy as well as anybody else. When he left the State Department, Hillary Clinton and Barack Obama called him and asked him to take a job as Vice President Biden's national security advisor. And he is there to this day. So somebody who is extremely well thought of in Democratic circles, and who is pretty young, he's still in his 30's, I think mid-30's right now.

HH: *Yeah, I think if people look back to the early days of Reagan when the troika—Baker-Deever-Meese—was there. If they look at Mills, Abedin and Sullivan, you're going to have the same sort of situation develop in a Clinton White House 2.0 if that happens. And do you quarrel with that assessment, Jon?*

JA: Well, you know, I wish that I was better at making that comparison. I think you know, having obviously watched that time period a lot more closely than I did as a youngster…

HH: Yeah, I lived it. I was there. It works, I'll tell you. But now let me ask you about Obamacare. You have a great section, and I'm not sure that they like the title "Obama Girl" of the chapter. And I don't know if you've heard anything about that, because you're referring to her all-in on Obamacare.

JA: That's where it comes in handy to have a female co-author. If you're going to title a chapter Obama Girl, you've got to…

HH: Yeah, and you quote the Secretary of State saying, "I believe strongly that the President needs to forge ahead," when there were rumblings about dumping Obamacare and pushed it through in 2010. On page 177, the first time she saw Obama after Congress passed the health care law months later, it was in the Situation Room. She told him she was proud of him, and she was uniquely positioned to affirm him. Now you know, that's a two-edged sword, Jonathan Allen. She owns Obamacare. I always call her, she's the grandmother of Obamacare. But here in your book is the record that she was all-in. She wanted it.

JA: Yeah, absolutely, and that's not something that had been reported before. I mean, if you go back to the time period, she was doing everything she could to demonstrate that she wasn't going to be involved in domestic politics. And frankly, Barack Obama was doing everything he could to demonstrate that she was not going to be involved in domestic politics. One of the reasons to make her secretary of State is to get her out across the world and not make her toxic to the things you're trying to do domestically, which I think he thought she would have been. But behind closed doors, she was advising Jim Messina and Rahm Emanuel about how to approach health care. She even lobbied a few members of Congress on behalf of the health care law. The way that she viewed it was when someone came to her, she'd give them her view as opposed to dialing 100 names. I mean, I have no idea what the truth of that is, but you know, she's acknowledged that she, in the book, that she did lobby some members. And of course, this cabinet meeting right after the Tea Party summer, if you will, in 2009, a lot of the cabinet secretaries were very angry about how much of the Democratic agenda was being subsumed into this maelstrom of health care. They wanted to get their things done, and they thought we're never going to get anything done, because everybody's stuck on this health care thing. The Republicans are against us. And there was a lot of grumbling going on, and she got up at this Cabinet meeting and basically said look, I've been through this before, and you know, I know what it takes, or I certainly know what it looks like to lose. I know what it looks like when the President's people abandon him. This is our time. It can get done. The Democrats have majorities in the House and Senate. Let's get behind the President, and let's move forward. And you know, people in the Obama White House thought that was a big moment if you think about it from the perspective of a Democratic Cabinet member, Democratic member of Congress. If Barack Obama and Hillary Clinton are both telling you you've got to do this, there's nowhere else to go in the Democratic Party. So it's a big, it's symbolic. It's not an actual vote on the floor, you know, but I think it mattered to the Obama people that she did that. I think for whoever she lobbied on it, I think it probably mattered to them. And now she owns health care that much more than she did before.

HH: Yeah, I mean, that's what the reporting of HRC comes clear to me, is that if Obamacare is soaring in 2016, as they're saying right now it's going to be, she's going to be in a great position. But if it tanks like I think it is, she owns it as much as Obama does. And when we come back, we're going to talk more about the fascinating Obama-Clinton relationship, not just Hillary and Barack, but also Bill and Barack when we return....

HH: Okay, now look, there's a great story within a story here of how Hillary merged with Obama. And it's in the person of Capricia Marshall. There's also a warning for young women everywhere about wearing Manolo [Blahnik] heels to a formal state dinner. But in this person, you get how she operated the bridging of the rift. Tell people about it.

JA: So Capricia Marshall is as diehard a Hillarylander as it gets. She's as close to Hillary as any of the women around her. And when Hillary came into the State Department, she wanted the president to appoint Capricia Marshall to this job of chief protocol officer. And if folks don't know too much about that, it's the job at the State Department where you do all the protocol, and it's actually something appointed by the President. It's an ambassador rank. And the person travels on all the foreign travel that the President does, not necessarily the secretary of state, but actually travels on

Air Force One with the president. And the Obama people were completely against Capricia Marshall coming into their fold. They hated the idea of one of Hillary's best friends being sort of in the inner circle on these foreign policy trips, of actually being on Air Force One with her. And they had a vote. His vetting team had a vote about it. And they all voted no. And then Jim Messina tells the group, breaks the bad news, and says look, guys, this is a Hillary Clinton pick, and we're going to have to take it to the president. Hillary Clinton goes to the president, goes to his aides, and says look, you guys, you have her all wrong. Once she's working with you, you'll understand she's great. Obama decides to back down. He promised to let Hillary Clinton appoint her people. Capricia Marshall gets the job. She turns out to be somebody that the Obama people really like. They appreciate her on Air Force One. They watch dirty movies with her on Air Force One, as we tell the story in the book. And there's even a point, as you note, at a state dinner where she falls down. She's at this formal thing. She's in a nice dress. She's got these Manolo heels on. She's leading the president and the first lady out, and she catches her heel. And she goes down, and you know, it's being photographed, and it's being videotaped. And the president says to the press, don't take that picture. And then Michelle Obama says don't print that picture. And they're trying to save Capricia Marshall the embarrassment of this fall. And then later on, the next time they have a state dinner, they're lining up to go out again, and Capricia Marshall can hear behind her the president lowering his voice like a golf announcer and says, "Here she is on the approach. Will she fall down?" And Michelle Obama says, "Shut up, Barack. Leave her alone."

HH: It is a great story, but it's also, they, Hillary put inside the Obama circle one of her best people who served well, and as a result, built a bridge that helped smooth this relationship out. But what's going to happen with people like, look, Samantha Power called Hillary a monster. You quote that on page 95. One Clinton aide referred to Dan Pfeiffer as a " zero who had ended up in the White House by happenstance." You quote that on page 100. You say on page 116, Tom Donilon is scared blankless of her. That's the Obama national security advisor. There's a lot of that still left over percolating. And then Biden wants to be president. When do all the knives start to get thrown at each other?

JA: Well, I think the Clinton people are very much hoping that they don't have to throw knives in a Democratic primary. I mean, their view is, I believe, they'd like to stomp everybody down so much that there isn't a contest. They may not have that luxury. You know, Joe Biden and Hillary Clinton get along well. Joe Biden and Bill Clinton get along well. That'll be tested if they run against each other. But I don't know necessarily that it would be nasty. They've run for president against each other before. Their friendship has survived it. You know, some of the other, you know, I really would not expect to see Sam Power in a Clinton administration unless it was in some ridiculously cold outpost like ambassador to Greenland or something.

HH: Moldova, yeah.

HH: I want to cover just a couple more things with him. On page 180 of the book, you quoted Glenn Kessler of the **Washington Post** *interview where he asked Hillary about 2016, and she says please, I will be so old. You detail her broken elbow, which you said was a metaphor for her first year. You detail her concussion. You detail her explosion before the Senate Benghazi Committee. Is age a factor here? I mean, she seems relentless. She seems a force of nature. At the end of HRC, as I told you, I called an old Clinton hand and said wow, she's just as tough as leather. But I mean, 69 is 69, Jonathan Allen.*

JA: It is. You know, you'll recall President Reagan was running for president at 69-years-old, I believe. It's, I think it's more of a factor for the American voter than it is for Hillary Clinton herself. I don't think she's going to make that decision based on age. I think she might make a decision based on health if there's some health issue that makes it difficult for her to run. But I don't think age is going to stop her. I do think that it might in voters' minds. If she gets up on stage, and she looks old, or she looks infirmed, or she looks like she's not all together there, then yes, age will be a factor for voters. If she seems vibrant and capable, then you know, I think that'll recede in most voters' minds. But that's the important place, and it's one of those things that's I think almost impossible to poll. How many people want to tell a pollster they feel like they're not going to vote for the person because they're too old? I mean, you know, there are worse things to say to a pollster, but I don't know that you would get real read on that in polling.

HH: Yeah, when she said that, I will be so old to Kessler, I thought maybe at that moment she was thinking that. But in the background here, there are two very strong women–Huma Abedin and Chelsea Clinton. And Chelsea, of course, you treat her very gently, and I think appropriately so. She's not an official person. She's a child of. Huma

is a public figure, and you deal with her less gently, though not, you
know, sledgehammer or anything like that. And you leave the worse
charges against her out. What do those two women want her to do?

JA: That's a great question. You know, we did not talk to Huma for this
book, or to Chelsea Clinton for this book, so I can't speak, and can't claim
to know their mind. But you know, I think generally speaking, the people
around Hillary Clinton want her to do what she wants to do. I mean, and I
don't think many of them think that they're going to be able to talk her out
of doing whatever she wants to do. I think most of them think she's already
two feet into a race. You know, the way we put it in the book, and I think we
lay out the case for this in the book over the course of the chapters, is she's
been running ever since the 2008 campaign. And it's just a matter of whether
she says stop at some point, and I don't see that happening right now.

HH: *Let's go back to what will be the most famous clip used in the*
2016 campaign if she get in, cut number 1:

> Sen. Ron Johnson: We've ascertained that that was not the fact,
> and the American people could have known that within days, and
> they didn't know that.
>
> HRC: And with all due respect, the fact is we had four dead
> Americans.
>
> RJ: I understand.
>
> HRC: Was it because of a protest? Or was it because of guys out
> for a walk one night or decided to go kill some Americans? What
> difference at this point does it make?

HH: *Now Jonathan Allen, you reveal on page 349 that Philippe*
Reines plants this seed at a briefing. "Everyone is briefed or testified
as wanted to stand up and scream what the hell difference does it
make," he said during a prep session. Well, it made a lot of difference
to her political future. That is a damning quote.

JA: It is. It's, you know, I think people watched that and they thought, look
at this reaction. Somebody got under her skin, and she got angry, and it's
raw emotion. And to some extent, that's good for Hillary Clinton, because
there's so many people who see her as robotic. So even if it's not the reaction

that they would like to see, generally speaking, the show of emotion can be a good thing for her. But in this case, what Philippe is telling, is saying behind closed doors to her is an acknowledgement that this was preplanned, or at least it was something she was thinking about ahead of time. And it gives it a manufactured feel once you know that.

HH: And it also, but it makes it more damning, because it was such a bad strategic choice. Let me ask you about...

JA: That's it. Right, that, too.

HH: Yeah, I mean, just, yeah, okay, preplanned. Preplanned like the red button's button was preplanned, and that was another Philippe question. Bill Clinton – Page 249. Bill offered his opinions for Obama. It was too much for Obama, who said he could only take Bill in doses. Can they contain him? I mean, the whole Clinton rewrite speech, we talked about it yesterday, he took her concession speech, rewrote it without telling her. He goes places, he does things. He is a force majeure in American history. People, as you write, she got great advice about her numbers will plummet the moment she starts running. His whole eight years come back. He left with that endless press conference with the pardons of Marc Rich. I mean, there's so much. Can they contain Bill Clinton?

JA: You know, it's one of those great questions, and I think it'll be, if she runs, I think we'll get the answer to that. I think it's hard to contain him, and I think it's particularly hard to contain him if you're Hillary Clinton. She's shown no aptitude for that in the past, although I do think during her years at the State Department, he did recede a little bit. I think he's starting to learn how to be if not secondary, at least not sort of tromp all over the scenery behind her and take all the attention of the public. Al Gore in 2000 distanced himself from President Clinton, and that was a terrible mistake. President Clinton's approval ratings were pretty high. He should have found a good way to use him.

HH: Now you write in here that when Osama bin Laden was killed, the president called Bill Clinton. I think it was the President. Maybe it was Panetta, to tell him, and he said I don't know what you're talking about, implying that Hillary had not told him that the raid was going down. Do you believe that?

JA: I do believe it. Maybe that's naïve of me, but yeah, I can believe. Look, the two of them have kept a lot from each other and from the public over the years, so the ability or the desire to keep a secret doesn't necessarily surprise me. And the other thing is one of the things that Hillary Clinton was very worried about behind closed doors was how many people had been informed that we were seeking out a potential bin Laden raid, and that we were doing all the preparations for it. She was very concerned that if it didn't happen soon, it was going to leak out. So there's something to be, there's something to be said for there being a little bit of evidence at least that that was her feeling, that it should be shared with fewer people, not more. But who really knows what goes on in the conversations?

HH: It's a fascinating bit of reporting, one of the many. One last segment with Jonathan Allen.

HH: I want to thank my guest, Jonathan Allen, who along with Amie Parnes, have produced really a terrific book, HRC: State Secrets And the Rebirth Of Hillary Clinton. I want to close, Jonathan, by going to an obscure part of the book, page 151. When Hillary got to State, she knew about the QDR, which Defensenicks know about—the Quadrennial Defense Review. And she wanted to produce, and got organized, the Quadrennial Diplomacy and Development Review, which has turned out to be, and I'm quoting now, "In the end, they had a 242-page blueprint for elevating diplomacy and development as equal partners with military force in the conduct of American foreign policy. The first QDDR's goals included making ambassadors CEOs for American agencies in foreign countries, bolstering soft power tools like economic assistance, improving the lives of women and girls around the world, reorganizing the Department's bureaus to better reflect modern challenges, insuring that diplomats had up to date computers and handheld devices, reforming the Foreign Service exam to bring in sharp, new diplomats, increasing diplomat direct-engagement with the people of their host countries, not just their governments, and using technology such as social media platforms for diplomacy. The exercise was aimed at strengthening the institution, even if the medicine tasted bad going down." And my margin note is that's it? They did a strategic review, and they came up with handheld devices? And it goes to my biggest critique. I don't think she has a strategic vision.

JA: Yeah, I think of her biggest problem in 2008, I would agree with you. I think her biggest problem in the 2008 campaign is she didn't make an argument for why she should be president. And Barack Obama went around the country and he gave speeches, and he would give out his policy prescriptions. And then at the end, he would say and that's why I'm running for president. And the people believed that he had a vision, and I think not only Democrats, I think there were independents and even Republicans who didn't agree with him or agree with his vision, would say look, this guy…and a lot of people would say he didn't live up to it in the presidency. But I think you know, in 2008, people looked at him and said here's a guy with a vision. Here's a guy with a way that he wants to do things that is different than what we are doing. And he can make some sort of explanation of how you get from where we are to his vision. And she failed at that in 2008.

HH: Well, my last comparison, I wrote a column in the **Washington Examiner** *that made this argument.* **She's George Herbert Walker Bush.** *She's the one who was bested, who comes back eight years later, gets hit on the vision thing, but wins 40 states and 424 Electoral Votes, because after a revolutionary figure, Reagan, the Republican case, and Obama in the Democrats' case, you want a consolidator. You want a pro's pro, and they're not exhausted. They still have the team.*

JA: Hugh, I'll tell your listeners. I sent you a note when I read it. It's a brilliant column. I think it made eminent sense. There's a really great parallel there. It is a, George H.W. Bush was somebody who had been entrusted with a lot of jobs in the past, was a pretty competent manager of them, did not have a big vision for where he wanted to take the country, and in a lot of cases, disagreed with his own party where he wanted to take the country. And so it was a great column. I think everybody should read it.

CHAPTER 42

An Interview with *The New York Times'* Nicholas Kristof, March 5, 2014

HH: *Now yesterday, former Secretary of State Clinton compared the Russian aggression to actions taken by Hitler in the run up to World War II. What do you think of her assessment?*

NK: In the narrow sense, I mean, there is some analogy to the seizure of Sudetenland in 1938 in the sense that, you know, it was with the excuse of protecting the Germans in the case of Sudetenland and Russians in the case of Crimea. So that parallel in terms of the excuse holds. I don't think the parallel holds in terms of where this is going to go. I mean, I don't think that the seizure of Crimea is the first step toward Russia waltzing into Western Europe, for example. But it is, you know, absolutely a violation of Russia's international obligations. And it also bodes ill for Russian-American coopera- tion in all kinds of things. I mean, it's going to make it harder to, Russia is going to be less cooperative, even though it hasn't been very cooperative, on Syria, on Iran. It may work a little more closely with China. And ultimately, I think this is going to be bad for Putin, because he doesn't want a pro- Western success on his borders, and I think ultimately this is going to mean that Ukraine is going to be more of an anti-Russian force on his borders, and ultimately, it may take a while, but it is going to be a success, and that is going to undermine the Putins or the Putin successors in Russia.

HH: *Well now there are two lines, then, that follow. One is geopo- litical, and one's political in the United States. Let me take the latter first. For former Secretary of State Clinton to use that language, she's the one that presented the reset button.*

NK: Right.

HH: *It's sort of like Samuel Hoare condemning the Hoare-Laval Pact five years after he signed it. Isn't that odd for her to be doing this?*

NK: Well, I mean, I think the Russian reset may have been, I don't know that there was a huge downside in trying to reset things. We do need to work with Russia. I do think it's important even now to continue to talk to Russia about Iran, about Syria, about North Korea. It kind of depends on how much faith she had that it was going to work or that she could trust Putin. And I just don't have a sense of that.

HH: *When she made that declaration five years ago and gave the reset button, your colleague, Peter Baker, told me yesterday, Nicholas, that the Russians simply do not have much respect for President Obama and his team. Do you agree with that assessment?*

NK: You know, I just don't know. It's hard to know. I do, I mean, the only time I met Putin I was just struck by the fact that he really seemed to be kind of in his own world, and living in his very kind of strong ideological world. Very, very smart guy, but getting information from his advisors, and with a very kind of skewed view of the world, so I think it probably is fair to say, though, that Russia and China and in the Middle East, there is a sense that Obama has focused inward and focused on American domestic problems, and I think that there is some feeling there. I don't think that would have changed Putin's judgments about whether to grab Crimea. I mean, after all, he grabbed parts of Georgia on George W. Bush's watch, and Bush was very engaged worldwide. But there may be something to that.

HH: *Now when you look at it, though, at the former Secretary of State, she's clearly running for president, but we've got Putin unleashed, Libya in shambles, Syria using gas, Egypt is alienated from us, the PRC is cresting, the Norks are nuking up, the mullahs are on the brink, did she get anything done as secretary of State that was good?*

NK: You know, the gains were, in many ways, fairly modest. You had the success in Burma, which as you say, sort of pales next to some of the difficulties. On the other hand, we did deescalate, we did move down from a mess in Iraq, and for now, it's a somewhat better mess than it was. That may also be true of Afghanistan. And the crisis in the Middle East was, I don't know that it was handled brilliantly, but it was a mess for anybody who would have been dealing with it. Likewise, China, North Korea, you know, I don't think that those are shining successes. I don't think they're shining failures. In the case of North Korea, I would, and maybe China, I would say that they were perhaps [handled] marginally more successfully by Hillary than in the Bush administration, although it kind of depends on the moment.

HH: Yeah, because what I'm getting at is the five years that we've had of the President Obama-Clinton-Kerry approach, I think the world is much worse off than we were post-financial crisis. The financial crisis is a standalone event that we can debate endlessly, but geopolitically, isn't America screwed around the world right now?

NK: I don't know about that. I mean, I think that al Qaeda is less of a threat now than it was before, although, I mean, it's all complicated. And in North Africa and West Africa, you have more localized al Qaeda-related affiliated threats. You have the Middle East in greater instability than it had been. On the other hand, in the case of Iran, you have a process that may lead to resolving that crisis, and Iran is no longer kind of rushing on a trajectory toward a nuclear weapon, which it had been for years. And in the case of North Korea, you have a regime that for a long time had, and North Korea is one of the things that really worries me the most. I think now we have a really unstable leader with Kim Jong Un, and he's one of the people I would really lose sleep over. And we'll see where that goes.

CHAPTER 43

An Interview with Maggie Haberman, then of *Politico* now of *The New York Times*, October 28, 2013

HH: Joined now by Maggie Haberman of Politico.com, who had a huge story this morning on Hillary Clinton's potential 2016 run. Maggie, welcome. It's good to have you on **The Hugh Hewitt Show.**

MH: Thanks for having me.

HH: Did the reaction to your column flow in today and raise questions about whether or not she's actually running? Or does everyone assume she's running?

MH: I've heard a mixture of reactions. I think that most people think the preponderance of evidence is that she is running. I had actually been among those who had thought she wasn't running, and I no longer think that. It's hard to think it after some of the speeches she's given recently. I think most people think that there is a chance that she won't run, that those would be for, you know, mostly personal reasons, or the unforeseen. But that chance seems pretty small at the moment.

HH: Now this is a process story that turns primarily on the argument that the biggest complaint about Clinton in 2008, and I'm quoting now, was that she ran a campaign of entitlement, showing feistiness and emotion only after Obama had surged when it was already too late. Is that what you consider, or what your sources consider to be her biggest potential problem this time around? Or is it her record as Secretary of State?

MH: Well, I think that there are two different issues. And I certainly think that her approach to a campaign will be very significant in terms of how she handles it. I think that her record as Secretary of State is obviously her most recent, and it is one of the pieces of her curriculum vitae that have been the least looked at, certainly in terms of repeated, in terms of the crux of a campaign and the crucible of a campaign. And I think that it's relevant. I think that it's going to come up a lot. I think that people around her are certainly prepared for that, or at least prepared for it to be an issue. How they handle it remains to be seen.

HH: *What is her biggest achievement as Secretary of State?*

MH: I think that the folks around her believe that among the biggest achievements was, and you've seen this pointed to a lot, was the amount of travel time she logged. They felt very good about the Chinese dissident, and how the disposition of that case went in 2012. I think that what they, and what most people are prepared for is a lot of questions about the aftermath of Benghazi, and I think there was a *60 Minutes* piece about that, that went out yesterday. I think there's going to be a lot more of that. I think that this is where the fact that most people believe she is running, but she has not set up a team of any kind in any meaningful way, potentially becomes problematic, because if her folks believe that they have something to say in response to that and they're not, they're sort of letting time slip away from them.

HH: *But pause for a moment with me on the achievement side.*

MH: Sure.

HH: *Articulate further. What is it that people say is her achievement? That she logged a lot of miles? What, is she running for George Clooney's role in* Up In The Air?

MH: (laughing) That has been certainly one of the focuses that her folks have talked about. They've also talked about how she ran a functional effort at State. Look, I think that when you hear from her world about what her accomplishments were, I think that they genuinely believe that she had made progress in terms of how America was perceived. People can agree or disagree with that. I think that that is obviously been coming into question now, and this is again something I think she's going to have to talk about more. She's clearly aware of that, but she's not saying much about it so far, on the NSA issue. It's very, very difficult for a former Obama administration official to run a sort of smoke and mirrors campaign on foreign policy. She's going to have a very hard time doing that.

HH: *Well, I know all the critiques, because I'm a conservative talk show host. So I know what all the vulnerabilities are.*

MH: Right.

HH: *I'm just curious as to what they think her strengths are, other than, you know, frequent flyer miles.*

MH: Look, they think that she was an effective diplomat. They think that she was good at helping America's image globally. They have a couple of cases like the case of the Chinese dissident where they think that State played a very effective role. She was among those who was pressing for more action in Syria of a restricted type earlier on than what you saw the Obama administration ultimately do this year. But you know, look, she was not, she certainly was not part of the team that, say, was dealing with Israel. She was not integral in that way, and so I think for some of the issues that are the hottest right now, globally, she was not a key factor in them.

HH: *So a Chinese dissident? That's it?*

MH: Well, I think we will see what they issue as her biggest strength as Secretary of State. That has not been a case they've been emphasizing so far. You've, I'm sure, read the *New York* Magazine piece, like everybody else, where they talked about again, her time as Secretary of State which was largely mechanical, at least in the focus of that piece, and how they thought she had run an effective effort. Everything with Hillary Clinton gets looked at through the prism of how she manages whatever team she's running, and that's been where a lot of the focus has been.

HH: *Well, it's very interesting to me, though, as you report early on, they are going to try, Team Clinton is going to try and give you the talking points, which they hope then enter into the bloodstream, and into the circulatory system of Washington, DC that is* Politico, *and then out through the rest of the country. And what I'm hearing you say is they've got a Chinese dissident.*

MH: No, I think, but I think that when you've asked me off the top of my head what are some of the things that her folks have pointed to over the last two years, that has certainly been one of the cases.

HH: *Anything else, Maggie?*

MH: Yes, there are others, but I'm just not coming up with them at the moment, but, and I'm not trying to avoid the question.

HH: Oh, I know you're not. I just don't think there's anything there. I think, actually, her biggest problem is that there is no there there. She occupied the State Department, and there's nothing to show for it. I guess there's this Chinese dissident, but I'm, that's not, that's not a name that's tripping off of my tongue right now. Do you know his name?

MH: I think that, no, at the moment, I actually cannot think of his name. I think that they're, I think this is going to be an ongoing problem for her. I think that showing sort of a body of work at State is going to be something that she's going to be pressed to do increasingly, and I think that running sort of a shadow campaign through paid speeches and free speeches over the course of the next year, I think is going to not cut it eventually, not just for conservative critics, but I think on the left. I think she's going to have a problem.

HH: But doesn't this sort of underscore the major problem? Here I am, a conservative critic, and I know the critique. And you're a mainstream reporter, and as far as I know, you have no ideology. You're one of the people at Politico *that I don't put on the left or the right, you're just down the middle.*

MH: Yeah.

HH: And neither of us can come up with any claim that she has to having succeeded at anything, and they are not able, they didn't spin you, because they've got nothing to spin you with. It's like the washing machine's broke.

MH: Well, we'll see. I mean, I think we need to see what they ultimately come up, to be fair. I think that since she's not yet running, I think looking at how they present her and present what she did there is an open question.

HH: They'll come up with something. What I'm getting at is, how long have you been with Politico, *five years?*

MH: Four years, three and a half years.

HH: Okay, so almost her entire tenure at State, and I've been on the air since 2000. And I can't think of anything, and I'm giving you the floor. If you can come up with anything for her case, lay it out there. Just from the top of mine, it should be front shelf, right?

MH: It certainly is not, there is not a giant list that I think people can point to.

HH: There is no list.

MH: There are a couple. And I think there's a couple of reasons for that like I said. With the major issue of dealing with Israel, she was not front and center. And she certainly received criticism early on in terms of how the US dealt with Russia. I think these are all going to be issues that she is going to have to address, and I suspect she is going to get asked about them repeatedly, and by many, many outlets.

HH: I mean, it's just a big, we're done, but go around the bullpen at **Politico** *and ask them what did she do, and it's going to be a giant whiteboard, and there's not going to be anything on it, Maggie.*

MH: I like the invocation of whiteboard, though.

HH: It is a whiteboard. Maggie Haberman, great piece today, great process piece. But boy, she's got problems if after writing it, you don't have the list at the tip of the tongue. The Clintonistas had better come up with a list, because there's nothing on it. Really, nothing.

CHAPTER 44

The Fear Factor

"Upon this a question arises: whether it is better to be loved or feared or feared than loved? It may be answered that one should wish to be both, but, because it is difficult to unite them in one person, it is much safer to be feared than loved, when, of the two, either must be dispensed with."

This is the most famous "conclusion" in all of Machiavelli's old book. It was controversial when it was first written, and is now, 500 years later. This conclusion is still true, at least for rulers and even statesmen.

Indeed, if you are not feared you cannot be loved. But you are hardly interested in that love in any event, except from Chelsea and all of her children, and, of course, Bill. I would not write that you don't care about love. You just don't allow it to interfere with your plans, except for Chelsea and Bill—and there your plans and their love do not conflict.

The fact is that the country is in real peril, and would be no matter if you had a stroke and were disabled or died today or were elected tomorrow. Our enemies—emphasis on "our"—are numerous and many are fanatics. Some may believe as a result of their theology that war and even holocaust are very good things, earnestly to be sought after regardless of the cost. Some may wrongly conclude that President Obama's deep weakness is not unique, but endemic throughout America, and especially among its leadership elite, and that his fecklessness is a foreshadowing of an accelerating trend not merely an exception to the rule of American strength and purpose.

They might be right, but if you want to win you will have to assert with believable conviction that they are wrong and that only you and the changes you urge can keep America safe and its prosperity secure.

To argue for fundamental change you have to make a case that the fundamentals of the world have changed. President Obama has so crippled the country's position that this will not be a difficult case to make and carry, especially for you.

The GOP will remind people that in the last month of 2014 alone a terrorist struck in Sydney, a massacre of school children took place in Pakistan—a country with about 100 nuclear devices up for grabs— Ebola ravaged West Africa, hundreds of girls were abducted in Nigeria, slaughter and counter-slaughter shook Syria and Iraq, racial tensions peaked in America even as the price of oil plummeted and Russia's currency and the Euro wobbled on the brink of panicked devaluation with markets teetering like the good old days of 2008, and a series of cyber attacks brought Hollywood to its knees.

In the first six weeks of 2015, the GOP will remind people of the march of Russia across Ukraine, and especially of the brutal assaults of the Islamic State, its beheadings and burning alive of dozens—the "jayvee team" on a rampage, as America stood by impotent, but for some airstrikes to stop them, and headlong on a rush to bless a nuclear Iran even as the president you helped guide in his Iranian policy blesses a near-nuclear Iran.

Three month's events two years before your election and who knows what President Obama will cause or allow to happen before the election of 2016 unfolds? Who knows what he will do in the interregnum between that vote and his departure? Your husband's pardon of Marc Rich left no lasting scar but one lasting lesson: After a decent interval nothing is remembered; and everything is, if not forgiven, at least forgotten. You have been on the public stage about as long as Betty White and can carry-off her camp about age with equal aplomb. Laugh off the old scandals. Be suitably outraged about the more recent. Communicate that you won't forget those who crossed you and yours.

Above all, dismiss as crack-pottery your bigger plans. Gillibrand to the Supreme Court? "Haven't thought about that, though she is certainly qualified." Chelsea in the Senate? "She is master, actually co-pilot, of her own ship. If she decides to serve that way she will certainly have our support, but right now she is totally focused on my grand-daughter—she'd better be!—and when she has time this election. I think she also wants to see what the Obama girls and the Bush girls did to the rooms!" Remove the two-term limit and abolish the Electoral College? "A conservative talk show host suggested that? Wonders never cease and both of those ideas have a lot of support in progressive circles and among those who study our Constitution in the modern era."

Above all you must make this a "first of firsts" elections. And not just about your being a woman.

There have been strong women leaders before, and if Angela Merkel, Maggie Thatcher, Golda Meir and Indira Gandhi are not always in your speeches, fire the writers. Own that lineage, not for their ideas, but for their courage. Be sure to pay homages to the assassinated Benazir Bhutto and to Corazon Aquino, the wife who succeeded the assassinated Benigno Aquino, but reserve most of your praise for the big three of Merkel, Thatcher and Meir. They are the leaders who will resonate with the center-right voters you need to woo.

The most important "first of firsts," though, is that you will be proposing the first major changes in the Constitution since women's suffrage. Sure, arranging an orderly succession mattered, as did lowering the voting age. But Prohibition was a failed and costly mistake and the income tax amendment was probably unnecessary as the income tax was constitutional to begin with. No, not since the vote for women and before it the abolition of the privilege of selecting senators by state legislators and the Civil War amendments has such a profound change been publicly advanced as ending the Electoral College. You will argue against its deep prejudice against the "one person one vote" equality embedded in the Declaration of Independence. You must turn the bedrock truth "that all men are created equal," Lincoln's "electric cord," against the Republic Party Lincoln founded. ("That is the electric cord in that

Declaration that links the hearts of patriotic and liberty-loving men together, that will link those patriotic hearts as long as the love of freedom exists in the minds of men throughout the world." —July 10, 1858.) You must present yourself as did Jefferson and the other signers of 1776—as a revolutionary for equality. Barack Obama represented the end and indeed the completion in fact of the flawed First Founding, a First Founding which was by necessity a moral compromise that brought about, in the words of Harvard's current president, "A Republic of Suffering" through a horrible civil war but which was, once repaired of this awful original sin, also a country strong enough to defeat fascism, then communism and now Islamism, but only if it continues to grow stronger itself in the cause of the equality of men and women.

Laugh off the attribution to you by me and others of vaster ambitions, by far, than the mere launch of a Second Founding. Mock dynasty in the face of dynasty. As was said in Part III, transparency, properly understood, is the key in which you must speak.

But, finally, let no one doubt that the paybacks are in fact coming—and not of the gentle sort. You will ruin people and sow ashes in their fields. Bill can deliver the message. Others can as well. But it must be delivered.

Abroad, as well as at home. There is no sense in winning the White House to see the country eclipsed by the PRC or devastated by terrorists sponsored by any of a dozen suspects. Follow through on rebuilding the military. And then use it. In these matters keep portraits of Thatcher and Meir close at hand, and of Lincoln. As George W. Bush was fond of saying to Oval Office visitors when pointing first to his chest and then to a portrait of Lincoln hanging on the wall: "41 is closest to my heart but 16 is always on my mind."

What, after all, is the point of establishing a dynasty if it has nothing to rule, no greatest Republic ever to preserve, even as its Republican veneer thins and thins into something quite different but perhaps necessary.

On that subject, perhaps another book, if you use the lessons of this one.

CHAPTER 45

The Nukes

President Obama has done his worst damage to our most important strategic asset —our nuclear arsenal.

Yes, there are still 450 Minutemen III missiles spread across Colorado, Montana, Nebraska, North Dakota, and Wyoming. Yes, we still have a fleet of 18 Ohio-class submarines ("SSBNs"). 14 of them carrying submarine-launched ballistic missiles ("SLBMs"), four with other capabilities, and all of them together making a total of about 28 "deterrence patrols" annually, each lasting about 70 days. "Deterring what?" the Steelers' fans but not you might ask. These subs are the strongest part of our nuclear deterrent, but we have always believed in a three-legged deterrent structure, the so-called "nuclear triad." In addition to the missiles in the ground and under the sea, we still have 94 nuclear-capable heavy bombers, both B-2s and B-52s.

All told there are between 700 and 778 deployed ICBMs, SLBMs, and nuclear capable bombers as of the middle of last year, though experts expect that total number to fall to 700 before President Obama leaves office.

The United States has not conducted a nuclear test since 1992. The new START treaty limits deployed strategic weapons to 1,550.

The annual cost for maintenance of this nuclear deterrent is approximately $16 billion—the most important $16 billion the federal government spends.

The Brookings Institution—your people—estimate that it would cost a trillion dollars to modernize our nuclear deterrent, to both extend the life span of our aging weapons and to develop new delivery systems like a new SSBN.

Jon B. Wolfsthal, Jeffrey Lewis, and Marc Quint, who are with the James Martin Center for Nonproliferation Studies in Monterey, California, issued a key study in January 2014, a study which you should carry around with you as a marker of national security seriousness, a cleaver to cut the cord between you and President Obama, the worst president ever when it comes to preserving and protecting America's national security.

"It is unclear how long the nation's nuclear weapon program can defy budgetary gravity," the Martin Center report concluded.

"Because there is no stand-alone life cycle budget for these programs, the administration and Congress are now only beginning to recognize the full scale of the investments being contemplated and have not yet made a public case for this level of commitment," it adds.

"The result may well be budget chaos," it continue, and "[i]n the worst case, an attempt to simultaneously rebuild all three legs of the strategic triad" could "imperil either the ICBM force or the nuclear mission for the follow-on bomber." The authors also noted that the Ohio-class SSBNs are scheduled to begin retiring in 2027, at a rate of one per year through 2042, and that procurement of a new nuclear weapon carrying submarine —the "SSBN(X)"— has already been delayed until 2021 "for costs and other reasons."

"As a result, the Navy now plans to operate fewer than twelve boats for more than a decade from 2029-41, dropping to 10 deployed boats for the majority of that period."

The report is rich in other alarming details, and you should spend hours with it, soaking in those details, displaying a command of them, highlighting again that "both Presidents Bush and Obama have utterly failed to preserve our strategic defenses even as strategic threats arise again in Russia and gather strength in the PRC and other countries quest to deploy them."

JFK ran on a "missile gap," and so should you, but this time the gap is real and primarily though not exclusively the consequences of actions by a president of your own party.

Madame Secretary, as the last chapter noted, what is the point of a dynasty and a Second Founding and a "Second Founding" if that dynasty and its founding fades almost immediately because of a refusal to take care of the most important assets of national power?

When you campaign, if you speak clearly on this issue, you will splinter the GOP and draw the serious people to you if they believe you are sincere. Once elected, demand—demand— the money for the "Clinton-class SSBN(X) submarines" (you can say they are named for Bill but you will build them and history will record that) and accomplish the laying of the cornerstones of the country's security and your legacy all at once.

This, the last chapter, is as straightforward as a nuclear bomb, and I hope as as bright. If you don't rebuild our nuclear deterrent—or if the Republican who beats you doesn't do this— it is all for naught anyway. The world has always respected the legions or their equivalent. If you want to be a Queen, you have to have the power to stay on the throne.

THE

QUEEN

ACKNOWLEDGMENTS

I owe thanks and continuous expressions of public appreciation to many people but especially Kate Harston, who edited this book and Craig Wiley who, as my agent, found it a home; Lynne Chapman who kept it organized and Snow Philip who proofed it; and, of course, the Fetching Mrs. Hewitt who encouraged it, as she did me, every day of its making.

In my last book before this one, *The Happiest Life*, I included both a chapter on "Friendship" and a lengthy set of genuine, deeply-felt acknowledgements for the joy in my life, to which I refer the genuinely interested reader, and from which I nevertheless reproduce all the people who make the radio show possible, beginning with Ed Atsinger and Stu Epperson, Dave Santrella, Greg Anderson, Phil Boyce, Tom Tradup, Russ Hauth and 100+ GMs and PDs, plus the A-team of broadcast, in order of their appearance in my radio life, Duane Patterson, Anthony Ochoa, Adam Ramsey, Russ Shubin, Danielle Hitchens, Marlon Bateman, Daniel Roberts, Tony J. Black, C.J. Morton and Dylan Kasperowitz. Who would have thought a voice over the air would require so many talents?